Rebuilding the Rural Southern Community

Rebuilding the Rural Southern Community

Reformers, Schools, and Homes in Tennessee, 1900–1930

Mary S. Hoffschwelle

The University of Tennessee Press / Knoxville

The paper in this book meets the minimum requirements of the American National Standard
for Permanence of Paper for Printed Library Materials.

∞ The binding materials have been chosen for strength and durability.

♻ Printed on recycled paper.

Library of Congress Cataloging-in-Publication Data

Hoffschwelle, Mary S., 1955–
    Rebuilding the rural Southern community : reformers, schools, and homes in Tennessee,
1900–1930 / Mary S. Hoffschwelle. — 1st ed.
        p. cm.
    Includes bibliographical references and index.
    ISBN 1-57233-021-X (cloth: alk. paper)
    1. Rural development—Tennessee—History—20th century. 2. Rural renewal—Tennessee—
History—20th century. 3. Education, Rural—Tennessee—History—20th century. 4. Rural
schools—Tennessee—History—20th century. 5. Home economics, Rural—Tennessee—History—20th century. 6. Tennessee—Rural conditions—History—20th century. I. Title.
HN79.T23 C666   1998
307.1'412'09768—ddc21   98-9096

For my mother and father

Contents

Acknowledgments / xi

Introduction / 1

1. The Progressive Impulse and Southern Rural Education / 13

**2. Consolidation and New School Buildings:
Reforms for White Rural Schools / 34**

**3. "Building an Ideal":
Model Schools for African Americans / 61**

**4. Building a Bridge between School and Home Life:
Home Economics for Rural Schools / 90**

**5. Better Homes on Better Farms:
Home Demonstration and Domestic Reform / 104**

**6. Domestic Consumption and Competition:
A New Ethic for Rural Homes / 127**

7. Legacies of Rural Reform / 145

Notes / 151

Selected Bibliography / 211

Index / 229

Illustrations

1. "Design No. 1 of a Model One-Room School" / 25

2. Anderson County's Consolidated School Buildings / 38

3. Doak Consolidated School, Greene County / 41

4. Afton School, Greene County / 42

5. "Fourth Grade Studying Health Rules" / 46

6. Community Pride School, Obion County / 47

7. Bowers Consolidated School, Obion County / 49

8. Cloverdale Consolidated School, Obion County / 49

9. "One-Teacher School—To Face East or West Only, No. 1-A" / 53

10. "Six-Teacher School—To Face North or South Only, No. 6" / 54

11. Meriwether Lewis School, Lewis County / 56

12. Bryant's School, Rutherford County / 68

13. Spring Hill School, Shelby County / 69

14. "One-Teacher Community School Plan No. 1-A" / 72

15. "Two-Teacher Community School Plan No. 20" / 73

16. "Floor Plan No. 8-A, Community School" / 74

17. South Fulton Consolidated Rosenwald School, Obion County / 79

18. Old South Fulton Colored School, Obion County / 80

19. Augusta Rosenwald School, Shelby County / 82

20. School Abandoned for Oakville Rosenwald School,
Shelby County / 83

21. Kitchen Furniture Made from Scrap Lumber / 120

22. Girl's Bedroom Exhibit / 122

23. Mrs. Bert Erwin's Kitchen, Maury County / 134

24. Living Room Improvement Exhibit / 137

25. Interiors of the Williamson County Better Homes
Demonstration House / 139

26. Worley Manor, Shepherd, Hamilton County / 141

Acknowledgments

Progressive reformers believed that families, communities, and institutions could create environments that would make life better for all Americans. As I studied some of those reformers and the rural people they tried to reach, I followed the Progressive model, relying on family, communities of scholars, and institutional support to reach my goal. Now it is my pleasure to thank them all.

Several institutions provided funding and time for this project. I am grateful to the Spencer Foundation for a Dissertation-Year Fellowship in 1991–92, and to the Rockefeller Archive Center for a research grant in 1992. A grant of released time in 1996, and the daily support and encouragement of the History Department at Middle Tennessee State University brought the project to its final destination in this book. Portions of chapter 4 appeared in the *Journal of Southern History*. I thank editor John Boles for permission to reprint this material.

My research also benefited from the assistance of several librarians and archivists who patiently helped me through their collections, including Erwin Levold at the Rockefeller Archive Center, Wayne Moore at the Tennessee State Library and Archives, Anne Allen Shockley and Beth Howse at the Fisk University Special Collections, Sara Harwell of the Vanderbilt University Special Collections, and Bill Eigelsbach at the University of Tennessee Archives and Special Collections.

Many scholars have given me inspiration and counsel at various stages through this project. I am deeply grateful to my dissertation committee at Vanderbilt University, in particular Samuel T. McSeveney and Dewey W. Grantham, for their guidance and wisdom. Sally McMurry, Mark Wetherington, and Deborah Fink offered insightful comments on versions of this manuscript, giving me fresh perspectives on my work and valuable suggestions for its development. Jan Leone and Susan Myers-Shirk kept me focused throughout the process of writing and rewriting, as we shared our work in weekly sessions in Murfreesboro. By long-distance telephone from Minneapolis, Patty Dean provided a sympathetic ear, as well as citations to the *Farmer's Wife*. I also want to thank Meredith Morris-Babb for bringing me to the University of Tennessee Press, Joyce Harrison and Scot Danforth for guiding the project to completion, and all the staff there for their support of this project.

My family has been the most important, continuous influence on my life and work. Carroll Van West has done double duty as husband and critic; my work would not be possible without his personal support, scholarly judgment, and editorial advice. Our son Owen arrived just as this project began, and our daughter Sara arrived for its conclusion; they made its progress a joyful one. This book is dedicated to my parents, Sara K. Hoffschwelle and John W. Hoffschwelle, who created my first home.

Introduction

"The South presents right now the Nation's No. 1 economic problem," announced Franklin D. Roosevelt in 1938. Addressing a conference on southern economic conditions, Roosevelt offered a litany of the region's problems—the destructive exploitation of agricultural and industrial resources, as well as of female and child laborers, the prevalence of farm tenancy and paucity of farm income, the inadequacies of public education, health, and housing. Yet he recalled southerners' equally distinctive legacy as descendants of combatants at King's Mountain and Shiloh. Tennessean Samuel L. Smith, one of the conference participants, well may have appreciated the references to his state's heroic military history.[1] But as one of Tennessee's veteran rural reformers, he knew that these southern problems had their own long history.

Progressive reformers like Smith had spent the first thirty years of the twentieth century attempting to reshape country life. This book uses the rural reform movement in Tennessee from 1900 to 1930 as a window through which to view the southern Progressive campaign to create a better country life. This campaign engaged a wide variety of reformers, educators, designers, intellectuals, and, just as important, many different types of rural residents. Each group assessed its own needs and desires and, when possible, pursued its own agenda. Rural reform generated vigorous debate in the American South because many reformers assumed that this impoverished region was in dire need of change, while country people did their best to ensure that change fit their own perceptions of a better life.

Tennessee provides an especially valuable perspective on the nature and significance of Progressive reform in the rural South, because of the diversity of its geography and rural socioeconomic patterns, and because of the significant reform institutions established in the state. Tennessee's traditional three Grand Divisions—West, Middle, and East—offer a range of agricultural and demographic regions representative of the rural South. West Tennessee's cotton-producing counties with large black populations were similar to those of the Deep South. Middle Tennessee's mixed-farming counties with small but still significant black populations were representative of many other Upper South and upland regions. East Tennessee's corn and grain–producing counties, with overwhelmingly white populations, reflect general patterns found throughout Southern Appalachia.

By birth or residence, Tennessee itself was home to a number of leading educational reformers, such as Charles W. Dabney, University of Tennessee president and educational historian; Philander P. Claxton, United States Commissioner of Education; Wickliffe Rose, director of the Rockefeller Sanitary Commission and later president of John D. Rockefeller's General Education Board; Bruce R. Payne, president of George Peabody College for Teachers; and Fletcher B. Dresslar, Peabody's professor of schoolhouse architecture and an authority on rural school buildings.

Tennessee also hosted a broad range of key regional institutions dedicated to rural reform. In the early years of the century, the leading southern educational reform organization, the Southern Education Board, largely underwritten by Rockefeller's General Education Board, established a bureau at the University of Tennessee as a clearinghouse for educational crusades throughout the South. The bureau's personnel created the University of Tennessee's Summer School of the South to promulgate new educational theories and methods. In 1914, a second key institution was created, with the opening in Nashville of the George Peabody College for Teachers, funded by the Peabody Education Foundation and the General Education Board. Peabody's presence, along with the tradition of African American activism and reform represented by Nashville's Fisk University and Tennessee Agricultural and Industrial Normal School, attracted the southern headquarters of the Julius Rosenwald Fund Rural School Program to Nashville in 1920 and the Interstate School Building Service in 1928. By the time of the Great Depression, then, Tennessee was the home base of a regional Progressive infrastructure for rural reform. These organizations joined the usual complement of officials from the state education department, agricultural university, extension service, and normal schools to keep Tennesseans in close contact with national and regional developments.

Country people were not overawed or overwhelmed by the onslaught of reform programs initiated in Tennessee during the early twentieth century. This too makes the state typical of the region, even the nation. Far from being passive beneficiaries of Progressive reform or stubborn opponents of change, rural Tennesseans decided for themselves whether reform proposals would transform their schools or homes. They adopted new ways of living when the proper combination of reform agitation, local needs, personal aspirations, and economic circumstances came together in their families and communities.

Rural people had good reason to pick and choose among the various reform packages offered during these decades. Tennesseans already had weathered an intense era of change in basic patterns affecting land, labor, and politics during their parents' generation from 1860 to 1900.[2] Now adults themselves, country people in the early twentieth century were coping with rapid developments in the state's agriculture and in its transportation systems.

Tennessee farmers, many of whom had savored the market boom of the 1850s, found their hold on the land weakening in the aftermath of the Civil War. In 1860, the average farm size in Tennessee was 251 acres, while the average value of a farm acre was $16.45, an increase in value of more than 100 percent since 1850. In the post–Civil War and Reconstruction decades, however, the size of farms and the value of an average acre fell markedly. Across the landscape, ever smaller farms proliferated, as larger plantations and farms were broken up and the white farm population expanded; on those farms, more acreage was improved than ever before. But it was not until the turn of the century that the average value per acre again reached 1860 levels. By 1900, the average Tennessee farm acre was worth $16.77, but the average farm measured only 90.6 acres.[3]

Not only were Tennessee farms much smaller, with acreage worth little more than in the immediate pre–Civil War years, but many farmers were tenants or were on the brink of tenancy. In 1900, just over one-third of white farmers were tenants, while more than two-thirds of black-operated farms were worked by tenants, who faced an increasingly bleak present and future. These numbers represented a steady increase over the previous twenty years, as both white farm workers and formerly enslaved black farm laborers moved into tenancy. As historian Robert Tracy McKenzie has demonstrated, share-cropping slowly emerged as the dominant form of tenancy and only in the years after 1880 came to characterize black tenancy. But for farmers of both races, their lack of resources and the poor market prices for their cash crops—still primarily corn, cotton, and tobacco—threatened their livelihood.[4]

The late nineteenth century was particularly bleak for African American farmers, for whom freedom had seemed to promise so much. Emancipation offered African Americans the opportunity to rebuild their lives in freedom, yet newly freed people were given few resources, let alone equal opportunities, for achieving personal independence and community advancement. The "official" disbanding of the Ku Klux Klan did not end white violence against blacks, the threat of which loomed over the development of free black communities and institutions. Tennessee's legal system steadily became less and less favorable to African Americans. The state's 1870 constitution, which authorized a poll tax and mandated segregated public schools, canceled out most of the fleeting opportunities created during Reconstruction. Though black men temporarily regained access to the polls when the poll tax was suspended in 1873, funding and facilities for public education became increasingly unequal. In 1881 came Tennessee's first Jim Crow legislation, requiring separate accommodations for first-class railroad passengers. Ida B. Wells challenged the state's railroad segregation law in 1884 and launched her anti-lynching career from Memphis after the murder of three African

American businessmen there in 1892. Other black Tennesseans chose to follow Booker T. Washington's self-help philosophy instead. Black activists joined white racial moderates to chart better paths for black progress and racial harmony that would flower in the early twentieth century in reform programs for new black schools and in groups such as the Commission for Interracial Cooperation.[5]

These changes in African American rights and political opportunities were part of a general transformation in Tennessee politics from 1870 to 1900. As a significant block of voters, the male heads of farm households seemed well positioned to defend their interests in these difficult years. Yet state politics during the Victorian era was wracked by regional and political partisanship—struggles between white Democrats in West and Middle Tennessee, white Republicans in East Tennessee, and black Republicans in urban areas and southwestern Tennessee. The Republican party remained a significant opposition party, capable of exploiting divisions among Bourbon, New South, and Agrarian Democrats to bid for state power in the 1870s and 1880s. African American legislators served in the Tennessee General Assembly during these years, as black Tennesseans struggled to maintain a political presence despite growing and vocal opposition from both white Republicans and white Democrats. Farmers' political clout reached high tide with the Agricultural Wheel and its successor, the Farmers' Alliance, which mobilized a political movement among white and black farmers that won the governor's office and significant minorities within the General Assembly in 1890. Agrarian successes, and pitched battles over the leasing of convicts to coal mine operators, unified the state's planter and industrial elites, who used race-baiting and disfranchisement to undercut the Alliance and diminish the ranks of poor white and black voters.[6]

By the turn of the century, a quiet "gentleman's agreement" divided the state between a safely Republican East Tennessee, and safely Democratic Middle and West Tennessee. This arrangement papered over the political, economic, and cultural divisions of the previous decade. As Tennessee's rural blacks found themselves formally excluded from the state's political system, many poor rural whites found that their roles, too, had been curtailed. Political controversy shifted to prohibition, a divisive issue cutting across party lines, that dominated state politics and pitted rural drys against urban wets even after the state officially went dry in 1909. Urban political machines overcame legislative and legal obstacles to keep the liquor flowing and the poll tax receipts handy for white and black voters who would keep them in power. At the same time, the state's woman suffrage movement began a campaign that would lead to the state's ratification of the Nineteenth Amendment in 1920, overcoming apathy, internal disagreements, opposition from industrial and liquor interests, and even the racial barrier.[7]

Southern rural reformers generally avoided explosive questions of political power such as alcohol, woman suffrage, and partisan loyalties when dealing with country people. Southern Progressives and their wealthy supporters, like the rural southerners they sought to reform, had grown to maturity amid the political disruptions of Reconstruction, Redemption, and farm and labor protest. Associating turn-of-the-century politics with the potential instability of class-based agrarian movements, mindless partisanship, and corrupt urban bossism, rural Progressives refrained from political controversy and partisanship to a large extent. Instead, they aimed their programs at convincing country people to exchange local control, and tax dollars, for centralized government expertise represented by new bureaucracies. These government agencies designated new experts to whom farm families should defer—teachers and extension agents who themselves lived in the rural communities. These experts, in turn, looked to schools and the women in farm homes as conduits for the expert knowledge and attitudes that would create a modern life. They would pitch their programs to country people, especially women, without addressing questions of racial or gender equity or political power. To secure local support, reformers insisted that their programs would redress the growing disparity between industrial and agricultural fortunes yet would not threaten established orders of class and race or the domestic hierarchy.

Most rural people brought open but skeptical minds to Progressive reform initiatives. They were skeptical because of what had happened to their parents in the late nineteenth century. But they were open because the decades of 1900 to 1920 witnessed, finally, rising agricultural fortunes that could not be entirely dissociated from the many reform programs implemented in those years, even when those fortunes sagged in the 1920s. A new highway system, together with the earlier consolidation of the state's railroad systems into the Louisville and Nashville, Southern Railway, and Illinois Central lines, by the late 1890s steadily expanded market opportunities for individual Tennessee farmers. Road building was slow in the first decade of the twentieth century. In 1913, however, county governments were authorized to issue road bonds; two years later, the State Highway Department and State Highway Commission were established. County governments began to purchase private turnpikes for public use, and they cooperated with the state commission in providing support for new state highways, such as the Memphis-to-Bristol Highway and the Dixie Highway. When Gov. Austin Peay reorganized the state highway commission and department in 1923, Tennessee had 4,644 miles of highways, of which 1,537 were primary federal highways, 1,585 were secondary federal highways, and 1,522 were state-funded roads. For Tennessee farmers, the benefits of the new roads were immediate. In 1918, the state highway department estimated, it cost 30 cents a mile to move a ton of wheat by wagon; cotton cost 48 cents a mile. Five years later, in 1923, a truck could move that same weight of wheat for 15 cents a mile, and it only cost 18 cents a mile to move cotton.[8]

Urban growth and improved transportation infrastructure led more farmers to produce new commodities for expanding agricultural markets. While corn was always the largest crop in Tennessee, and cotton remained the state's major cash crop, tobacco production boomed in these years, especially in the cultivation of burley tobacco, used largely in the making of cigarettes. Greeneville, in East Tennessee, where the state department of agriculture would locate a burley tobacco demonstration farm, became the largest tobacco market in the state, replacing the once-dominant Middle Tennessee dark-fired tobacco market.

Livestock became more important, beginning with purebred beef cattle in 1917 and booming Jersey dairy cattle production in Middle Tennessee during the 1920s. By 1925, dairy products in Tennessee were valued at $25 million; by the end of the decade, the federal government had established a U.S. Dairy Experiment Farm in Marshall County. Wealthy industrialists developed private experimental livestock farms. Frank Mars, for example, established the Milky Way Farm in Giles County as a dairy experiment farm. Hobart Ames of Boston turned the Ames Plantation of Fayette County into one of the state's largest purebred livestock farms. Poultry production also increased in these years, as an extension service–designed chicken coop became a fixture on Progressive farms in Tennessee. Morristown in East Tennessee and Cookeville in Middle Tennessee ranked among the major poultry-shipping centers in the nation.[9]

Tennessee farmers by 1920 owned land much more valuable than that of their fathers and mothers. The average value per acre of all farm property had jumped from $16.77 in 1900 to $64.17 in 1920; values of farm land, buildings, implements, and machinery doubled in the decade 1910–19, while livestock values climbed steadily throughout the two decades. In terms of personal experiences, however, these trends meant different things for different farm families. Average farm size continued to decrease—it would reach 73 acres by 1935. Farm ownership and tenancy rates remained constant from 1900 to 1920 for whites, with one-third of white-operated farms worked by tenants. Black tenancy continued to increase, however, from 72 percent of African American farms in 1910, to 74 percent in 1920 and 77 percent in 1930. Yet rural blacks could point to some new causes for hope, especially in education. After the passage of the state's General Education Act in 1909, black school attendance stood at 49 percent of the school age population in 1910. By 1920, this had increased slightly to 54 percent; but during the 1920s, the percentage jumped to 64.6 percent of the school-age population.[10]

For Progressive reformers, such statistics demonstrated more than skewed rates of land ownership or the success of the state's 1913 compulsory school-attendance law. Such figures were only some of the more obvious manifestations of serious problems in rural southerners' values, personal and community relationships, work methods, hygiene, health, and intellectual development, caused by defective social and economic conditions. To change those fundamental conditions, rural reformers again sought no fundamental restructuring of political and economic power. Rather, they sought to reach farm families directly, where they lived and learned. Progressives looked to such essential social institutions as the home and the school for answers. Although they alleged that these institutions had failed, reformers still believed that they possessed unfulfilled potential. Better educational programs and home environments eventually would transform country life, producing happier, more productive country people.

Such Progressive prescriptions contained a strong dose of environmental determinism, assuming as they did that the physical environment expressed and implanted ideas and values. Progressive reformers held an optimistic view of human beings as capable of improvement by their own volition or with outside intervention, but as vulnerable to social and economic forces beyond individual control. Like many social activists before and after them, they argued that living and working environments could be manipulated to produce desirable values and behavior in their inhabitants. Reformers sought to sanitize, beautify, and organize the rural environment in ways that would exert a continuously benevolent influence over its inhabitants, allowing them to triumph over disorder, dirt, and ugliness. Better school conditions would encourage students to associate academic progress with orderly, efficient ways of learning and living.

Reformers saw the school as a bridge to the rural home, the linchpin of an improved country life. School buildings were object lessons, explicated by a teacher to pupils who would share their knowledge with parents. In effect, the redesigned rural school was a demonstration intended to spark imitation at home. The new rural school, better constructed, furnished, and cleaned, could provide a physical model of the ideal rural dwelling. Consequently, home economics education and girls' clubs assumed particular importance in the reformed rural school. Such programs would transmit new standards of domestic production and consumption through girls to mothers at home.

My own interest in these rural reforms began here, with Progressives in the emerging field of home economics. Their assumptions about how different environmental conditions, especially in the home, would influence a family's quality of life seemed the logical extension of so many other reforms directed at working and living conditions. Home economists perceived—and wished to strengthen—meaningful connections between the home and school. They and other Progressives were fascinated with the power of education in general, and vocational education in modern school buildings in particular.

Their common cause became the Country Life movement, with its emphasis on vocational education as the key to revitalized farm production and nurturing farm homes.

To understand the importance and the meaning of reformed rural environments, I have used publications by Progressive reformers in the Country Life movement, education, and home economics, as well as the official records of both governmental and private philanthropic agencies. Such documents showed the interconnections between reformers and their agencies at the regional and national level, and the place of Tennessee within the rural reform movement. For a statewide perspective on rural reform, I consulted monthly and annual reports from Tennessee's rural school and Rosenwald school agents, and home demonstration agents; and I examined the material culture of the new buildings and domestic environments themselves. What the reformers built and demonstrated to country people is as important in assessing the successes and failures of their initiatives as what they said and did in rural communities. Indeed, how rural people adapted the new environments to their lives speaks directly to the degree of acceptance they gave to Progressive reform ideas.

To investigate that range of acceptance, six counties have been studied in greater detail, two from each Grand Division. In 1923, the state education department published a survey of Tennessee's ninety-five counties, providing a guide to general socioeconomic trends that can serve to introduce the selected counties and their reform experiences.

From East Tennessee, traditionally a region of small farms, Greene and Hamilton counties illustrate the agricultural prosperity and urban expansion that predisposed some rural people to embrace Progressive ideas. In 1920, Greene County, with fertile valleys between its rocky ridges, boasted 5,313 farms producing corn, wheat, oats, tobacco, and livestock. Farmers moved those crops on the Southern Railway, three hundred miles of pike roads, and another two hundred miles of graded roads. Thanks to the recent tobacco boom, the county seat of Greeneville possessed six tobacco warehouses, a tobacco factory, and a stemmery and redrying plant, as well as four banks, a hosiery mill, chair factory, two wagon factories, and three flour mills.

Hamilton County, with its county seat at Chattanooga on the Tennessee River, in 1920 had 2,480 farms producing grains, grasses, fruits, and vegetables, as well as cattle, hogs, and poultry and dairy products. Farmers engaged in extensive truck farming around Chattanooga and marketed their vegetables out of state as well on the Nashville, Chattanooga and St. Louis, Southern Railway, and Cincinnati Southern lines, or via other connections southward at Chattanooga. New roads helped, too, and the Dixie Highway Association located its headquarters in Chattanooga.[11]

In Middle Tennessee, Lewis and Rutherford counties demonstrate that local attitudes, as much as economic conditions, determined the course of reform. Lewis County, although "not blessed agriculturally as most of the counties of Tennessee," profited from the phosphate and iron deposits found in the state's western Highland Rim. In 1920, 537 farms yielded corn, wheat, oats, grass, livestock, and peanuts. While the Nashville, Chattanooga and St. Louis rails cut through the county, the Lewis County seat at Hohenwald was isolated from major transportation routes.

By contrast, the rich soil of the Central Basin supported Rutherford County's 5,254 farms, which produced corn, cotton, wheat, sorghum, peas, clover, and grass; this also was "one of the best livestock counties in the state," with a rapidly developing dairy industry. Murfreesboro, the county seat, sat on the NC&SL line, as well as at the junction of the Dixie and the Memphis-to-Bristol highways. Agriculturally blessed or not, residents of these Middle Tennessee counties expressed only limited interest in rural reform initiatives.[12]

West Tennessee's Obion and Shelby counties shared the economic benefits of cash crops and market access from the northern and southern ends of the state's Mississippi River boundary. Though both embraced reform, Obion relied on outside experts, while Shelby raised its own crop of activists. In both cases, river access long had been supplanted by railroad connections to markets on the Illinois Central, Mobile and Ohio, and other lines, as well as turnpikes and highways such as the Memphis-to-Bristol road in Shelby and the newer Jefferson Davis Highway in Obion. With 3,378 farms producing cotton, corn, wheat, oats, and livestock, Obion was "one of the best wheat-producing counties" and "one of the richest agricultural counties in the state." Reelfoot Lake, on Obion's western boundary, had been contested by local fishermen and commercial interests in a series of night-riding attacks in 1909 that led to state control of the waters.

Downriver, Shelby County and the commercial hub of Memphis would gain notoriety as the personal fiefdom of political boss Edward Hull Crump. Yet Shelby was "one of the best cotton-producing counties" and also cultivated corn, lumber, and hogs on its 8,204 farms, many of them worked by black tenants.[13]

This study of Tennessee reformers and rural people is divided into sections on schools and homes, connected by a discussion of home economics—just as the Progressive reformers envisioned. I consider white and black school programs in separate chapters because they operated with different goals, strategies, and outcomes, for both the reformers and the rural people involved. The two chapters on homes are not divided by race, but in accord with two different initiatives for domestic reform. The first is the home demonstration program advocated by the Tennessee Extension Service. The educational network created by extension officials, county home demonstration agents, and members of rural women's clubs was crucial to the success of the second major domestic reform program, the "better homes" campaigns, which involved rural women in public events and competitions to promote greater consumption of consumer goods. Together rural women and women reformers fostered a new vision of the rural home: in its amenities comparable to any middle-class urban home, but a place where farm women juggled an increasing workload of productive and reproductive roles.

As Tennessee indicates, the early-twentieth-century impulse for improving country life yielded mixed results, for both Progressives and rural families, largely because the dynamic of reform was interactive and multifarious. Progressive reformers preferred to impose their ideal of rural life, since they assumed that a top-down strategy would produce uniform results. That assumption was not groundless but was based upon urban, industrial models that did not necessarily fit rural reality. Country people had their own values and their own goals; they were willing to listen to Progressive ideas, but then they proved selective about which initiatives they adopted. They embraced those changes that promised to meet rural aspirations and largely ignored the rest.

Second, the responses of both Progressives and country people demonstrate that race and gender issues were integral to reform and its dynamic. Progressives argued that the South's racial hierarchy trapped African Americans in poverty and tenancy, and thereby lowered living standards for all southerners. Reformers' paternalistic racism and acceptance of legal segregation, however, allowed for retention of separate school systems and curricula for rural white and African American Tennesseans. Simultaneously, rural whites and blacks evaluated reform initiatives by their own different needs and aspirations.

Reforms aimed at country homes followed the same double track. Home economists, home demonstration agents, and home improvement campaigns encouraged rural women of both races to expand their roles in the family and community by adding new tasks, such as interior decoration and club work. They also suggested new market products, such as rugs, to enhance the ability of farm women to pay for modern domestic consumer goods. The reactions of rural women varied, from indifference to excitement, across racial and community boundaries; the leap from domestic to community improvement that seemed so novel to white women already was the norm for African American women.

Finally, changes in the material environments in which Tennesseans lived and learned illuminate both the dynamic of reform and its relationship to race and gender issues. Indeed, Progressive reformers counted on reformed environments to inculcate the values and standards for an improved country life. They believed that modern schools and modernized homes could induce rural Tennesseans to embrace the modern educational and consumer values of urban and suburban America. When adopted, school consolidation and construction initiatives created standardized, specialized buildings that represented the exchange of local autonomy for a corresponding increase of state authority. White and black country people recognized, and sometimes resented, that they were being asked to give up local autonomy and identity, but rural African Americans, the most disadvantaged rural group, also saw those modern schools as essential vehicles for advancement.

Domestic programs also reveal country women's diverse responses to new prescriptions for home life. Home improvement campaigns encouraged rural women to measure themselves and their homes by the material standards of the national consumer culture developing in the 1920s. Farm women adopted new methods or household goods that might either increase or diversify the sources of their cash income for new home furnishings, or reduce domestic drudgery and improve living standards at minimal cost. In so doing, they adapted home economists' ideals to the material conditions of southern farm life.

Together, Progressive reformers and rural Tennesseans participated in the movements that made the countryside a different place in 1930 than it had been in 1914, or 1900. Why did some people want these changes? Why did their plans to induce change succeed or fail? What did Progressive reformers and rural Tennesseans do about schools and homes, and where did those changes take them? The story begins with Progressives' discovery that rural America had gone astray, and the creation of a broad array of reform instruments with which they could rechart its course in the South and in Tennessee.

• 1 •

The Progressive Impulse and Southern Rural Education

Why did some Americans pursue Progressive reform, and why did they target schools and homes in rural communities? Many intellectuals, government officials, and educators of the late nineteenth and early twentieth centuries believed that key social, economic, and political values were dissolving in the United States. These were predominantly native-born, white, middle-class Americans, who mourned the demise of an earlier (and probably imaginary) community in which everybody, regardless of status, felt a common bond of interest. Yet they embraced progress, optimistic about the potential of scientific methods to solve the nation's problems, and the power of private and public agencies to effect change. Historians have identified these reformers collectively as Progressives. Progressives proposed an array of sometimes conflicting diagnoses and prescriptions for America's ills, ranging from the direct primary to vocational education and child labor laws. Their "search for order," to borrow Robert H. Wiebe's telling phrase, invoked traditional ideals of community identity and the supremacy of public over private interests, in order to transmit the humanistic values of the past to a scientific, efficient future.[1]

Progressive reformers also shared a common background of personal roots in rural communities and a yearning for the agrarian myth of a yeoman democracy. They found urban, industrial America lacking in humanity in comparison with the countryside of their memories. Yet, even as they called for a return to the rural values of citizenship, dignified labor, and social interdependence, they traced the roots of many urban problems to the inadequacies of life in the countryside. Increasing rural migration, for instance, swelled unruly urban populations. Food was too scarce and expensive for urban workers; reformers blamed lazy and inefficient farmers for rising agricultural prices in the years between 1910 and 1919. Making matters worse, reformers believed the most intelligent and productive farmers were the ones who migrated; agricultural innovation seemed to have little future. If more rural families could fulfill their needs for personal fulfillment and advancement, reformers imagined, they would stay on the farm and out of the city.

The Country Life movement attempted to meet those needs. It followed in the wake of numerous projects aimed at increasing farm production or improving the lives of farmers, including agricultural education and research in the 1862 and 1890 Morrill Acts and the 1890 Hatch Act, and farmers' movements such as the Grange and Farmers' Alliance. What was novel about the Country Life movement was its alliance of urban-oriented Progressive reformers and agricultural interests, whether in the Commission on Country Life, appointed by U.S. President Theodore Roosevelt, or in the American Country Life Association. Members of this movement agreed on little more than the need for better education and scientific agriculture. Some saw increased production and farm income as ends in themselves; others believed that higher incomes would improve living conditions, which, in turn, would restore an ideal of community identity to isolated and impoverished people.[2]

The rural South attracted much attention from Progressive reformers. Southern reformers identified with national trends in political reform and economic regulation, thanks to the growing influence of business and professional elites from urban centers.[3] Yet, in a region still dominated by agriculture and crippled by poverty and racism, the countryside posed a Progressive dilemma all by itself. In the first three decades of the twentieth century, reformers aggressively sought the causes of, and possible cures for, the apparent backwardness of southern rural life.[4]

Education emerged as the first and most popular panacea.[5] Schools could teach more than literacy and numeracy skills: they could teach rural people how to live properly. Progressive activists prescribed education as the remedy for almost every ill they diagnosed, and their attempts to redefine education and expand its social functions have fascinated historians. Inheriting a traditional notion of the public school as dispensary of the knowledge and culture necessary for a democratic society, reformers found that contemporary southern schools failed this standard. For generations, southern public education had been poorly funded and under tight local control; the system required massive change.[6]

In the first decade and a half of the twentieth century, a coalition of southern Progressives and Country Life reformers joined with northern philanthropists to create an infrastructure of private and public reform agencies devoted to the rural South. They expected government regulation and social services to produce the "order, morality, benevolence, efficiency, and development" which Progressives deemed essential for better rural citizens.[7] Their preferred reform tool, education, promised social uplift through the power of the state. Expanded public school systems dedicated to training model rural citizens, reformers proclaimed, would generate economic development, improve social conditions, ameliorate racism, and pave the way for honest (meaning all-white) politics.[8]

Compared to other regions, reformers believed that, as a result of local politics and indifference, southern school systems were stunted. Southern schools had one-half to one-third the funding of other public schools. Those southern children who attended school did so for an average of about 70 days a year, compared to between 100 and 130 days elsewhere. Although literacy rates had improved recently, in 1900 over 20 percent of southerners were illiterate, the highest ratio in the country.[9]

Most rural public school programs in the South would have to be constructed almost from scratch. Far from being discouraged by the enormity of their task, Progressives leapt at the opportunity to form the environmental conditions essential for improved country living. Southern Country Life reformers and Progressive educators argued that reorganizing rural schools and promoting vocational education in agriculture and home economics would break the South out of its agricultural stagnation.[10]

Educational change, however, would not proceed unless reformers gave special attention to issues of race and poverty. In an era when many whites imagined African Americans as "beasts" and when a division existed between followers of W. E. B. DuBois and those of Booker T. Washington, white reformers often seemed little concerned with racial reform. In the South, however, where the vast majority of African Americans lived, race was a factor in any reform proposal. Paternalistic white reformers saw racial divisions as a cause of their region's economic and social problems, but they also assumed black inferiority.[11] Middle-class and professional black southerners, although largely excluded from Progressive organizations and from political power, conducted parallel reform campaigns in their own communities.[12]

In the southern countryside, racism, combined with farm tenancy, limited educational opportunities for African Americans. White planters discouraged the construction, operation, and maintenance of schools for their tenants' children. Rural whites correctly interpreted blacks' desire for education as a pursuit of social and economic advancement that threatened the racial hierarchy of their society. Educational change in the South proved possible only when rural and educational reformers outside the region tailored their programs to southern racial sensibilities.

One way of gauging the importance of racial issues to southern educational reform is through the annual encounters among educators, ministers, and business leaders at the Conferences for Education in the South from 1898 to 1914.[13] The first conference, at Capon Springs, West Virginia, brought together ministers and college educators for a discussion of black education. Their ranks included the former Confederate officer, Jabez Lamar Monroe Curry, who, as agent for the Peabody Education Fund and John F. Slater

Fund, administered two northern-based philanthropies funding the expansion of public education and teacher training for whites and blacks. The 1899 conference broadened its scope to include public education for whites and blacks, and its membership to include northern businessmen such as New York merchant Robert Curtis Ogden, president of the Board of Trustees of the Hampton Institute. Curry and Ogden became mainstays of the early conferences, with Ogden's chartered trains bringing in northern associates and picking up southern conference members en route to the meeting. In 1901, at the fourth conference, held at Winston-Salem, North Carolina, Ogden brought a group of friends who included John D. Rockefeller, Jr.

The 1901 conference members created the Southern Education Board (SEB) as a propagandizing agency for their work. They elected Ogden as SEB president and Alabama child labor activist Edgar Gardner Murphy as executive secretary. Curry served as supervising director and campaign committee chair. The SEB established a Bureau of Information and Investigation at the University of Tennessee as a clearinghouse for state-wide campaigns for education legislation. This conference also inspired the creation of the General Education Board (GEB). Upon his return from the meeting, John D. Rockefeller, Jr., urged his father to join the cause of southern education. In the spring of 1902, the elder Rockefeller placed his advisor, Baptist minister Wallace Buttrick, in charge of what would become the nation's largest educational philanthropy. The General Education Board made public education in the South its first priority, and the SEB among its first beneficiaries.

Under Ogden and Curry's leadership, participants in the Conferences on Education in the South and the SEB quickly adjusted their focus from a special concern for black education to the goal of universal white public education, supplemented by a limited black curriculum. The race-specific portion of the conference's reform agenda followed the model of industrial education set by Samuel Chapman Armstrong at Hampton Institute and Booker T. Washington at Tuskegee Institute, with a curriculum of mechanical arts, agriculture, and domestic science.[14]

Progressive white southerners defended this curriculum as both practical and realistic. Industrial education best suited blacks' supposedly innate capabilities and social status, they argued. It also was the only approach acceptable to white voters and taxpayers. Reformers' own paternalistic racism informed their claims. At the 1901 conference, Charles Dabney spoke of blacks as "a child race" requiring industrial training as part of the region's program for universal public education. J. L. M. Curry further insisted that whites must be given highest educational priority to enlighten their racial outlook and elicit their support for black education and uplift.[15] If white southerners needed further assurance that educational reform would not threaten their social order, Edgar Gardner Murphy pledged that "there are some questions which the South has decided, which the South has the right to decide, and which it is neither desirable nor necessary to debate."[16] Acting upon these beliefs, the SEB, GEB, and philanthropies such as the Slater Fund used their financial contributions to force the industrial curriculum on African American educational institutions.[17]

As William A. Link has observed, the Progressive indictment of southern schools arraigned the rural South itself. The region's rural schools could not even meet the traditional ideal of the one-room school as American democracy in action, an ideal that Wayne Fuller has documented as reality for many midwestern farm communities in the same period.[18] Country schools segregated by race, staffed by teachers hardly more knowledgeable than their students, and conducted for brief sessions in dirty shacks furnished with the barest essentials, revealed provincial, racist, poorly educated, and cash-poor school officials and parents. More than school systems would have to change, social reformers argued, for southern progress to happen. The very character of rural life must change, beginning with the rural home as the basis of the rural community.

Reform programs for southern education aimed to create schools, homes, and communities that would make country people more contented and productive and, consequently, keep them on the farm. School, home, and community would reform each other in a spiral of uplift, once a close relationship was established between the rural school and the rural home. Rural educators fondly described schools as the "entering wedge" into rural homes. At best, rural schools could reach adults by serving as community centers for extension education and voluntary group activities; at least, they could send better informed children home to shame their parents into uplifting themselves.[19]

Progressives coordinated educational and domestic reform to strengthen the link between school and home. Louis R. Harlan has written that "the local literature early in the century reveals the rural schoolhouse and the small farmer's or tenant's dwelling house as products of the same culture."[20] Writers of this "local literature" realized that rural culture was grounded in the home, that in order to improve rural schools they would have to improve the rural home, and that to improve the rural home they would have to reach rural women.

Women played important roles as instigators and subjects of Progressive social reforms. A new concern for the adjustment of middle-class and working-class males to industrialism, and for children's health and education, buttressed women's traditional duties as wives and mothers. Simultaneously, middle-class homemakers and home economists claimed professional status through scientific housekeeping and home consumption management, as well as through careers in education, research, and institutional settings such as hospitals.[21] Their domestic reform movement, like women's voluntary organizations engaged in "municipal housekeeping," tried to extend female authority into educational, economic, social, and political arenas.[22] In the South, what Marjorie Spruill Wheeler has called the "noblesse oblige" of the white "southern lady" denoted the influences of class and race on the region's female activists. White and black women reformers formed their own Progressive organizations, from clubs to settlement houses and suffrage leagues.[23]

Home economists, rural educators, and architectural reformers concurred on the importance of environmental conditions in determining the quality of life. They searched for women capable of running the ideal country homes and schools that would save rural communities. The members of the Commission on Country Life described the home as "the center of our civilization." They proclaimed, "The school is capable of changing the whole attitude of the home life and the part that women should play in the development of the best country living." Rural sociologist John M. Gillette argued that a new outlook on life would benefit country people more than the acceptance of scientific agriculture. Modern, comfortable, and sanitary homes with labor-saving devices could elicit proper attitudes and modern ways of living.[24]

Home economics and extension education consequently gained important places on the southern rural reform agenda. Helen Campbell, a founding member of the National Home Economics Association and a prolific writer on home economics and social reform, prescribed such programs for what she described as "the frowsy shiftlessness of the poor white in the South." Others included black women in their vision, seeking to transform the domestic environment of black families for racial uplift and to provide better-trained servants for white households.[25]

Like other Progressive issues, these educational programs combined progress with tradition. Home economics classes for schoolgirls and women thrived on conventional concepts of the home as a feminine preserve and as the foundation of social values. At the same time, such programs were agents of a new order in which women could gain status within the family and society by updating their domestic tasks and redirecting community life. At the sixteenth Conference for Education in the South, held in Richmond in 1913, J. L. Whitfield, president of the Mississippi Industrial Institute, indicted the rural school for its failures in training women. Whitfield insisted that vocational training alone would not solve the problem. He called for a complete reorganization of rural female education, revamped training for rural teachers, and a congenial community atmosphere, as well as church support and the introduction of labor-saving devices in the home. These changes would reinforce classroom training in health, citizenship, and home life by supplementing the usual sewing, cooking, hygiene, and agricultural lessons with training in parenthood, home leisure, and home decoration.[26]

Progressives across the South indicted rural schools and proposed sweeping visions of school, home, and community uplift. Better public schools, vocational education, and domestic reform were essential, and related, elements of the Progressive agenda for improving country life. They would serve as the foundation for rebuilding rural communities across the South in the first three decades of the twentieth century. These basic tenets, in turn, shaped the first campaigns to rebuild rural communities in Tennessee.

First on the Progressive agenda was the state's inadequate public school system. The cataclysm of civil war had torn apart Tennessee's rural communities; rebuilding the agricultural economy, biracial society, and bipartisan politics of their regions preoccupied most country people for decades. Interest in public education gradually increased in the late nineteenth century. The Peabody Education Fund had been active in the state since 1868. It distributed funds to public and normal schools, as well as supporting scholarships, teachers' institutes, a state education journal, and Peabody Normal College. The fund also employed an agent who worked for the state superintendent of education. Rural protest in the late 1880s and 1890s, culminating in the election of a Populist governor in 1890, made greater support for public schools an issue in state politics. Yet many rural whites saw little utility in public schools and distrusted education in general as the province of the white elite and as an opportunity for blacks to progress at their expense.[27]

Tennesseans actively participated in the Southern Education Board's quest to overcome this apathy and distrust. The University of Tennessee's President Charles Dabney was a founding member and officer of the SEB; his university hosted the SEB's Bureau of Information and Investigation. Dabney hired native Tennessean and UT graduate Philander P. Claxton to head both the bureau and the university's education department. Claxton had worked closely with North Carolina educational reformers at graded schools in that state and was an original member of the Conference for Education in the South.[28] Dabney and Claxton made common cause with the staff of the state's Department of Education, who, like all rural reformers, believed "that many of the institutions peculiar to country life are on the decline; that the country church is weakening, the glamour is being lifted from the old-time country home, rural population is declining, and there is manifest a general decay of country life."[29]

Tennessee's educational crusades began in 1903, with Dabney and Claxton assisting State Superintendent Seymour A. Mynders. In successive biennial campaigns between 1903 and 1913, many of them managed by Claxton, state reformers focused on the most basic issue, the construction of a system of public schools. Financial support was essential; the greatest achievements of the crusade were those provisions of the General Education Act of 1909 that set aside 25 percent of gross state revenue for education and empowered county governments to levy school taxes. A 1913 amendment increased state support to one-third of gross revenue and specifically appropriated the additional money for rural schools. Other legislation addressed control of local schools and school funds by abolishing district boards in favor of countywide boards of education (1907) and authorizing those boards to consolidate local schools (1913).[30]

Improved teacher training also was essential to the new public school system. Dabney made teacher training a priority at the University of Tennessee, in 1902 appointing Claxton as the director of an annual Summer School of the South. The summer school offered courses intended to improve the quality of public school teaching and to recruit teachers for local educational campaigns. For the next decade, it attracted teachers from across the region and the nation to courses and guest lectures by leading educators and public figures. Beginning with the second session in 1903, the school's education courses included one focused on rural school problems. The influence of the Summer School of the South waned after 1911, when, in the wake of Claxton and Dabney's departures, tensions between summer school staff and the rest of the university erupted into open hostility. Declining enrollment, as students chose competing state teacher institutes, combined with intramural politics to close the school after its 1918 session.[31]

More enduring was Dabney's creation of a College of Education within the university, which opened in the January term of 1903. Dabney's appointments to his new educational faculty included Philander Claxton and, for a brief time, former Peabody Normal College professor Wickliffe Rose. Dabney had chosen well: both men would gain national stature, Claxton as U.S. commissioner of education and Rose as secretary of the Rockefeller Sanitary Commission and later as president of the General Education Board. Dabney also hired instructors of manual training and domestic economy, two of the "special subjects now demanded in the newer and more progressive schools."[32]

Apparently demand for teacher training outstripped the university's commitment and resources. The 1909 General Education Act authorized construction of three normal schools for the preparation of white teachers. These opened in 1911 in Johnson City, Murfreesboro, and Memphis. The same act authorized creation of an Agricultural and Industrial State Normal School for black teacher training, as well as permanent state funding for the University of Tennessee.

The opening of the Agricultural and Industrial Normal School in Nashville in 1912 finally brought the state into compliance with the 1890 Morrill Act requirement that states provide land grant colleges for all students, with separate facilities for whites and blacks permitted if properly funded. In the wake of the second Morrill Act, University of Tennessee President Charles Dabney negotiated a new contract with Knoxville College, which had functioned as Tennessee's land grant institution for African American students since 1884. Knoxville College then established an industrial department, which fit with Dabney's biased assumptions about black educational standards but not with the views of Tennessee's black students or leaders such as Nashville newspaper publisher Henry Allen Boyd. Boyd's editorial agitation in his Nashville *Globe,* combined with the efforts of Philander Claxton and state superintendent Robert L. Jones, won inclusion of a bona fide black land grant institution in the General Education Act of 1909. Henry Boyd, banker James C. Napier, and state capitol porter Benjamin Carr secured the normal school for Nashville. Tennessee A&I's first president, William J. Hale, used his school's agricultural and industrial designation to promote black education among white legislators and citizens, as well as with more conservative African Americans.[33]

As public teacher-training facilities expanded, regional reformers and northern philanthropists planned a private university for white teachers and school administrators to serve the entire South. The trustees of the Peabody Education Fund, in accordance with George Peabody's testamentary requirement that the fund cease operation after thirty years, in 1905 voted to devote the one million dollars left in the fund to a new George Peabody College for Teachers in Nashville. Nashville, the "Athens of the South," offered the legacy of the well-respected Peabody Normal College, the cooperation of Vanderbilt University, and a state appropriation to secure the new teachers' college for the city. It also was no accident that the last Peabody fund agent was Wickliffe Rose, a native of rural Saulsbury, in southwestern Tennessee. He served as executive secretary of the Southern Education Board from 1909 to 1913. His SEB position and membership in the General Education Board netted the new Peabody College one million dollars in GEB contributions by 1914.[34]

Wickliffe Rose's most important contribution to George Peabody College for Teachers was the Seaman A. Knapp School of Country Life. On a train ride with GEB Executive Secretary Wallace Buttrick, Rose mentioned his dream of an institution devoted to reclaiming country life through a revamped rural education. Buttrick urged Rose to prepare a formal proposal, which in May 1912 led the GEB to offer George Peabody College President Bruce R. Payne $250,000 for a school of country life. Rose planned "a clearing house for the rural communities of the South" that would combine rural sociology, agriculture, and home economics education and demonstration work, and rural public health, to create a complete Country Life college program. The Seaman A. Knapp School of Country Life dominated the early work of George Peabody College. Payne believed it would make the college "the center of the most conspicuous and most important educational movement in the history of American education."[35] The teacher training revolution in Tennessee soon would influence the ways of rural life as its graduates tackled country schools.

In a 1902 address to the Peabody Education Board and the Southern Education Board, Charles Dabney called for "educated leaders, public-minded citizens, as well as teachers, who know how to construct, direct, and maintain good schools." It took Tennesseans a decade to implement Dabney's vision. But Progressive educational reform involved more than better trained teachers. It also involved the construction and maintenance of new schools designed in a contemporary style. After studying 1,580 schools in twenty-eight southern counties in 1904, the SEB Bureau of Information and Investigation found that 1,107 were single-room, one-teacher schools, 938 of which were "old, dilapidated buildings." Of these dilapidated schools, two-thirds were unpainted, and over half were not weather tight; almost half had homemade desks, and twenty-seven had no desks at all.[36]

Proper rural school buildings, equipment, and grounds ranked among the top items on the reform agenda. John W. Brister's survey of the state's rural schools, published by the Department of Education in 1911, condemned the typical one-room school as expensive to operate and educationally "inferior" and "inefficient." Brister's report called for the consolidation of one-teacher schools to provide better facilities, teachers, and incentive for pupils to attend. Consolidated schools, he contended, would keep farmers in the country by offering the same quality of education given in urban schools, albeit with a rural vocational emphasis. They would foster community identity as "constant object lesson[s] in cooperative effort."[37]

Brister further emphasized how improved rural school facilities could uplift pupils and their parents:

> What is needed is local public sentiment that . . . will look upon the rural school as a part of each home, a place where the character of the child is to be greatly influenced, where its life and destiny is to be determined. The buildings and grounds should be made just as attractive as means will allow. The buildings should be properly lighted; the desks should be comfortable, and adapted to the size of the students; good, beautiful, and elevating pictures should adorn the walls; . . . the ventilation of the buildings, the water supply, the toilet rooms, the floor dressing, the screening of the doors and windows, should be models of sanitary arrangements for the entire community. . . . The arrangements and planning of the grounds should be such that not only the students but the parents as well, will be interested in carrying out the same kind of work in their homes.

With a photograph of a small rectangular board-and-batten school, the author asked, "Is there much inspiration in this for the country child?" Brister's lobbying met with success; in 1913 the General Assembly increased public funding for rural schools.[38]

Educational activists could take heart from the results of their efforts to construct a system of decent school buildings. Between 1899 and 1913, Tennessee increased its capital investment in school buildings and their furnishings by almost $5.5 million. Wood framing remained the construction material of choice; two-thirds of the state's log school buildings were abandoned in these years. These probably had represented the most ancient and decrepit structures, and their replacement by consolidated schools accounted for most of the overall decline in the number of school buildings.[39]

Campaigns for rural school consolidation and construction generally focused on elementary education; however, secondary schools also came in for support and criticism. The General Education Board funded a professorship in secondary education at the University of Tennessee, as well as in other southern state universities. Professor Harry Clark spent most of his time lobbying county courts for increased financial support. While construction of new consolidated high schools was his primary mission, Clark also labored for high schools in counties where none existed at all. His 1912 map of state high schools, distributed as a broadside, showed that only forty-five of the state's ninety-six counties had one or more high schools. Of the 111 high school programs in the state that year, almost half offered only a two-year course. Seventy-four were housed in forty-one frame and thirty-three brick or stone high school buildings; the remaining thirty-seven high school programs shared facilities with elementary classes.[40]

Constructing a state system of public education offered an exciting opportunity for the reformers of school architecture. They campaigned through a broad range of private voluntary and philanthropic organizations and public agencies. Following the lead of other states, in 1907 Superintendent Robert Lee Jones convened a Cooperative Education Association to promote educational legislation. Jones painted a grim picture of rural school conditions, observing that "as a rule, public school property is much neglected. The houses and grounds are poorly cared for and kept. The walls are bare and often dingy and dirt-begrimed." Although it dissolved after the passage of the 1909 education bill, the Cooperative Education Association spawned the School Improvement League, a partnership of local groups dedicated to school-building improvement. The Southern Education Board paid the salary of a school improvement organizer, Virginia Pearl Moore, a Gallatin teacher, who began work in September 1908.[41]

A School Improvement Association sought the "better physical surroundings[,] good books for all[, and] art in the school room" that it deemed essential to the realization of its motto of "health, comfort, beauty, and attractiveness." Each association devoted committees to the schoolhouse, the grounds, and sanitation. The state organization provided detailed hints for local committees, including painting or tinting walls "a cheery and restful tone," hanging sash curtains for a homelike appearance, providing individual drinking cups, and hanging copies of fine art masterpieces in plain frames.[42]

Moore photographed improvement projects in Sumner, Lauderdale, and Bradley counties. She documented a cloakroom in a rural Sumner County school, where rows of sanitary tin cups hung neatly beside a tin water cooler, denoted improving health conditions. "Before and after" photographs of the Curve School in Lauderdale County and the Mouse Creek School in Bradley County showed new, tightly framed, white-painted buildings replacing unpainted, poorly kept clapboarded buildings. The Curve School even boasted a belfry and a millwork spandrel at the peak of its central gable. In 1912, Moore turned over school improvement work to the newly formed Tennessee Congress of Mothers and Parent-Teacher Associations. In her final report, she claimed to have 1,500 groups with a membership of 60,000.[43]

Moore's local organizations paralleled state-level efforts by officials at the Tennessee Department of Education, who joined architects and college professors in promoting improved rural school architecture. In 1907, the state legislature authorized the superintendent of public instruction to issue model school plans, albeit without granting any power to enforce their adoption. Adams and Alsup, a Chattanooga architectural firm, drew up the official *Plans and Specifications for Public School Buildings,* which featured some of their designs for Hamilton County schools.[44] The architects argued their case for combining architectural beauty with sanitation and economy in construction. Following then-current school architectural standards, they emphasized classroom lighting and ventilation, setting out formulae for the ratio of window glass to floor surfaces (1:4–6 square feet) and cubic feet of fresh air per pupil per minute (30–40 cubic feet) required in each room.

Adams and Alsup's illustrations of large schools designed for Hamilton and Montgomery counties depict elaborate, highly decorative structures. Plans of model buildings for one to four teachers, like the "Design No. 1 of a Model One-Room School," which served as the plan for the new Mouse Creek School photographed by Virginia Moore, were more likely to be used for country schools (fig. 1). They exhibit more restrained Bungalow and Classical Revival influences, reflecting American architects' longstanding assumption that a rural setting demanded simplicity in form and plain decoration.[45]

The Country Life movement's assumptions about rural character and the corruption of urban influences reinforced this premise, and Progressive aesthetic values of simplicity, rationality, and naturalness guided its expression. Thus, Fletcher B. Dresslar, a leading writer on school architecture, asserted that a plain country school building taught good taste to rural girls and boys, who otherwise, deluded by "gingerbread decorations," would seek the "glare and tinsel of city life."[46]

While not an architect, Dresslar apparently taught himself technical matters concerning school hygiene and construction. He led a small group of activists who were interested in extending the principles of urban school architecture to rural buildings. As a consultant to the U.S. Bureau of Education, Dresslar prepared the bulletin *American Schoolhouses* (1910), in which he summarized current thinking on the relationship between school archi-

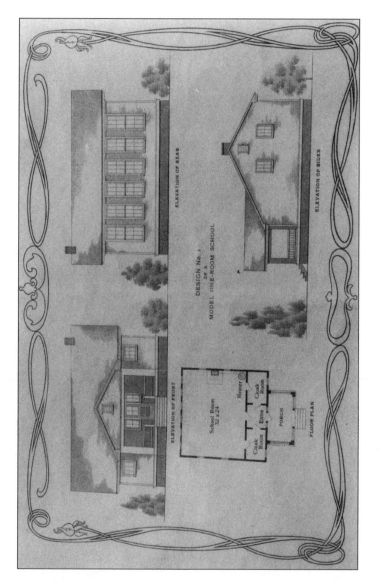

Fig. 1. One of the first model school plans issued by the Tennessee Department of Public Instruction, this design was used for the Mouse Creek School in Bradley County. Adams and Alsup, "Design No. 1 of a Model One-Room School," in *Plans and Specifications for Public School Buildings* (Nashville: Tennessee Department of Public Instruction, 1907), [14].

tecture and school improvement. "The problem, then, of building a school-house to-day," conceded Dresslar, "is in no small sense complicated by the growing tendency to use schoolhouses for all sorts of attempts at social betterment." He called for building design to be correlated with both educational and community needs. Using rural schools as an example, Dresslar invited architects, art leagues, and all "those who have better taste" to provide schools as proper aesthetic models for average citizens.[47]

Better school construction promoted health as much as taste. Dresslar constantly emphasized the relationship between building conditions and student health. Besides the standard warnings about drinking water and toilet facilities, he cautioned school officials about inadequate lighting, which hampered instruction and damaged students' eyesight. Single flooring drew his ire for allowing dirt and drafts into the classroom, inviting illness by making classrooms difficult to clean and chilling pupils' feet in winter. Double flooring would assure warm feet in winter, he argued, and adjustable windows would lower classroom temperatures and increase air circulation in summer. Dresslar's growing professional stature secured his early appointment to the faculty of George Peabody College for Teachers, where he supervised campus construction projects. His bulletin on *Rural Schoolhouses and Grounds,* which won him national recognition, appeared just as the college opened in 1914.[48]

The University of Tennessee already promoted better school architecture through the Summer School of the South. Its first course devoted to school architecture appeared in the 1909 catalog, and state superintendent Seymour Mynders taught the class in the 1910 and 1911 sessions. Courses in school sanitation supplanted architecture after 1913. At the 1913 session of the Summer School of the South, teachers resolved to implement building reform in their own schools:

> [W]e shall all go home to work for better school conditions in our respective states until it can no longer be charged that our faulty school lighting is ruining the eyes of one third of our children, that our faulty school desks are bringing spinal curvature, that unsanitary school conditions are blighting the futures of a host of children, and that the farmer's barn is more modern than his school. To that end be it resolved, that we shall each of us carry on in our neighborhoods a campaign for better school conditions in lighting, ventilation, sanitation, beautiful school grounds, artistic school interiors, and for medical inspection in both country and city.[49]

Public health reformers participated in school improvement campaigns as well. Their prescriptions for ventilation and lighting were mainstays of school architecture reform. The public health Progressives' obsession with sanitation, however, was the key to their influence with other reformers. Sanitary concerns prompted the use of individual drinking cups and protected water supplies, as in the Sumner County school cloakroom, rather than a communal open bucket and ladle. George Peabody College planned special courses for teachers on how to instruct their pupils about home sanitation, germ theory, bacteriology, and proper ventilation; they also would study how to incorporate health guidelines into school buildings and equipment.[50]

The campaign against hookworm, led by the Rockefeller Sanitary Commission (RSC), likely offered the best model for overlapping efforts in public health and school improvement. The RSC employed state sanitarians and field agents throughout the South. Because persons contracted hookworm by contact with fecal matter, primarily by walking barefoot in areas without toilet facilities, RSC officials aggressively promoted the construction of sanitary privies, emphasizing that a cleaner environment was a more effective cure than medicine. If adults would not listen, reformers used rural schools to reach as many children as possible. RSC officials lectured at teachers' institutes and harangued administrators on the need for sanitary privies, pure water supplies, and individual drinking cups.[51]

In Tennessee, where hookworm infection was detected in every county, the RSC established thirty-nine county dispensaries to diagnose and treat hookworm. Field agents issued broadsides, made stump speeches in rural villages, gave demonstrations on sanitary privies using scale models, lobbied county officials for matching funds to operate dispensaries, and promoted school sanitation.[52] State Sanitarian Dr. Olin West cooperated with state agricultural and educational departments. He reported that the health car on the 1911 Tennessee Agricultural Train, sponsored by the state's Department of Agriculture and by railroad corporations, exhibited "Floor Cleaners and 'Dustless Dusters,' . . . models of sanitary closets, . . . Pneumatic Cleaners, Individual Drinking Cups, Sputum Cups and Flasks, [and a] Fly Exhibit" promoting domestic hygiene.[53] Yet "there are no 'sanitary conditions'" in rural Tennessee, West complained. "They are all unsanitary, in the rural homes, schools, churches, industrial plants, etc." Although nothing came of his proposal, West even suggested that the State Board of Health seek joint control with the Board of Education over school buildings and grounds.[54]

All of these programs, however, omitted country schools for black Tennesseans. Increasing public support for rural schoolhouse improvement generally ignored the needs of black country schools. When change did occur, it followed the general pattern of white-supported black educational and self-help programs: promoting industrial education, making few demands on white citizens, and relying on the efforts of black families. The task of improving school buildings and grounds for African Americans fell largely to a small group of black educators, the Jeanes Foundation supervisors working in a number of Tennessee's rural counties, and their constituents. Established in 1907 and administered by the General Education Board, the Anna T. Jeanes Foundation supported the work of industrial supervising teachers in rural schools. All supervisors were black, and most were female. Some taught in one school, while others divided their time among a county's several black schools.

At first, Jeanes supervisors focused on training in simple manual and domestic skills such as basketry, but school improvement quickly joined industrial training as their primary task. Like the white school improvement associations, the Jeanes supervisors organized students and parents to repair and build new school buildings and enhance their interiors and grounds. Unlike the white organizations, they had no opportunity to mount local campaigns to pressure county governments for increased education funding. Tennessee's first Jeanes supervisors went to work in 1909 in four counties. By 1914, six supervisors were at work. One served in the largely black Shelby County in West Tennessee, and two operated in the East Tennessee counties of McMinn and Loudon, where black residents were not numerous. Two of Middle Tennessee's three supervisors worked in Davidson County, home to the state capital of Nashville, and the other worked in adjacent Williamson County.[55]

The Jeanes Fund's Director James Hardy Dillard also headed the John F. Slater Fund, which had been brought under the General Education Board umbrella by former Slater agent and GEB Executive Secretary Wallace Buttrick. The Slater Fund promoted secondary education for blacks in what came to be called county training schools. The curriculum of Slater-supported schools generally stressed vocational education, a central objective of the Slater Fund. Eligible schools received $750 for salary support to encourage construction of county training schools by lessening counties' initial financial outlay.[56]

Nevertheless, the construction of adequate public schools for blacks in Tennessee, as in the rest of the South, awaited the development of an experimental rural school building project at Tuskegee Institute, initiated by Julius Rosenwald and Booker T. Washington in 1912. Rosenwald had provided funds for school buildings for black students in rural Alabama, a pilot project that Rosenwald and Tuskegee opened to other southern states in 1914.[57]

Parents were as essential to black and white school improvement programs as teachers, school officials, and experts. From a practical standpoint, especially in black schools, parents had to be recruited simply to provide labor and materials for necessary repairs and improvements. Parents also played a central role in reformers' strategy of using the rural school to reach the rural home and, in particular, rural women. Philander Claxton, speaking in 1913 as the U.S. commissioner of education at the Conference on Education in the South, asserted that both traditional academic and vocational subjects belonged in rural schools. He declared, "The school and the home must be brought closer together, not alone by bringing the work of the home into the school, but also by carrying the school into the home. . . . The principles and lessons learned in school should find immediate application in the work of the home, shop, and field."[58]

Home economics offered the necessary vocational training for homemaking in the school. One of many Progressive efforts at environmental and social uplift, the national home economics movement prescribed rational, professional housework methods to achieve stricter standards of domestic hygiene, comfort, and convenience. Higher education in home economics in Tennessee began when President Dabney hired Anna Monroe Gilchrist, formerly of Teachers College, Columbia University, for the education department in 1903. Three years later, Professor Gilchrist and an instructor offered a degree course in the subject within the College of Liberal Arts. In their view, home economics constituted "a truly educational subject . . . equally balancing thought and activity," not merely a component of teacher education. Graduate courses began the following year.[59]

The university's Summer School of the South also provided home economics instruction in foods, sewing, and household management. Gilchrist brought in Ellen Richards, the nation's leading home economist and an instructor in sanitary chemistry at the Massachusetts Institute of Technology, for lectures in the 1904 and 1905 sessions. Catharine A. Mulligan, Gilchrist's successor, directed the preparation of *A Brief Course in Domestic Science for State Institutes of Tennessee* for the State Department of Public Instruction, no doubt based on her experience with the Summer School of the South.[60]

Progressive white women jumped on the home economics bandwagon. Lizzie Crozier French of Knoxville, president of the Tennessee Federation of Women's Clubs and a suffragist, counted home economics among her causes. Speaking before the Tennessee State Board of Health in 1912, French called for increased home economics education. Recognition of homemaking as a profession, she argued, would promote the housewife's efficiency in caring for her family's dietary, hygienic, and moral needs.[61] Others applied home economics principles to country life problems, especially the role of the farm wife in encouraging or discouraging migration to the city. Like other reformers, they relied on the public school as their agent of change. In an address to the Tennessee Home-Makers' Association in 1913, Mrs. James C. Bradford favorably quoted a Country Life Commission report to support her argument on the power of education to transform the home and the role of women in rural life. "In this day and generation the school goes hand in hand with the home," she added. "In our development they have a most reciprocal influence."[62]

Interior decorating skills taught in home economics courses would produce an aesthetically and emotionally satisfying, as well as efficient, rural home atmosphere. Bradford observed that the home environment was central to the individual because it formed taste and character, and to society because it held the answers to the pressing problems of the day, including the power to anchor farmers on the land. How could a woman create the home environment that would keep a farmer in the country? Rather than making special provisions for the rural home, Bradford offered broad, Progressive principles of decoration: sound construction, cleanliness, and simplicity, expressed through good proportions and decorative restraint. These would create the "comfort and restfulness" craved by the hard-working farm man and essential to social stability.[63]

Rural white women's organizations circulated these ideas among a broader audience of Tennesseans. In 1910 and 1911, Virginia Moore organized white homemakers' associations as female auxiliaries to the three regional farmers' institutes. Their meetings included addresses on homemaking by members and guest speakers, as well as cooking demonstrations. Campaigning for improved education and preparing the woman's building at the state fair were their major statewide activities. At the sectional and county levels, the associations offered both technical and social benefits. Ada Cooke Settle, who chaired the Woman's Board of the Tennessee State Fair, claimed that these organizations encouraged cooperation among isolated rural women and, by allowing men to attend their meetings, fostered cooperation between farm men and women.[64]

Discussions that stressed domestic values over techniques dominated the published proceedings of the homemakers' associations. "Through the exercise of kindness and intelligence women bring to the detailed routine of household labor the magic aid of home-love, and it is the knowledge of how to apply love and method for which the Home-Makers Sections of Tennessee stand," Settle declared. Even fruit preservation could be presented as an answer to country life problems. Mrs. W. S. Bomar of Shelbyville extended her discussion of proper canning syrups to schools: "Something must be done for the advancement of the rural school; then we, too, can have our daughters educated in many lines with the city girls. Their cakes will be just as artistic, their preserves and jellies just as attractive."[65]

Farm families did not, however, rush to embrace the well-intentioned plans of either the homemakers' associations or rural reformers. At the 1912 convention of the East Tennessee Home-Makers' Association, Lizzie B. (Mrs. James A.) Reagan, its founding president, complained that, "if only" farm women would come to the meetings, they could learn methods that would lighten their workloads and permit them to become better wives and citizens.[66]

Perhaps Reagan glimpsed a potential remedy for her complaint in Virginia Moore's address to the same audience. Moore spoke on "The Girls Industrial Club Work," a program she had based on the demonstration methods pioneered by Seaman A. Knapp, where people learned by doing rather than by passively absorbing information dispensed by a teacher. Knapp had observed that farmers, whether out of ignorance, tradition, or individualism, generally ignored or disparaged new practices advocated by agricultural colleges and experiment stations. Only when they saw the effects in a neighbor's field could they be persuaded to try a new method.

Knapp believed that those same techniques could work with rural women, especially those who expressed little interest in formal homemakers' organizations. In the canning and poultry clubs advocated by Knapp, "the direct object [was] to teach some one simple, straightforward lesson to the girls on the farm, which will open the way to their confidence and that of their mothers, and will at the same time open their eyes to the possibilities of adding to the family income through simple work in and about the home. The indirect object [was] that of attacking this home problem on the farm."[67]

Demonstration work for girls and women seemed an ideal method for ensuring that the home economics lessons taught in school actually reformed the rural home. The demonstration method and club work soon became the principal strategy of a "thorough and definite constructive reorganization of the rural school course of study upon the basis of rural life." "We cannot wait," urged one writer, "until those now in the schools will be the men and women of the homes. . . . The homes as they now are, with their conservative adult members as well as boys and girls, must be reached, and what is known about making more efficient homes must be made available to those who cannot or will not be helped directly through schools. This must be done for the direct benefit to the adults; and if not done for them, their influence on what the schools may do for their children may make it more difficult to secure effective results."[68]

Knapp's work gained the backing of the General Education Board (GEB), which hoped to secure farmers' support for education taxes by increasing their income. GEB county agents supplemented the federal government's efforts in southern cotton regions. In Tennessee, government-supported agricultural demonstration work began in 1909, GEB-funded work in 1913. Thomas A. Early began organizing boys' demonstration clubs in 1910.[69]

The GEB also sponsored demonstration work among girls and women, which Virginia Moore incorporated into her school improvement campaigns. Moore met Seaman Knapp at the 1909 Conference for Education in the South and attended the discussion that proposed tomato club work as the first female demonstration project. She helped Thomas Early organize Tennessee's first tomato club in Shelby County in the fall of 1910. Thanks to a cooperative agreement between the GEB and the Department of Agriculture, Moore combined canning-club work with her duties in school improvement until she became a full-time club agent in January 1912, following her appointment as state collaborator for the U.S. Department of Agriculture. She hired the first four female county agents (also called collaborators) in the summer of 1911, using funds channeled through the

Southern Education Board by the GEB. Soon she expanded club work to include sewing and poultry and developed lesson plans that correlated club work with classroom instruction.[70]

Virginia Moore claimed that those who saw the club girls' work "declare it is the *greatest work in America* and will do more for the rural people than any work that has yet been inaugurated." By 1913, 1,900 white girls in eighteen counties had enrolled in clubs and produced goods valued at $39,693.50. Tennessee's club girls gained national recognition, including the filming of a canning team at work at the 1913 National Corn Show. Myrtle Hardin of Benton County won so many prizes for the exhibits, booklets, drawings, and recipes she developed from her 1913 canning project that she appeared as a role model in Martha Foote Crow's 1915 book, *The American Country Girl.*[71]

Like the adult members of her Home-Makers Associations, Moore saw domestic technical training as a means to the broader ends of domestic and community uplift. All the official goals of girls' club work aimed at the home, whether by promoting cooperation among family members, providing the family with cheaper and better food, or using the home kitchen as a school laboratory. Country life reformers taught girls that homemaking was not drudgery but rather woman's highest calling, and attempted to show girls that homemaking could be handled as a rational, profitable business. Club work provided "means by which the girls may earn money at home and at the same time get the education and viewpoint necessary for the ideal farm home." It made "the home attractive, interesting, and helpful to the entire family and render[ed] less possible the dissatisfaction so characteristic of the farmers' wives and daughters." While not questioning whether farm homes offered the best future for country girls, Virginia Moore realized that income from club work offered girls alternatives. As they walked through a Putnam County tomato plot, a fourteen-year-old club girl "looked up with an expression I shall never forget," recalled Moore. "A girl don't have to marry if she can make some money herself," she said, indirectly referring to the local custom of marrying at sixteen or seventeen.[72]

In her writings, Virginia Moore recounted a number of such anecdotes to underscore her goals for demonstration work. She emphasized club teamwork to foster cooperation and community identity. When a girl from a wealthy home in the "bluegrass" area of Sumner County remarked favorably upon a club meeting at the home of a tenant family's daughter, for instance, Moore took it as proof that democratic values were promoted by club work. She gladly repeated a claim made by Jennie Moore, Unicoi County collaborator, that isolated mountaineers forgot their feuds while canning together.[73]

Moore's primary responsibility was to girls, yet, just as reformers had hoped, the girls led her to their mothers and homes. Her observations about country women were sympathetic but blunt: "Women were not in the habit of 'getting out'. They were of a resigned, hard working class, with a dull, hopeless look—feeling a pride in being 'porely' and feeling 'broken down.' They took it as part of their duty as a good wife, it seemed[,] to be dull, stay at home and raise a large family of puney, ill fed children." Canning work, Moore claimed, gave women "a larger realization of the home in its entirety. They also realize that the home is not four square walls, but that their influence is needed in the community, in the county, in the State, in the Nation. [They have] learned to have an open mind for men and progressive things."[74]

Moore was sensitive to the most ticklish problem facing middle-class reformers like herself: how to uplift without seeming to dictate or presume superiority. She demanded that her collaborators be women with "gumption" who could talk to country women and girls and understand their needs without pity or condescension. Her own work exemplified this approach, as she tactfully showed the women of a mountain family in Polk County how to make more digestible biscuits; she praised collaborators who could casually switch into a fly-trap demonstration when the insects got too thick around a woman's canning table.[75]

Virginia Moore was not alone in realizing that rural women, in addition to girls, must be served by an organized demonstration program. At the national level, home economists, Country Life advocates, and educational reformers battled to include home demonstration work in proposed federal legislation for a national extension service. Moore herself, at the request of Walter Hines Page, then editor of *The World's Work,* lobbied legislators and USDA officials in Washington on behalf of federal funding for home demonstration, an obvious complement to her work in rural homemakers' associations and canning work.[76]

The creation of the USDA Extension Service mandated by the Smith-Lever Act of 1914 marked a turning point in rural reform across the nation.[77] In Tennessee, the extension service and its canning clubs joined an array of reformist institutions to seek a revitalized and modernized rural environment to improve the quality of life for country people. With public schools as their selected points of entry, Tennessee reformers in 1914 sprang into action. The expansion of the state extension service, the hiring of state agents for rural white and black schools funded by the GEB, the opening of George Peabody College for Teachers and its Seaman A. Knapp School of Country Life, and the development of a regional program of black school construction by Julius Rosenwald promised a new era for rural Tennesseans.

• 2 •

Consolidation and New School Buildings: Reforms for White Rural Schools

Rural public schools built in Tennessee between 1914 and 1930 testify to the Progressive faith in the power of education and new school environments to transform and uplift country people. Reformers who addressed white public schools looked to consolidation as their basic strategy. Consolidation, in theory, would replace inefficient small community schools governed by district boards with large graded elementary and secondary schools administered by a county school board and a professionally certified superintendent. A consolidated school system, consequently, would be more amenable to state control and more open to Progressive programs in agriculture and home economics. Reformers assumed that, over time, school consolidation would inculcate in rural people a broader definition of community and a greater willingness to accept centralized authority. Rural Tennesseans recognized that these school initiatives offered both state interference and opportunity. The schools they built reveal how rural leaders and citizens chose to remodel community institutions.

Reformers understood that convincing country people to surrender their traditional local schools for a consolidated, professional educational system was not a simple task. But the Progressives offered a potent lure: financial incentives for the construction of new schools. State money made consolidation more palatable to rural people, while state-mandated designs would ensure that the new buildings served as laboratories for change. Rural educational activists believed that modern classrooms, auditoriums, laboratories, workshops, gardens, and playgrounds could mold the minds and behavior of rural children and adults. Specialized spaces within the new school environment were simple in design and decoration, orderly in arrangement, clean, and bright, not only to set proper aesthetic standards for students, but also to meet scientific health standards. The standardized appearance of the new schools also conveyed the unmistakable presence of a consolidated school system, where each school fit into a larger machine for modern education.

As consolidation proceeded and Progressive reforms matured, Progressives in Tennessee reevaluated their assumptions about the value of new school buildings. Progressive reformers initially combined idealistic moral and social goals with an abiding faith in the power of science. By the time of the Great Depression, scientific methods came to be seen as ends in themselves rather than as means to a broader social agenda. In Tennessee, this shift resulted in the creation of private and public agencies for professionals in school building—the Interstate School Building Service and the Tennessee Division of Schoolhouse Planning.

George B. Tindall has labeled this trend "business progressivism," the application to government and society of the principles of rationalization and scientific management associated with industrial production. Alliances between rural reformers shattered as they shifted their attention from improving rural life to raising the technical and interpersonal skills of country people.[1] Educators relinquished their role in social welfare for improved teaching methods and professional training of school administrators.[2] Rural reformers abandoned community revitalization for increased farm production and income; they turned to professional institutions and administrators as the best way to direct, manage, and perpetuate change. Walter Burr, in his 1929 study of rural towns, made the business progressive argument typical of the 1920s, contending that social movements were enthusiastic but spasmodic; only institutions could change society fundamentally.[3]

Reexamining southern progressivism, historians William A. Link and Jeanette Keith have argued that reformers turned to institutions and coercive measures because their structural reforms met with limited success and because country people rebuffed reform. In this scenario, Tennessee reformers' search for professional and bureaucratic power in the 1920s can be viewed as a strategic retreat. But as Joseph Kett has noted, the South's relative slowness in developing centralized bureaucratic institutions also preserved social progressivism in that decade.[4]

That same slow development of coercive state power allowed rural people flexibility in dealing with reformers and their programs. Typically, educational Progressives in Tennessee, whether federal, state, or foundation officials, followed their sponsors' lead in business progressivism, shifting from rebuilding communities toward professional administration. Reformers did so in part because they encountered country people who were as intransigent in 1930 as they had been a generation earlier. Yet they also identified allies among white rural Tennesseans, who, with the support of their fellow citizens and the state's persuasion, transformed the state's educational landscape.

Rural School Consolidation

In 1914, the General Education Board assumed responsibility for rural school projects from the Southern Education Board and the Peabody Education Fund. The Tennessee Department of Education now received GEB subsidies for two rural school agents, one for white and one for black schools. The rural school agents bore primary responsibility for elementary school programs and buildings. Two additional agents, also supported by the GEB, tackled high schools. The GEB financed the University of Tennessee's professor of secondary education as a high school campaigner and, after 1919, a state agent for secondary education. Because many high schools shared their buildings with elementary programs, secondary school agents also lobbied for new buildings, though they left the question of school architecture to the rural agents.

When Abraham Flexner announced the GEB program in 1914, he directed that rural school agents first address the conditions—"organization, taxation, length of school terms, salaries, training of teachers, etc."—for better rural schools.[5] S. H. Thompson, the state superintendent for public instruction, instructed white rural school agent John B. Brown to survey the state's rural schools with a view to future consolidations, and gave the agent "almost entirely" the authority to approve "plans for new buildings."[6]

Brown's first published report in 1915 set a precedent for urging consolidation of white schools as the principal tool for uplift in rural Tennessee. Brown charged that "unattractive, uncomfortable, unsanitary" rural schools, with outhouses "such as you might expect to find at a construction camp," produced "physical and mental cripples, and moral perverts." These malignant conditions were typical in the state's one-room schools; the best—perhaps the only—solution was consolidated schools in "more attractive, more comfortable and more sanitary" buildings.[7]

The consolidation process was under way. In dispensing tax dollars for consolidation, Tennessee's education department gave priority to counties in greatest financial need. Through its aid criteria, the state also promulgated new standard school plans. Each year the state's Department of Education distributed consolidation incentive funds to counties where new schools met minimum school acreage requirements and used approved building plans and construction techniques.

Brown quickly proclaimed consolidation a success. By 1916, he claimed, rural people had embraced "the spirit of the new education." They supported consolidation and construction of new schools: "New buildings and better buildings, attractive in design, convenient, commodious, properly lighted, heated and ventilated are being provided in even the most rural sections." State financial incentives, combined with local fundraising, prompted the construction of 123 consolidated schools in the 1915–16 school year. The new schools, according to Brown, reflected "a standard type of schoolhouse that will meet the requirements of modern school architecture." According to a 1916 state bulletin on rural school supervision, local officials interested in construction or consolidation could obtain plans and specifications from the Department of Public Instruction, including model one- and two-teacher school designs.[8]

The department's biennial report for 1915–16 featured photographs of new consolidated schools, juxtaposed with pictures of the buildings they replaced (fig. 2). In each case, sturdy brick structures had supplanted framed buildings in varying states of repair. Even the form of the buildings had changed. With only one exception, square-shaped, two-story schools with centrally located entrances replaced one-story rectangular buildings with entrances at the gable end.[9]

Many local educational leaders, however, remained unconvinced that consolidation and new schools met their community needs. Lewis County Superintendent John A. White reported in 1914 that his constituents militantly opposed consolidation: "When all the other counties get their schools consolidated and consolidation has been shown to be a modern necessity, when all the arguments against it have been 'shown up' as falsehoods, then look out for us. We will consolidate with a boom—but until that time comes, let us alone. You may have trouble insuring your houses if you don't."[10] Two years later, White admitted that consolidation remained controversial and had "met with stern opposition in this county."[11]

Nor did rural people immediately accept the aesthetics of the new schools. Citizens took pride in their small schools, constructing between one and three one-teacher frame schools annually as replacements for deteriorating structures. Superintendent White in Lewis County claimed in 1914 that "never in the history of the county have the children been so comfortably housed, or so well seated, as at present." Rural people apparently felt more comfortable in buildings that blended with the vernacular idiom of their built environment. "Few counties in the State have their one-teacher school buildings in better shape than we," the superintendent boasted in 1916. "[Y]et our people complain that the types advised by the Educational Department are not as good as the old styles."[12] Citizens did not see any correlation between a new school building and better education. A correspondent from the Topsy community expressed neighborly pride in the two one-teacher schools serving local children. Their excellent teachers had inspired an "educational energy, fit or spasm" that boded well for the future, if "our sons and daughters have the brains to rise above a common clodhopper."[13]

Judging from the scant surviving buildings and photographs, Lewis County's small rural schools had a distinct vernacular flavor. The 1922 Garrett School was a one-story wing and gable frame structure, similar to many country cottages of the late Victorian era. It exhibited some Progres-

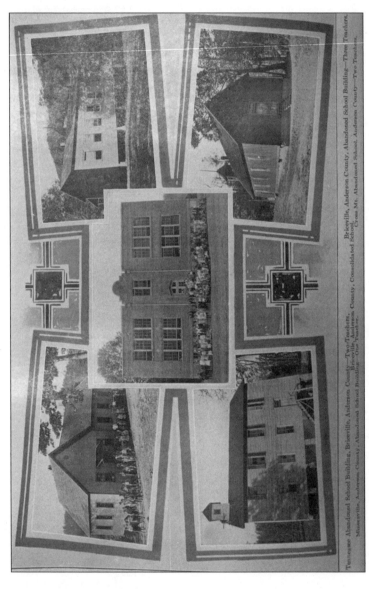

Fig. 2. In its 1915–16 biennial report, the Tennessee Department of Public Instruction contrasted Anderson County's consolidated school buildings with the deteriorated structures they replaced. *Biennial Report of the State Superintendent of Public Instruction of Tennessee for the Scholastic Years Ending June 30, 1915–1916* (Nashville: Baird-Ward Printing Company, 1916).

sive design principles in two banks of tilt windows hidden at the rear of the building. Three other earlier schools documented in 1935 followed a standard pattern of local design, not those found in any state-sponsored standardized design book. The Lawson (after 1923), Loveless, and Springer (1922) schools resembled rural churches, consisting of frame rectangles with two doors at one end and either three or four regularly spaced windows along their sides. County residents apparently preferred schools that corresponded to their own standards and values rather than those of outsiders.[14]

School finances suggest another reason for a county's reluctance to construct consolidated schools. As one of Tennessee's poorest counties, Lewis had little money to spare even for matching state funds.[15] Elementary school terms for white students fluctuated between six and nine months, depending on tax revenues for a particular year; at times only contributions from business leaders in the county seat of Hohenwald kept schools open for a full term. Even so, Lewis County spent 18.39 cents per student per day of the 1920 school year, one-half cent higher than the state average, ranking it seventeenth among Tennessee's ninety-five counties. In 1923, 34 percent of the county's property tax collections went to elementary schools; two years later, elementary and secondary schools received 70 cents of the $1.22 tax rate.[16]

At least one Lewis resident associated schools with high taxes. Tom Willis warned his neighbors, "Now listen tax payers, the schools will soon ruin the county just as fast as it can. We don't need this much school, we are getting it [the tax rate] too high now." That winter, Robert Fain, a county court candidate, denied the rumor that he would slash the high school's programs and reduce the school term to four months, yet he recommended that voters seeking lower taxes cast their ballots for him.[17] Despite the state argument that consolidation would save money, until the late 1920s local pride in one-teacher schools, along with reluctance to fund an expanded school system, made consolidation inconceivable in Lewis County.

In Greene County, in a much more prosperous East Tennessee farming region, citizens and school officials constructed an intriguing network of both consolidated and one-teacher schools. "The school spirit in this county is fine," proclaimed Joel N. Pierce, Greene County school superintendent in 1914. Greene had just increased its tax support for elementary schools and reinstated a high school tax levy. With a $25,000 bond issue and $65,000 in private contributions, the county had built nineteen new school buildings, each with two or more teachers. Pierce estimated that, if the county court would allocate another $50,000, he could raise a matching sum for school equipment.[18]

At the end of the 1913–14 school year, Greene had 113 white schools, 80 of them one-teacher facilities. Consolidation quickly reduced the number of one-teacher white schools to 54 by the end of the decade. In the 1920s, the number of white one-teacher schools hovered between 46 and 49.[19] School construction followed the same pattern of activity, with a rapid period of construction in the middle years of the century's second decade, and another burst of activity in the early 1920s. Greene County built between one and three white schools annually between the 1914–15 and 1929–30 scholastic years.[20] Over the same period, the number of consolidated schools fluctuated between 34 and 42.

Consolidated school construction transformed the educational landscape of Greene County. In 1927, for example, officials combined the Afton and Doak schools into Doak Consolidated School, the single school reported built that year. More elaborate in its design than any known state-approved plans for rural consolidated schools, Doak Consolidated was a two-story Classical Revival brick building, with a central pedimented block raised above and in front of the two sections of classrooms that stepped back from its sides (fig. 3). The Classical Revival style inspired the façade's arched doorway and windows and pilasters under the dentil molding and roundel of the pediment.

As an architectural statement representing a school as a classical temple of formal instruction, Doak Consolidated offered a striking contrast to the unadorned wing-and-gable vernacular style of the old Afton School, which was similar in form to a country cottage (fig. 4). Afton's distinguishing characteristics were its bell tower and double entrances, features common to rural churches and schools alike. This overlapping vernacular architectural vocabulary had unified homes, schools, and churches in the rural built environment. To farm families looking at Doak Consolidated School, the historical pretensions of pilasters and pediments, or the health concerns inspiring unilateral lighting, probably meant little. But they could have seen instantly that talk of new schools and revitalized rural life meant breaking with the past as they had known it.

Consolidated schools signaled reform in Greene County, but they were not the only school buildings constructed during this era. The school board deliberately created a network of schools that balanced consolidation against the needs of small communities, so that reform took place within the context of local tradition. Schools like Doak Consolidated joined more commonplace new buildings such as the Cedar Creek High School, with its frame structure built against the slope of a hillside, which the county converted from a church. Cedar Lane School, with its bell tower and shady porch, and the barnlike school at Newmansville, also preserved continuity with rural building traditions.[21]

Not only did Greene County combine such old-fashioned buildings with more up-to-date facilities within its school system, it also maintained a significant number of small schools concurrently with consolidated ones. Although, at forty-two, one-teacher buildings fell to their lowest level in 1929–30, they still amounted to over 40 percent of the county's white elementary

Fig. 3. One of Greene County's Progressive school buildings, the Doak Consolidated School (1927) introduced a classical temple into the rural landscape. Photograph 495, box 29, Tennessee Board of Education Records, Record Group 91, Tennessee State Archives, Nashville. Used courtesy of the Tennessee State Library and Archives.

Fig. 4. The Afton School was abandoned for Doak Consolidated School. Its bell tower and double entrances were traditional features of vernacular rural schools and churches. Photograph 498, box 29, Tennessee Board of Education Records, Record Group 91, Tennessee State Library and Archives, Nashville. Used courtesy of the Tennessee State Library and Archives.

schools; one- and two-teacher buildings accounted for 80 percent of white elementary schools.

Greene County's high schools blended with this network of elementary schools. Greene expanded its secondary school system from four first-class high schools and two second-class (three-year) high schools to between eight and ten schools in the early 1920s, and then to twelve or thirteen after 1926.[22] According to high school agent Joe Jennings, this program reflected a deliberate policy of making high schools more accessible. Combining elementary and secondary enrollments also made the county's construction program more cost-effective. In 1923–24, for example, only one high school had a brick building exclusively for its own use; other high schools shared facilities with elementary programs. Whether or not Greene's secondary programs enjoyed independent housing, their instructional quality failed to impress Jennings, who found their equipment and teachers "weak."[23]

Greene County thus instituted consolidation and expanded academic programs with careful attention to local identities. Its mixed system of Progressive-inspired consolidations and neighborhood schools were housed in a variety of buildings that accommodated traditional and modern sensibilities. Other agriculturally prosperous counties followed suit, rebuilding virtually all white school facilities between 1914 and 1930.

Shelby County, in the southwestern corner of Tennessee, also instituted innovative educational reform programs in the early twentieth century. Leadership for change, however, came from county officials rather than through state intervention. Shelby County was one of Tennessee's most urbanized counties in the early twentieth century, thanks to its county seat of Memphis. But surrounding the urban core was a large countryside, where wealthy white farm families supported one of the state's most comprehensive educational improvement programs.[24] Under the guidance of County Superintendent Charl Ormond Williams, Shelby quickly subscribed to the state consolidation program. In 1914, when Williams took over the superintendency from her sister, Mabel Williams Hughes, Shelby reported sixteen one-teacher and eleven two-teacher white elementary schools.[25] Fifteen years later, just three one-teacher and one two-teacher schools for whites remained, while the county transported over three thousand students to twenty-seven consolidated schools.

Shelby's new school buildings for whites reflected the county's prosperity and its commitment to education. The prominent Memphis architectural firm of Jones and Furbringer designed the buildings at Bolton College (an agricultural school), the Rosemark, Arlington, and Cordova high schools, and the Lucy and Capleville schools, all constructed before 1916.[26] The 1913 Cordova School exemplified the standard set for school architecture for whites in the county. The Classical Revival styling of its central block, with Corinthian pilasters flanking the entrance, provided a dignified anchor for the classroom wings, where only the battery windows and a stone string course embellished the front elevations.

Four other "Beautiful Shelby County Schools," Bartlett, Bolton, Ellendale, and Whitehaven, featured in the Memphis *Commercial Appeal* in 1926, demonstrated a continuing emphasis on classical brick structures like that at Cordova. Bartlett stood as a two-story brick block, with an adjoining one-story wing, probably a gymnasium. Ellendale and Whitehaven shared a common entrance design, with stone Classical Revival pediment and pilasters.[27]

John Stansell, Shelby County's agricultural agent, noted at the end of 1916 that "several" new schools had been built that year, each valued at between $30,000 and $85,000 and equipped with steam heat, electric lighting, and running water. Evidently these were consolidated schools, for the county transported some students to them in wagonettes. Later consolidated schools at Leewood, constructed in the 1919–20 scholastic year, and Collierville, built in 1921–22, at the modest costs of $6,000 and $6,250, respectively, inclusive of state aid, may not have enjoyed all of those amenities.[28]

The high school movement also appealed to Shelby County officials; Shelby had been one of the first two counties in the state to establish a high school in 1906. By 1915, Shelby County had fourteen secondary programs in operation, a situation that Professor Harry Clark found "unfortunate," because, he contended, the county had created too many inferior secondary programs crowded in with elementary grades. State officials like Clark fretted when counties embraced new educational initiatives too zealously. The problem could be corrected, Clark believed, by abandoning substandard programs and consolidating others.[29] Apparently the Shelby County school board and staff disagreed; fifteen years later, the county still operated three two-year and twelve four-year secondary programs.

Standardized School Plans

Consolidation progressed rapidly in Shelby and Greene counties and other prosperous Tennessee communities during the years between 1910 and 1929. Those counties not so wealthy, however, more closely resembled Lewis County, in that they slowly embraced and instituted consolidation and new school construction. The uneven pace of change across the state frustrated Tennessee's Progressive educators, even though their efforts had met with some success. For example, more counties were establishing high schools. In 1922, the *Tennessee Educational Bulletin* reported that over the previous decade, the number of high schools had risen from 111 to 533, the number of high school buildings had jumped from 74 to 499, and enrollment had almost quadrupled. But in reformers' eyes, too many of these new high schools existed with inadequate programs and inferior buildings. True enough, only 202 of the 500-plus high schools were four-year schools; 34 schools still housed both elementary and secondary programs.[30] Secondary school agents called for more consolidation and more new buildings.

A 1920 survey of Tennessee's rural schools by the Tennessee Child Welfare Commission also documented a reform record of success mixed with failure. While new schools were in operation, too many older buildings, and some of the new ones, had substandard siting, lighting, ventilation, heating, sanitation, and water supplies. Three years later, Commissioner of Education Perry L. Harned regretted that the need for new rural school buildings and equipment had "failed to impress itself on the minds of the people in rural sections." While counties issued bonds for new roads and courthouses, "they left the poor little uncomfortable, unsanitary school house as a marker of the lack of interest in the school home of their children."[31]

The condition of schools in Union County, in northeastern Tennessee, supported Harned's observations. Martin Leander Hardin surveyed the county's schools and found that 80 percent were one-room buildings, with one log school still in use. Two buildings came close to meeting modern standards, a five-classroom school that included secondary grades and a three-classroom consolidated school with an industrial room. Almost two-thirds of the schools lacked any toilet facilities; 80 percent drew their water supplies from nearby unprotected springs, and 57 percent served that water from an open bucket. Students sat at homemade desks in one-third of Union schools, their work poorly lit by the insufficient and improperly placed windows present in 95 percent of all classrooms. Hardin sadly concluded that Union County was not atypical of the region, but he remained confident that education could convince local people to change: "If people knew standards and demanded that their school buildings conform to them," Hardin remarked, "the right type of school plants would come into being without further effort."[32]

Officials at the state Department of Education shared Hardin's optimism. If they made modern building designs available free of charge and provided state financial incentives for their use in construction, officials believed, local communities would embrace both new standards for school architecture and the call for consolidation in elementary and secondary education.

Funding for school consolidation always was contingent on state approval of building plans. When Tennessee revised its consolidation program in 1919 and again in 1921, it strengthened requirements for school architecture. Counties could receive up to $1,250 for a building that replaced two or more existing public schools, if it adopted one of twelve "Community School Plans" designed in 1920 by Samuel L. Smith, the state agent for black rural schools. In addition, the school site had to be at least two acres and deeded to the county school board, and the building had to be painted and furnished, and pass a state inspection.[33]

Samuel Smith had prepared the "Community School Plans" in consultation with his mentor, noted rural school architecture reformer Fletcher B. Dresslar of George Peabody College for Teachers. Smith spent most of November 1919 working with Dresslar on plans for new schools and for remodeling existing buildings.[34] These plans probably exhibited Dresslar's fundamental concern for simple functional design, as well as his standards for orientation and fenestration. According to Dresslar and other school planners, buildings should be designed and sited properly to provide unilateral lighting. All light in the classroom must come from the left, preferably the east, through windows grouped in a "battery" to obtain the best natural lighting for the right-handed majority of students. To allow students' eyes to remain focused on their work, windows should be set no less than four feet from the floor and extend up to the ceiling (fig. 5).[35] Battery windows for unilateral lighting would mark all of Smith's designs for rural schools.

In 1922, the state's Department of Education asserted that "the best authorities on school house architecture have been consulted, and plans worked out combining the most modern ideas on lighting, ventilation, economical arrangement of space, sanitation, heating and attractiveness." The *Tennessee Educational Bulletin* described these buildings as similar to one-story bungalows, "made up of simple plain lines, but so arranged as to be attractive in appearance."[36]

Teachers adopted state standards in judging their own schools and planning improvements. In 1922, a committee of the state educational associa-

Fig. 5. This Rutherford County classroom exhibits the characteristic elements of Progressive school design. Sunlight streams in from battery windows on the left, lighting the blackboard and patent desks. The windows, with adjustable shades, rise from the wainscot to the ceiling, and the upper walls are painted a lighter color than the wainscot to keep the room light at students' eye level. Appropriately, this is a "Fourth Grade Studying Health Rules." Harry S. Mustard Photograph Album, Tennessee Historical Society Collection, Tennessee State Library and Archives. Used courtesy of the Tennessee Historical Society.

tion developed a scorecard for rating elementary schools that allocated sixty points to the school building, its grounds and outbuildings, and equipment. Criteria included closed foundations, unilateral lighting, adjustable shades, adjustable desks, pure water and equipment for drinking and washing, blackboards, and equipment for domestic science or manual training. "At least three good, well-framed pictures in each room" and "neatness and attractive arrangement" served both pedagogical and aesthetic purposes.[37]

Where local officials and residents wanted new schools, the designs of the state's Department of Education made modern school architecture affordable and spurred a dual process of standardization within the state educational bureaucracy and across the rural landscape. Obion County, in northwestern Tennessee, almost completely overhauled its school system and literally set a standard for other counties.[38]

In 1918, the creation of the Obion County Board of Education, which superseded district boards comprised altogether of 276 members, largely ended the prevailing practice of building one-room schools for rural white students. Centralized school administration paved the way for the first of two ambitious school consolidation and construction programs in 1920–21, conducted by Superintendent B. A. Vaughn. John W. Brister, the associate state high school inspector, participated in dedication ceremonies at three "splendid new consolidated schools" at Troy, Rives, and Obion in the fall of 1920.

Another consolidation, Community Pride School, opened in October for grades one through ten. Patrons from the former Beech, Old Republic, Maple Grove, and Houser Valley schools had donated money and labor toward the construction of the new school. Community Pride—a name to warm the hearts of rural and educational reformers—received its name from one of its patrons (fig. 6). Its design may represent one of the state-mandated "Community School Plans" devised by S. L. Smith in 1920. A one-story frame building in an "H" plan, the school stood on an enclosed brick foundation with brick steps and pillars on its incised central porch. A low dormer of five windows stretched across the bar of the "H."[39]

A second wave of consolidation in white schools swept over Obion County beginning in late 1924. In December, the three-teacher Obion School and five-teacher Troy School each received state consolidation grants, after an inspec-

Fig. 6. Community Pride School (1920), one of many schools for white children in Obion County, built according to standardized plans. Photograph 1165, box 36, Tennessee Board of Education Records, Record Group 91, Tennessee State Library and Archives, Nashville. Used courtesy of the Tennessee State Library and Archives.

tion by rural school agent Ollie H. Bernard. Bernard was the state agent for black rural schools, but Smith's legacy and his own zeal for school building reform meant that Bernard also assumed the duty of inspecting all state-supported school construction. Troy Consolidated was a long, narrow block with a central gable marking the entrance. Two batteries of double-sash windows, six in each group, punctuated its façade to either side of the door. A smaller central door afforded direct access into the right side classroom. Bracketing under the roof eaves and the overhang above the side entrance offered the only hint of decoration. The building was finished with stucco, for a final cost of $13,925.[40]

The smaller Bowers Consolidated—a blocky frame rectangle with a projecting porch gable at one end—was built for $5,000 (fig. 7). Clusters of double-sash windows marked the classrooms. Bernard's photographs of Bowers documented the subsidiary structures accompanying a consolidated school: a basketball goal, three small sheds behind the school (one of which clearly is an outhouse), and a ventilated well house. These outbuildings reinforced school lessons about the benefits of a sanitary environment.[41]

Obion officials, pleased with these schools, decided that consolidation deserved more systematic effort. A survey of Obion's schools, conducted in the summer of 1925 with Bernard's assistance, identified thirty white schools for consolidation and replacement by twenty-one new buildings. Bernard reported that he, the superintendent, and the Board of Education took special pains to determine "not only the logical but the geographical location" of each new school. He proudly noted that the county board of education acceded to his every recommendation, down to the design of individual buildings. A special bond issue for $185,000 partially financed the consolidation program, with the rest coming from local donations.[42] Twenty-one white schools, built within a five-month span, resulted in the abandonment of twenty-nine schools, sixteen of them one-teacher structures.

Bond proceeds also supported new buildings at existing schools. Bernard engineered this portion of the building program in response to local requests for additions to overcrowded schools. Using this approach, Bernard ensured that each building project resulted in a new school—"modern in every way and equipped with modern furniture"—rather than perpetuating older, less formal schoolhouse patterns by additions or renovations.[43]

Construction materials displayed the county's commitment to a centralized system of white rural schools. Durability and solidity distinguished the sixteen stucco and four brick veneer schools from the sole new frame building. Several took their design cues from the earlier Troy consolidated school, amplifying the anchoring effect of the central gable by projecting it several feet from the rest of the façade. Larger schools in this format assumed a "T" shape by placing classrooms along a rear wing, such as the brick Cloverdale Consolidated School (fig. 8). Alternative designs included the popular "H"

Fig. 7. Bowers Consolidated School, Obion County, was flanked by several outhouses, as well as a ventilated well shed and a basketball goal, reflecting the Progressive concern for health and hygiene. Photograph 1168, box 36, Tennessee Board of Education Records, Record Group 91, Tennessee State Library and Archives, Nashville. Used courtesy of the Tennessee State Library and Archives.

Fig. 8. Cloverdale Consolidated School, Obion County, illustrates the "T" plan, one of several forms suggested by Progressive designers for larger schools. Photograph 1174, box 36, Tennessee Board of Education Records, Record Group 91, Tennessee State Library and Archives, Nashville. Used courtesy of the Tennessee State Library and Archives.

plan with a small gable over a center door, used for the brick Woodland Mills High School, and the hipped-roof brick Obion Grammar School.[44]

"They are standard in workmanship and design, adequately and completely equipped and in every way measure up to the standards fixed by the state," remarked O. H. Bernard, who approved of their modern, standardized appearance. Bernard measured local compliance to "the standards fixed by the state" with terms such as "adequately" and "completely." In comparison, the schools abandoned by consolidation met few, if any, of these same modern standards of construction, lighting, and maintenance. For example, Crittendon Grove, a frame building standing on brick piers, probably had been a two-teacher school, judging from a repeated arrangement of window-door-window along its length. At least its bell tower identified it as a school, unlike the four intersecting gables that told nothing of the old Elbridge School's purpose.[45]

To Bernard and other reformers, one of the benefits of new consolidated schools was that their superior facilities and modern curriculum would attract, and retain, the interest of rural youngsters, especially secondary students. Obion County found this a mixed blessing, as successful consolidation and high school programs strained public school resources. In 1928, T. C. Callicott, a member of the county board of education, anxiously reported to State Superintendent Perry Harned: "In building our school houses in Obion County in 1925 we thought they would be large enough to take care of the children for years but we find in some localities that we will have to make some other arrangements. . . . In some cases the schools have grone so that we have made four year high schools of them so much that we need more room, have we the right to build on the grounds of these high schools rooms for grammar schools." Harned replied that the local board exercised full authority over rural elementary school construction funds from the state but left Obion officials to figure out how to deal with overcrowded secondary schools.[46]

Consolidation also exacerbated local conflicts, putting school officials on the hot seat. In January 1928, State Superintendent Harned received a letter from Obion County resident J. S. Glover, complaining that "our Rural Schools are getting in a desperate situation . . . our county children need some schooling." Even at new schools, Glover continued, teachers remained dissatisfied, due to the irregular schedule of the school calendar—stopping school for nine weeks during cotton-picking season—and inadequate funding. Glover explained, "There is people in every neighborhood that want to send their children to school and there are people in every neighborhood that do not want to. They know by cutting down the attendance they will stop the school and are doing that."[47]

Redirecting the letter to Obion's superintendent, Fowler, Harned acknowledged the demand for labor during the cotton season, but wondered "if you superintendents of cotton counties are making an effort to solve your problem." Fowler claimed that he was "studying" the cotton versus school problem. As for Glover's letter, he found that it had little merit and contended that it represented only the views of one disgruntled spouse. Mrs. C. C. Hill, wife of the teacher referred to in the letter, had written under her father's name.[48]

Yet, as Glover-Hill family members doubtless realized, Obion's consolidation and construction campaigns had not necessarily improved education. The county's school term had fallen from an average of 154 to 131 days (144 days for whites and 119 for blacks) between 1924 and 1928, well below state averages for both races, placing Obion ninetieth among the ninety-five counties on that standard. At the Elbridge-Cloverdale School, a three-teacher elementary and secondary school for whites, students in the 1920s began their school year after the summer cotton chopping in July, took a two-month break in the fall for cotton picking, and then went back to school for the rest of their eight-month term.[49]

Whatever its motivation, the Glover-Hill letter described genuine problems stemming from the disruption of cotton picking season and divisions between teachers and parents. This letter, and others sent by rural Tennesseans to the state's education officer, delineated the intertwining of personal and political issues in educational reforms at the local level. Rural residents complained of board members and superintendents who misused school funds, used schools for personal gain or as political pawns, favored one section of the county over another, or, in Glover-Hill's case, left teachers and schools at the mercy of the rural economy and local indifference.[50]

Recognizing that, by the later 1920s, many counties, like Obion, had reached the limit of local support and finances, the state increased its support for school construction programs. State Superintendent Harned and Gov. Henry Horton in 1927 convinced the legislature to appropriate a million dollars of tobacco tax receipts over the next five years for new rural school buildings. "This is the beginning of a building program, which, if carried on at the present rate will guarantee every community in the State, however remote it may be, an up-to-date comfortable adequate school home," promised the *Tennessee Educational Bulletin*.[51] Although the legislature's distribution plan favored wealthy counties, Harned hoped for the replacement of as many as seven hundred of the "worst" schools housing white and black students.

Once again, state aid hinged on higher building standards. To guarantee that the new schools would be "up-to-date," the Department of Education required that counties use its 1928 bulletin, *Building Plans for Rural School Houses,* which contained fifteen new building plans by Memphis architect George Mahan, Jr., or the 1927 edition of the Julius Rosenwald Fund's plans for rural black schools. Repairs to existing structures could be funded as well, but, as Harned and building agent Ollie H. Bernard warned county officials, "no money should be used to repair old, poorly lighted, inadequate or practically worthless houses."[52]

Mahan's elevations depicted brick and frame structures incorporating standard provisions for unilateral lighting and industrial rooms. He generally utilized rectangular, U- and H-shaped floor plans (figs. 9 and 10). In keeping with contemporary taste, Mahan embellished most of his structures with Colonial Revival details, such as broken pediments, trellises, arched "Palladian" windows, and columns.[53] A few carried the heavy bracketing common on Craftsman bungalows or used vertical clapboards in gables to create the feeling of traditional board-and-batten construction. Inside, each building had provisions for heating by stoves or a furnace, and blackboards. Either wooden or plaster walls and ceilings were permitted, and wainscoting was encouraged. Interior finishes were golden oak stained and varnished wood trim, with Sherwin-Williams Flat Tone Old Ivory paint on the walls and Flat Tone Ivory on the ceiling.

Mahan also provided a design for a school privy (a fairly decorative clapboarded and bracketed structure), a landscape plan for an outdoor water fountain, and two plot plans suggesting how the school should be sited on its property and landscaped. His site plans located the school in one corner of a two-acre rectangle, with a baseball field and tennis court occupying most of the remaining area. The elaborate nature of Mahan's designs suggests that these plans were intended for white schools; the incorporation of such elements as tennis courts suggests Mahan's limited experience in rural communities.[54]

The rural school construction initiative clearly encouraged building in the 1927–28 and 1928–29 scholastic years, after which time the legislature discontinued the program. While the number of city schools built in those years totaled 44, 1927–28 witnessed the construction of 176 rural schools, and 1928–29 set a record of 274 new country schools.[55]

Increased building funds also encouraged the spread of standardized school architecture that had already taken root in counties like Obion. In Rutherford County, home of one of the three state normal schools preparing white teachers, schools had been intolerable by Progressive standards in 1915, when state rural school agent John B. Brown visited all but 4 of the county's 118 schools. "The full story cannot be told," he had declared. "I have never seen such an exhibition, taking the system as a whole, of poverty in school grounds, building and equipment in my life." With disgust, he reported that "the lack of regard for cleanliness, to say nothing of beauty and attractiveness, is astounding, and the almost total disregard for decency with respect to toilet facilities for boys and girls in the majority of schools, is positively criminal. The forests afford their only places of retreat in at least 50% of cases."[56] School officials and taxpayers gave little attention to Brown's report. County Superintendent J. D. Jacobs reported to the state that the county's Board of Education refused to earmark school tax revenues for

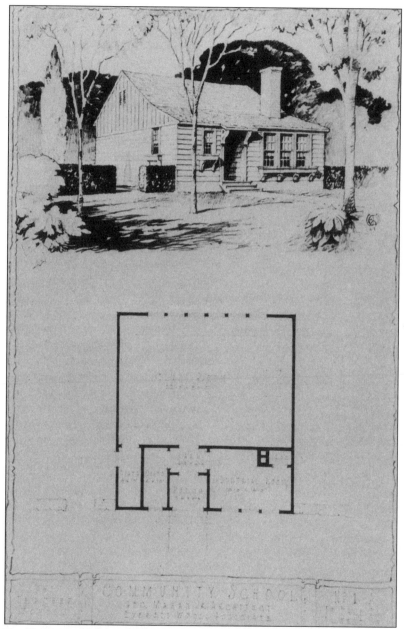

Fig. 9. George Mahan's designs for the Tennessee Department of Education used bracketing and clapboarding, evoking the Craftsman style that remained popular in 1920s bungalow homes. "One-Teacher School—To Face East or West Only, No. 1-A," in *Rural School Building Plans* (Nashville: Department of Education, 1928), 10. Used courtesy of the Tennessee State Library and Archives.

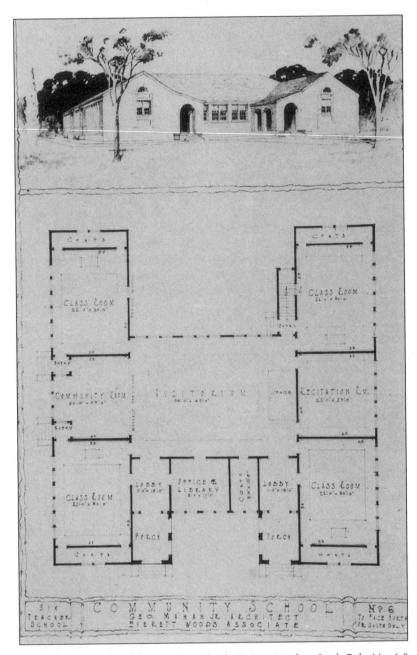

Fig. 10. George Mahan's "Six-Teacher School—To Face North or South Only, No. 6," embodied another style popular in the 1920s, the Colonial Revival. *Rural School Building Plans* (Nashville: Department of Education, 1928), 24. Used courtesy of the Tennessee State Library and Archives.

construction or maintenance, "leaving this to the community."[57] A decade later, William F. Walker, associate field director of the American Public Health Association, found that "child training is made subsidiary to cotton training." "It is surprising to see the low esteem in which school property is generally held," he marveled.[58]

Rutherford high schools, too, were substandard. In 1924, secondary education agent Joe Jennings found only one of Rutherford County's two-year schools worthy of state recognition as a high school. He considered the others "very badly organized from a high school standpoint," exhibiting such faults as a teacher who conducted seventeen classes.[59] Residents of Lascassas and Eagleville begged to differ, each community claiming that its high school was second to none in the county in the quality of instruction, building, and equipment. Yet neither Lascassas's frame high school, with its bell tower and gingerbread decoration, or Eagleville's 1915 concrete and stucco building, with a central bell tower and spaced window arrangement, met modern Progressive standards. Reformers would have approved of the new brick H-plan Eagleville High School, constructed after the older school burned in 1923. It followed one of the state-approved designs for consolidated schools distributed by the Rosenwald Fund.[60]

From 1925 to 1929, however, Rutherford County experienced a period of prosperity, with the establishment of a thriving dairy industry and the opening of better access to new markets on the recently completed Dixie Highway and the Memphis-to-Bristol Highway. Renewed promises of state assistance and the prospect of standardization helped to spur a limited building campaign.[61] Walter Hill's "nice modern" new brick consolidated school and the similar six-teacher frame Buchanan Consolidated School, both constructed in 1925, impressed state agent O. H. Bernard as the best of their respective types in the county.[62] Additional state funding resulted in the construction of nearly identical schools in nine communities. Influenced by the H-plan building constructed at Eagleville in 1923, the different schools shared many design qualities. A long horizontal front section, adorned by a columned porch with a simple pediment over the central doorway, housed the auditorium, school office, and library. Two rows of short windows squeezed between the roof edge and porch roof augmented the indirect lighting provided by windows under the porch. Two banks of classrooms flanked the central block.[63]

Treatment of the wings depended on the siting. In approved modern fashion, successive batteries of windows lit each classroom from the side. The front gable ends of those wings facing north-south featured decorative brickwork laid in herringbone or log-cabin patterns, while gables facing east-west inserted additional batteries of windows in their fronts. Other modifications, such as frame construction and the use of architectural details, depended on cost as much as the desire for variety.

Even Lewis County, reeling from financial losses incurred by official misman-
agement of county school funds, finally broke with vernacular tradition under
the influence of state largesse.[64] After years of local debate and inaction over
proposals for a new high school, during which secondary enrollment rose from
51 to 170 students, citizens voted overwhelmingly for a $50,000 high school
bond issue in July 1927. Their inspiration was a $75,000 windfall from the state
government, a reimbursement of local taxes used for state road construction.
Even so, the county took this step with a tight grip on its pocketbook.
Hohenwald's grammar and high school and the county courthouse exchanged
sites, county offices going into the remodeled school. With the $50,000 bonds
and a previously owned site, Lewis County in 1928 built a new brick school,
the Meriwether Lewis School, in Hohenwald. Its contemporary Colonial Revival styling broke with the preferred "old styles" that Superintendent White
had described in 1916. A two-story rectangular block, Meriwether Lewis School
balanced three banks of windows on either side of a central pediment highlighted
by a two-story colonnaded portico (fig. 11).[65]

Shortly after the vote for high school bonds, the county court in the fall
of 1927 approved an additional $1,100 for building and repair of schools
and then, in January 1928, brought its tax levy up to the requirements of
the new state rural elementary school building fund. The increased levy
qualified the county for matching state aid, although, because of its small

Fig. 11. Frugal Lewis County built the Colonial Revival–style Meriwether Lewis School in 1928
with an extraordinary windfall from the state. Photograph 905, box 36, Tennessee Board of
Education Records, Record Group 91, Tennessee State Library and Archives, Nashville. Used
courtesy of the Tennessee State Library and Archives.

population, Lewis County received only $6,825, far less than the official minimum state grant of $10,000. Presumably these monies supported the construction of three frame schools built in 1929.[66] Lewis County had stuck with familiar school buildings and held the line on school construction costs until unusual financial opportunities virtually guaranteed overall savings in return for its investment.

Where rural Tennesseans found the modern state-approved designs either aesthetically or financially compelling, hundreds of Progressive-inspired country school buildings by the late 1920s announced their willingness to change the countryside. With the need for new rural white schools apparently addressed, foundation and state government officials turned to new aspects of the reform agenda. In 1927, the General Education Board ended its financial support for the state agent for rural white schools. The following year, the state terminated the rural school building program, in part because of its success and in part because of abuses at the local level, including the use of rural building funds for past construction debts. But these funding decisions did not summarily end the Progressive effort to improve rural white schools. Instead, reformers believed that it was time to consolidate their gains by creating new institutions for building modern rural schools.[67]

Professional School Building Improvement

To continue the mission of designing and building modern school environments, rural reformers and Progressive architects established institutions to train the next generation of experts. The first was at George Peabody College for Teachers, which in 1927 introduced a degree program in school building service. The degree curriculum grew from the original school hygiene and building courses of Fletcher B. Dresslar.[68]

Dresslar's graduate students were his greatest contribution to southern school buildings. These men—he apparently trained no women—eventually dominated state school building divisions across the South. William F. Credle summarized his teacher's credo in his final term paper:

> It is important that we know that our schoolhouses are hygienically correct, that they are so orientated and the windows so arranged that glaring lights do not disturb the children at study, but that healthful sunlight can come in, that the walls are painted with the proper tints of cream or yellow, symbolic of cheerfulness, at the same time having the proper co-efficient of light reflection, rather than with colors that excite and tire the nerves. . . . Are the seats comfortable? Is the room heated properly? Is it well ventilated? Does the teacher know? Does she realize that the behavior, even the future lives of the children, is to be largely determined by these things?[69]

At George Peabody College for Teachers, school architecture and hygiene endured as independent courses, perhaps because of the presence of Dresslar and his close ties with the specialists he had trained.

Compared to Peabody, the University of Tennessee proved to be a limited source of school planners. Instruction in school hygiene began with the 1916 session of the Summer School of the South. The 1917–18 academic year added a class entitled "School Hygiene and Management," offered by education professor John A. Thackston.[70] By 1922, Thackston's "School and Mental Hygiene" course emphasized detection, measurement, and correction of students' medical or mental problems, although environmental factors were considered.[71]

In 1927, the UT Department of Hygiene introduced its own course on "School Health and Hygiene." Addressing the needs of students preparing to teach in rural schools, the class covered the school building and grounds, the hygiene of the rural home and community, and health education. Retitled "School Health Education" in 1929, the course reduced its scope to testing and corrective measures, bringing it closer to the education department's psychological approach. From this point on, school architecture was divided up among the disciplines, if it survived at all.[72]

The most important legacy of the school building initiative of the early twentieth century, besides the buildings themselves, was the creation of an agency devoted to school architecture reform, the Interstate School Building Service (ISBS). The impetus for the ISBS came from state agents for schoolhouse construction, many of whom had been trained by Fletcher Dresslar. Many, too, were subsidized by the General Education Board or were involved with the Julius Rosenwald Fund's school building program for black southerners. At the 1928 meeting of the National Council on School Construction, the seven southern agents present initiated a school building service, electing Dresslar, Samuel Smith, and Haskell Pruett of Oklahoma as an executive committee to find a sponsor.[73]

Smith first approached the GEB about extending its subsidies for schoolhouse construction agents to their professional organization. After the GEB declined, Smith turned to the Julius Rosenwald Fund, describing the project to Rosenwald Fund officers as a natural extension of their work: "As I see it, we would simpl[y] be assisting in greatly enlarging the service which we have been doing for almost 9 years, reaching a much larger group and tying up with the building program for Negro schools, this new group, which might otherwise feel it their principal duty to look after building white schools." The Rosenwald Fund appropriated five thousand dollars to establish the ISBS at George Peabody College for Teachers, under the aegis of Fletcher B. Dresslar. ISBS funding supported an annual fellowship for a state supervisor to attend Peabody for further study under Dresslar, while also handling the routine office work of gathering and circulating school plans.[74]

The ISBS was a private organization supported by private funds, yet most of its members were public officials with state departments of education. Members discussed school architecture at annual meetings and published and distributed school plans from a variety of state and private architects.[75] The importance of the ISBS lies not in the quality of the plans thus disseminated, nor its endless debates over wall laths and privy construction, but in the nature of the organization itself. The ISBS embodied the reform trend toward using scientific approaches to social problems.[76] It reflected the spirit of the times, centralizing the architectural work of the southern education departments and outside philanthropies into an agency that prevented duplication of effort and promoted ever higher standards of construction. The ISBS appealed to 1920s business progressivism by institutionalizing reform. Designs that once had seemed at the vanguard of rural school reform, including those which the Rosenwald Fund promoted for all-black schools, now became minimum standards for an entire profession.

External and internal reform movements also intersected in the creation of a state division of schoolhouse planning. Following the national trend toward using professional architects and school building experts, and the example set by Fletcher Dresslar at George Peabody College and S. L. Smith's Community School Plans, Tennessee Department of Education leaders began agitating for their own architectural staff as early as 1924. "Through the benevolence of the Julius Rosenwald Fund the Department has been able to supply general plans for a number of types of school buildings, but," they charged, "that is not sufficient." With a state-operated building service, Tennessee taxpayers could look forward to "standard regulation buildings" at great savings in architects' fees.[77]

In the fall of 1928, the GEB agreed to finance a school architecture service for Tennessee. Although the state's 1928 *Building Plans for Rural School Houses* had listed O. H. Bernard as the state's building agent, he combined construction inspection with his duties as black rural school agent until the new year. Bernard then became supervisor of rural schoolhouses, a new position directing the Division of Schoolhouse Planning. GEB appropriations continued for the next four and one-half years, in the expectation that, by the end of the period, "there will not be a single inadequate or dilapidated school house in any community of the state."[78]

After Bernard's death in 1929, J. B. Calhoun headed the division, working with draftsman J. C. Russell. They advised and inspected all schools constructed with state funds and designed new rural schools for black and white Tennesseans. Division of Schoolhouse Planning drawings published in 1932 depict simple school buildings. Like those designed earlier by Mahan, these buildings evoke domestic cottages with elaborate Colonial Revival styling.[79]

The creation of the state's Division of Schoolhouse Planning marked a distinct achievement for Tennessee's educational reformers and their philanthropic patrons in the GEB. Joint financing of rural school agents and building agents encouraged states like Tennessee to incorporate school improvement work into the education bureaucracy. The ISBS, as a private organization, and the Division of Schoolhouse Planning, as a public agency, took the final steps toward professional, state-administered control over school buildings.

Over a decade and a half of reform initiatives sponsored by outside philanthropists, together with activists in Tennessee's Department of Education and institutions of higher learning, had placed money and staff resources in the hands of those eager for a reconstruction of rural southern life. Yet, for all their early local crusades and campaigns, and for all the new schools, the final results of most programs affected their administrators as much as rural people. Reformers had created new bureaucratic structures and professional specialties that urged consolidation and standardized school construction upon rural Tennesseans. White citizens and taxpayers who ran the schools at the local level gave these proposals a mixed reaction, being fully aware of the potential and the pitfalls as they accepted the carrot of state tax dollars only to place themselves under the stick of state building regulations. Country people did not automatically correlate better education with consolidation and standardization; they used those programs as tools for advancement when local leadership could count on community resources and acceptance of change.

With the same optimism that inspired their work with white schools, the state's education officials and their northern supporters assumed that their bureaucracies would benefit both races by prescribing standardized curricula and building plans that introduced the same educational and social values to all students.[80] Nevertheless, state officials and African American Tennesseans would forge separate paths toward a better rural life.

• 3 •

"Building an Ideal": Model Schools for African Americans

Progressive reform in rural schools for African Americans confronted special problems. The law and ingrained racism were the most serious impediments to change. Tennessee law required that black children attend separate schools. These schools were supposedly separate from, but equal to, white schools. As child welfare advocate Gertrude Folks noted, however, "No one even pretends that the latter part of this requirement is observed." Indeed, in the early twentieth century, Tennessee's rural schools for African American children amply demonstrated how legal segregation and racism created what Louis R. Harlan has termed a "separate and unequal" system of public education.[1]

Within this context of tremendous racial prejudice and Jim Crow segregation, reformers approached reform in rural black communities with care. Southern Progressives identified the poor educational attainment of African Americans as a major impediment to their region's development, but they realized that prevailing white racism could block reform initiatives for black schools. Bowing to external racist pressure and reflecting their own paternalistic racism, participants in the Conferences for Education in the South had quickly deflected their reform agenda from black to white schools. As these Progressives continued their work in the Southern Education Board, they revived the issue of black education but couched their arguments for improved black education in terms of the benefits whites would reap from a black labor force that had better skills and was more contented, rather than emphasizing equal rights or justice.

More aggressive school reform campaigns in the years between 1910 and 1930 also stayed within the South's racial boundaries. The General Education Board, Anna T. Jeanes Foundation, and John F. Slater Fund subsidized state personnel and educational facilities for blacks within the confines of an industrial curriculum, reflecting their assumptions that African American males were suited only for the field or factory and that black females were suited largely for work in the field or as domestic servants. Nevertheless, elements of the reform agenda nudged whites ever so slightly toward equal, if separate, public education. The most important step was the school building program of the Julius Rosenwald Fund, which dared to suggest that black schools might become models for white schools to emulate. Philanthropies like the Rosenwald Fund forged partnerships with state governments by subsidizing the standard Progressive instruments of reform: new curricula ostensibly more suited to (African American) country life, standardized school architecture, financial incentives to county school boards, and official supervision.

In Tennessee, two individuals dominated these reform efforts for better black education: Samuel L. Smith and Robert E. Clay. Smith's blend of curricular and architectural reform guided his labors as the state agent for black rural schools and then as director of the Julius Rosenwald Fund's rural school building program. He placed school architecture at the center of Progressive education for rural black southerners; thanks to his labors, rural black schools became models for southern school architecture in the 1920s.

Robert Clay delivered the Progressive educational gospel to rural Tennessee. As the state's Rosenwald building agent, he was the only African American acting in an official capacity for the state department of education. Clay coordinated grassroots crusades for new school buildings aided by the Rosenwald Fund, mediating between black citizens and the white leaders who controlled local and state governments.

Both men's work rested on the shoulders of rural African Americans, who welcomed official gestures of support for black education as an alternative that, however limited, was better than neglect. For black Tennesseans, additional labor and money for school construction, and the loss of local control over consolidated schools, would not block reform. They embraced the Progressive rural school movement as a new opportunity for building community institutions that affirmed their right to a place in the countryside. As Samuel Smith phrased it, these Tennesseans were "building an ideal."[2] Inspired by visions of comprehensive social and economic change through education, they achieved only partial victories against the caste system in public education. Yet their dreams and achievements outlived both the exuberance of early Progressive reformers and the rationalization of reform under business progressivism.

Partnerships for Black Rural Schools:
The General Education Board Philanthropies

Tennessee's dual system of education mandated that the state use General Education Board funds to hire separate officials for black and white rural schools. Samuel L. Smith, former superintendent of schools for Montgomery County, accepted the position of state agent for black rural schools. Unlike the white school agent, who emphasized consolidation, Smith identified vocational education and the construction of model educational facilities as his priorities. When nominated for the position, he announced that an exhibit of industrial and agricultural work by black school children would be his "first effort" at recruiting white support for better black schools.[3]

To fund industrial education for African Americans, Samuel Smith pursued contributions from the General Education Board and both of its subsidiary philanthropies, the John F. Slater Fund and the Anna T. Jeanes Foundation. Smith directed the industrial education supervisors sponsored by the Jeanes Foundation. These supervisors, fourteen of whom were at work in Tennessee's black rural schools in 1915, guided the industrial curriculum in a county's black public schools, sometimes teaching the classes themselves, and organized school improvement campaigns among African Americans. By 1920, twenty-four Jeanes supervisors were "helping to make better schools and better homes."[4]

To Smith, the curriculum and the building were inseparable elements of a broader program of social reform that would strengthen community bonds among black Tennesseans and also between rural whites and blacks. Consolidation campaigns promoted by John B. Brown, state agent for white rural schools, offered state aid for both black and white school construction. Smith took this initiative one step further by leading the Department of Education's drive for standardized school plans.

Samuel Smith's approach reflected his training under Fletcher B. Dresslar at George Peabody College for Teachers and his personal interest in reforming education for black southerners. He injected his mentor's precepts concerning rural school architecture into projects for rural African Americans, believing that industrial education taught in properly constructed schools offered the best avenue for racial advancement. School buildings would dominate Smith's work during his six years as state agent for black rural schools.

In 1915, Smith helped select a site in Soddy, in Hamilton County, for an African American school. Completed that fall, the Soddy School exemplified Smith's educational goals in its three classrooms, an office, an auditorium, separate rooms for manual training and home economics, and a basement housing a furnace. Not only did the school provide space for boys' and girls' vocational instruction, but the principal was, in Smith's words, "as good an agriculturalist as can be found in Hamilton County." Smith described this as the prettiest, most modern rural school for either race in the state. It may have been the "colored school on the mountain side of Hamilton County" photographed for the General Education Board that year. This was a rectangular stucco building, the stucco rendered in three horizontal varicolored bands enclosing the batteries of five windows on the front and side. Its smooth façades, flat roof, and unilateral lighting added a taste of modern design to the mountain landscape.[5]

Another financial resource for Smith's programs was the John F. Slater Fund, which provided building costs for new construction and, after 1920, salary support for teachers in African American schools. In 1915, Smith inaugurated the Slater Fund's construction program for county training schools in Tennessee. Training schools offered at least eight grades and, as soon as possible, two years of secondary education, heavily slanted toward vocational subjects. These institutions chiefly trained teachers for rural black elementary schools—the very teachers who would become the Jeanes supervisors of the future.[6]

The Slater Fund intended its training school buildings to serve as model educational facilities, and they were equipped for classes in agriculture, manual training, and home economics. Provisions for "elementary pedagogy" also were required for their mission of preparing African American rural teachers, who would "inspire [students] to love the country and to remain on the farm."[7]

The Shelby County Training School at Woodstock certainly met these objectives when it opened in 1915. Built at a cost of four thousand dollars, this six-room frame building with gable end entrance replaced a "one-room dilapidated frame building" which had housed only one teacher, an assistant, and 150 students. The new school held seven teachers and over three hundred students.[8] Although the school stood on an enclosed, ventilated foundation and had guttering along the porch roof, the window spacing and churchlike bell tower would not have been condoned by Dresslar or Smith in their later work for the Julius Rosenwald Fund.

Shelby African Americans had raised the school construction funds, then contributed an additional $500 for the purchase of additional acreage for agricultural work and another $351 for industrial equipment. Led by Principal T. J. Johnson, male students built shops, a poultry house, and a playground. Mrs. Johnson presided over a "sensibly equipped," "sanitary" domestic science room, its furniture also constructed by male students. A grant from the General Education Board purchased books and maps, lumber for shop construction, and materials for vocational subjects that included carpentry, shoe- and harness-making, tin work, painting, and glazing for the boys; and laundry, sewing, and cooking for the girls.[9]

By the fall of 1917, the Johnsons were living in a cottage constructed by their black neighbors and male students with materials purchased by the county, and a dormitory had been built to attract pupils from outlying areas. Female teachers offered cooking classes at night for local mothers, while teaching their daughters canning during the day.[10] Johnson dubbed the training school "a big home." As he described it, the school served as a working model for a rural farm and home, including its division of labor between the sexes:

> Her [the school/home's] activities are the same as any other rural home. We have our teachers' cottage, farm, barn, cows, mules, garden, poultry house and chickens, and farm implements, including a sorghum mill. Thus we have an opportunity to put into effect the many things taught in the class room. The cottage is kept by the girls, they even use their own ideas in the arrangement of the furniture. They also have charge of the poultry and dairy. The farm is kept by the boys. They grow all the peas, beans, potatoes, corn, sorghum, and vegetables that the Boarding Department uses. They also care for the barn and live stock.[11]

Visiting officials praised Johnson's plan of industrial education, their comments revealing what white reformers considered to be appropriate black attitudes. When secondary supervisor Harry Clark and county superintendent Charl Ormond Williams arrived at the Woodstock School in October 1915, they found it "faultlessly clean" but closed for cotton picking. Clark considered this "an unavoidable condition with the poverty of the negro students." Williams, "deeply touched" by Principal Johnson's "earnestness," promised to raise money for a teachers' home from affluent African Americans in Memphis. Clark, too, was "touched" by "begging letters" to northern philanthropists being written as English class assignments, and by rural blacks' "affectionate attitude" toward Samuel L. Smith.[12]

Jackson Davis, the General Education Board's southern agent, inspected the school three months later, accompanied by Charl Williams and Samuel Smith. He found "a fine spirit on the part of all teachers and students." The visitors enjoyed watching girls make shuck mats and hearing students sing "old plantation melodies." Jackson's notes of his conversations with Johnson and Williams also reveal the white visitors' assumptions about black education and its purposes: "The Farmers' and Teachers' Convention met Oct. 28, 1915, bringing about 3,000 people to the school. It was quite an achievement in this community to get together such a large number of Negroes together without any semblance of disorder. Mr. Johnson wishes to return to Hampton this summer to learn mattress-making and to study poultry. He says he can help the people have more comfortable beds in their homes if he can learn mattress-making and teach it in his school." As for county superintendent Charl Williams, Jackson found her "intensely interested in the colored schools" and favorably reported that she had sent sixty-five of her black teachers to summer institutes, where "all of these took Industrial work."[13] Like Harry Clark, Jackson approved when local officials and teachers identified black education with industrial training.

Further support from the Slater Fund fostered the development of a small statewide system of black public high schools. County training schools receiving Slater Fund aid increased from three in 1915 to twenty-two in 1929.[14] As an ancillary goal, the Slater Fund urged the development of training schools into four-year accredited public high schools. By 1930, Tennessee had twelve state-approved two-year high schools and eighteen state-approved four-year high schools for black students.[15]

These programs for industrial education and secondary education benefited a minority of African American communities. In general, white-controlled county school boards generally ignored or minimized the needs of African American schools. Reform initiatives for white schools, in fact, often perpetuated disparities between white and black schools. In Greene County, for example, black students were part of a tiny and declining African American population, representing only 3.3 percent of the population in 1930, a decline of 9 percent from 1920.[16] Their schools' development followed the same trend as schools for white students, but on a much smaller scale. Thus, as with white schools, the number of black facilities dropped in the years 1910–19 and leveled off in the following decade, with the black schools numbering eight or nine. Yet all of these elementary schools were one-teacher buildings, and their value lagged far behind that of the white schools.[17]

In the East Tennessee countryside, otherwise reform-minded local officials did not use school construction programs to redirect rural black education, and black residents had neither the numerical strength nor the assistance of state officials to pressure white officials for better schools. In Middle Tennessee's Lewis County, white frugality and outright discrimination against the dwindling numbers of African American students only worsened conditions in black schools.[18] While the Lewis school board annually replaced between one and three school buildings for its white elementary students, there was no black school building program. Black schools dropped from five to three between 1921 and 1924; all were one-teacher schools.

School plant value provides stark evidence of the disparities between white and black schools. In 1924, Lewis County's three black school buildings and their grounds were worth an estimated $140 and their equipment $50, for a total value of $190. The thirty-four white elementary schools averaged $737.35 in value, over eleven times the average black school value of $63.33. This wide gulf would not soon diminish. In 1925, for instance, the Lewis school board decided to build a new white school at Gordonsburg and equip it with new furniture. They transferred the broken-down seats from the old school to "the colored school at that place, as they will have use of the old building that has been used by the white school."[19]

Significant change in black education would not happen until African Americans joined forces with reformers to bring blacks directly into the school building process. The Julius Rosenwald Fund's rural school building program provided the necessary combination of outside aid, state support, and rural black determination for change.

Model Schools for Black Children:
The Rosenwald Rural School Building Program

Upon assuming his position with the state's Department of Education in 1914, Samuel Smith learned that the Tuskegee Institute was in charge of distributing funds for black school construction that were provided by Sears, Roebuck and Company magnate Julius Rosenwald. Smith in 1915 secured aid for his first Rosenwald school, the Reaves School in Fayette County, a West Tennessee county with one of the largest black populations in the state. Tennessee received $1,500 in Rosenwald school funds from Tuskegee in the 1915–16 biennium. That figure jumped to $20,000 in 1918, when almost half the state's outside aid for black education came from the Julius Rosenwald Fund. By 1919, Smith received two or three applications for Rosenwald assistance each week.[20]

The Rosenwald Fund also subsidized the salary of a rural school building agent as Smith's assistant, beginning in 1918. That official, known as "the Rosenwald agent," was the only African American in the state education department. Although short stints were served by H. N. Robinson and W. L. Porter in the early 1920s, Robert E. Clay occupied this position for much of his professional life. Clay worked from an office at the black Tennessee Agricultural and Industrial College. He mediated between rural blacks and white officials of state and local governments, allowing the rural school agent to devote his time to administration and building inspections.

Julius Rosenwald's program constructed new learning environments for improved rural education and race relations.[21] In 1912, Sears, Roebuck and Company's president, Julius Rosenwald, authorized Booker T. Washington to construct six experimental rural schools with a portion of an earlier donation to Tuskegee Institute. Thereafter Rosenwald made annual contributions to Tuskegee for school construction projects. Then, in 1917, he created the Julius Rosenwald Fund to handle his philanthropic interests. Julius Rosenwald's initial reliance on Tuskegee had grown out of his personal relationship with Booker T. Washington. Like most philanthropists of his day who were interested in race relations, Rosenwald applauded the efforts of Washington and the Tuskegee Institute to train blacks as productive laborers. Both men hoped that Rosenwald's school building program would establish the Tuskegee model in public education and broaden its influence.

Some of Tennessee's early experiences with Rosenwald assistance led Progressive officials like Samuel Smith to believe that black school building projects could inspire both whites and blacks to support better educational opportunities for rural African Americans. For example, Rosenwald aid enabled Rutherford County to address black school needs a year or two before it tackled white schools. Nine of the fourteen Rosenwald-aided schools eventually built in the county were constructed between 1918 and 1920.

These buildings followed plans developed under Tuskegee Institute's supervision, rather than the "modern" principles of white school designers. Rutherford's early Rosenwald schools were like Bryant's School there: an unpainted frame rectangle with a steeply pitched roof, a center door in the gable end, and two windows (and sometimes a door) on each side (fig. 12).[22]

All but one of these first Rosenwald schools were one-teacher structures, each costing between $1,150 and $1,550. Patrons combined cash and in-kind donations for their required matching contribution; at Gladeview School, for example, parents raised $125 in cash, donated the $100 school site, furnished $75 in materials, and provided $25 worth of their own labor.[23]

By 1920, Rosenwald had several reasons to terminate the fund's association with Tuskegee Institute. Some white education officials did not want to participate in a program run by black administrators. Moreover, the General Education Board warned of Tuskegee's declining reputation as a teacher-training institution; an audit of the school construction program had alleged financial irregularities.[24] School architecture reformers found problems in the buildings themselves. Fletcher B. Dresslar, in a survey of Rosenwald schools

Fig. 12. Bryant's School, one of nine schools built in Rutherford County between 1918 and 1920 with Rosenwald aid administered by the Tuskegee Institute. Photograph in folder 7, box 559, Julius Rosenwald Fund Archives, Fisk University Special Collections, Nashville, Tennessee. Used courtesy of Fisk University Library.

built under Tuskegee supervision, documented haphazard construction standards and insufficient planning in siting and lighting. Dresslar inspected one of Shelby County's ten three-teacher Rosenwald buildings, the Spring Hill School (fig. 13). Although its plain surfaces and T-shaped plan met Dresslar's standards, it had many drawbacks, including the lack of sanitary facilities and the building's open foundation and single floor. These latter elements would admit cold drafts around the pupils' feet, resulting in chills and sickness. Dresslar probably cared little for the windows; they had adjustable double sashes of appropriate height but were not grouped in a battery for even illumination of the classroom. Dresslar concluded, "This place could be made attractive, but somebody with ideals must start the work. This building (and its environment) does not suggest a new sort of education."[25]

Dresslar's critique convinced Julius Rosenwald to focus his contributions on the promotion of standardized modern schools, with properly enclosed foundations, functional floor plans, adequate lighting, and sanitary facilities. Severing the building program's connection with Tuskegee Institute,

SPRING HILL SCHOOL, SHELBY CO., TENN.
1. Up on "stilts," with single floors.
2. No sign of a toilet of any sort.
3. This place could be made attractive, but somebody with ideals must start the work. This building (and its environment) does not suggest a new sort of education.

Fig. 13. Criticism from Fletcher B. Dresslar, an authority on rural school design, led the Julius Rosenwald Fund to adopt new plans for African American schools. Fletcher B. Dresslar, *Report on the Rosenwald Schools*, Bulletin No. 1 (Nashville, Tenn.: Julius Rosenwald Fund, 1920), 60.

Rosenwald in 1919 convened a meeting of leading reformers who formulated an enlarged rural school building program headquartered in Nashville.[26] The Nashville office would cooperate with state departments of education in fourteen southern states, dispensing allotments for schools, scaled according to the number of teachers employed. Rosenwald selected Tennessee's Samuel L. Smith to direct the southern office and serve as its general field agent. With Smith at the helm of the Rosenwald program, Tennessee became the headquarters for southern school building reform, especially in black schools.

Professional reformers continually emphasized black self-help, black community identity, and interracial cooperation as the most important features of the Rosenwald school building program. Rosenwald officials held that local commitments of labor and money were essential self-help strategies that would produce direct results in better schools, and indirect results as the new school buildings inspired blacks to improve the appearance and sanitation of their own homes.[27] Reformers also argued that black self-help in education would foster an appropriate black community identity, one that would encourage both races to work together in improving the quality of life for a biracial community.[28]

Building a Rosenwald school was, literally and figuratively, a constructive activity. A local Rosenwald school campaign began when African American school patrons committed themselves to matching the fund's allocation— from $400 to $2,100, according to the school's size ($150 for each room added to an existing building, $500 to $900 for a teachers' home, and $200 to $400 for workshops). By raising the money and contributing materials and labor, rural African Americans would make a commitment to each other and to their community's future.

At the same time, by subsidizing school construction and a subordinate curriculum, black southerners would be forging better relations with the white leaders who appropriated tax revenues for school construction. Official white support was essential, because Julius Rosenwald envisioned his schools as permanent additions to public education. The Rosenwald Fund required that state and local governments match the private contributions from his fund and from black southerners. Fund officials further insisted that schools be located on a minimum of two acres deeded to public school authorities, and built according to plans supplied by the Nashville office. Desks, blackboards, heating equipment, and sanitary toilets also had to be provided.[29]

Realizing that financial incentives might not be enough to prod white school officers into action, the Rosenwald Fund also played on white concerns about black mobility. Fund officials argued that new school buildings would tie students and their parents more closely to their locales, forestalling black flight to cities and enhancing the local labor force. The vocational education courses taught in Rosenwald industrial rooms allayed concerns that schooling "spoiled" African Americans.[30]

Samuel Smith earnestly believed that new learning environments could reform rural education and race relations simultaneously. Describing building campaigns under way in Rutherford and Shelby counties in 1918, Smith noted the sacrificial generosity of blacks in their pursuit of decent facilities, and how such schools would ground black community members in their proper roles in country life:

> It is wonderful to see how eager the Negroes themselves are for these new schools. They are ever ready to contribute generously in order to help build a good house. Many of them give until they are forced to do without many things they need.
>
> We are trying to encourage the erection of as many of these buildings as possible, feeling that it is the best way to keep the Negroes in the country prosperous and contented, and ultimately to help make "Democracy safe for the world."[31]

At least in his mind, Rosenwald schools in these counties resulted from the fusion of black demands for better education with white desires for a secure labor force in a period of black migration.

Smith's vision of how rural people could be transformed by school buildings perfectly suited the Rosenwald construction program, which emphasized Progressive design. The Rosenwald Fund intended that its schools set new standards for all rural schools, white as well as black. Smith applied the "Community School" designation that he had used for state-mandated designs to the plans that he disseminated on behalf of the Rosenwald Fund. The schools convey proportion and massing of form, accentuated by groupings of windows and occasional squared columns. These details reflected the simplicity and plainness typical of the earlier work of Smith's mentor, Dresslar. Smaller buildings exhibit little in the way of formal style, except to recall the Craftsman style in the bracketing under their eaves (figs. 14 and 15). Larger schools featured columns or dormers reminiscent of the popular Colonial Revival style (fig. 16).[32] Wood-framed schools suited country resources and sensibilities, meshing well with the Craftsman and Colonial Revival touches in their designs. Brick construction gave a sense of solidity to larger buildings and permitted relief designs to highlight their form.

Rosenwald Fund officials scrutinized painting, equipment, and furnishings. As exterior color schemes, they preferred white with gray trim or light gray with white trim for frame buildings, but they also permitted the use of "bungalow" or nut-brown stain with white trim. Interior color schemes featured light cream or ivory ceilings, walls of gray or buff above darker wainscots of tan or brown, and walnut or oak-stained wooden wainscoting and

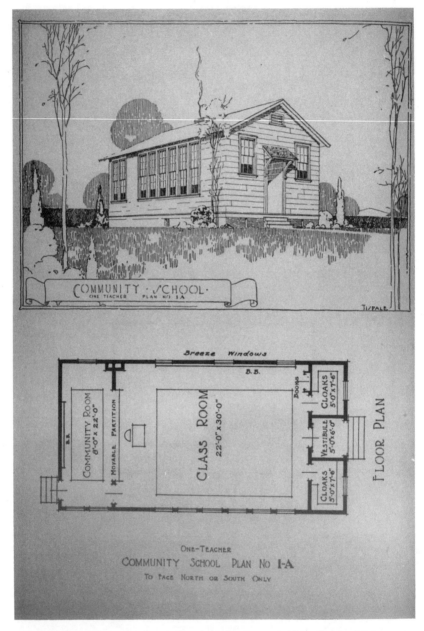

Fig. 14. Samuel L. Smith's designs for the Julius Rosenwald Fund met all Progressive requirements for school architecture, with few decorative details. "One-Teacher Community School Plan No. 1-A, To Face North or South Only," *Community School Plans,* rev. ed. (Nashville: Julius Rosenwald Fund, 1927). Used courtesy of the Tennessee State Library and Archives.

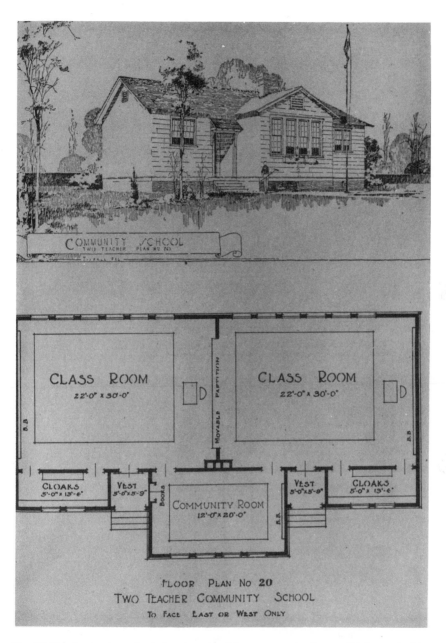

Fig. 15. This two-teacher school plan was one of the most popular Rosenwald designs built in Tennessee. Its window arrangement maximized natural light in the classrooms and industrial room. "Floor Plan No. 20, Two-Teacher Community School, to Face East or West Only," *Community School Plans,* rev. ed. (Nashville: Julius Rosenwald Fund, 1927). Used courtesy of the Tennessee State Library and Archives.

trim. The dual color scheme for classroom walls maximized light reflection at window level, while reducing glare for seated pupils.[33] Fund publications gave explicit instructions for installing light-colored (preferably tan) and translucent window shades, although raising and lowering of these to reduce glaring light, it was hoped, would be eliminated by correct orientation and fenestration. Equally important were decent blackboards for teacher and student use and modern patent desks to replace the ubiquitous wooden slabs and benches used by African American children (fig. 5).[34]

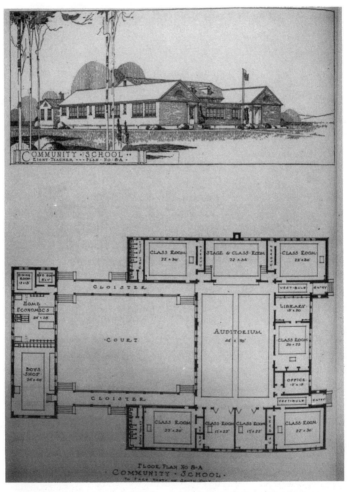

Fig. 16. Schools built on an "H" plan allowed unilateral lighting for all classrooms in larger buildings. "Floor Plan No. 8-A, Community School, to Face North or South Only," *Community School Plans*, rev. ed. (Nashville: Julius Rosenwald Fund, 1927). Used courtesy of the Tennessee State Library and Archives.

The Rosenwald Fund also dispensed funds for teachers' homes and shops. Since few county school boards would pay for such buildings, the Rosenwald Fund split the cost with black communities.[35] Citizens could choose among four plans for teachers' homes: two reformulations of a one-teacher school plan, a third in the popular "Bungalow" idiom, and a large home resembling a streamlined Colonial Revival cottage. The provision for workshops, however, was even more central to the Rosenwald plan. Every school design included an industrial room. State agents complained constantly that these rooms were either not being used, or not being used well. Many communities could not afford industrial equipment; overcrowded schools used industrial rooms as additional classrooms. To keep industrial education at the heart of the Rosenwald program, and to qualify for federal aid for vocational programs, the fund offered additional money for the construction and equipment of one- to four-room shop buildings.[36]

Some rural white southerners rejected the fund's designs as too good for black children; these schools looked strange, with their battery windows and unadorned appearance. But reformers asserted that Rosenwald plans set the standard for rural schools in the South and the nation.[37] Smith's successor in the Tennessee Department of Education, O. H. Bernard, claimed that Tennessee's "attractive, well-equipped" Rosenwald schools promoted "civic pride" among black patrons, visible in "better kept homes, better farms, and higher standards of living."[38]

Smith's Nashville office constantly revised plans and sent them free of charge to state departments of education, where they could be distributed to county boards of education and used for white and black schools. As reformers focused more attention on the design of rural schoolhouses, the Rosenwald plans remained among the simplest in design and least expensive in construction.[39] Such frugality reflected the fund's desire to build as many schools as possible; it wished not only to stretch its own money, but also to accommodate the limited resources of rural southern communities. In so doing, the fund implicitly acquiesced in white school officials' reluctance to expend tax revenues on black education, placing an even greater burden on rural blacks as the price of progress.

Rosenwald Schools and Tennessee Communities

The Rosenwald Fund made a considerable contribution to the physical expansion of Tennessee's black school system: the fund assisted in constructing over 350 new buildings with a total school plant value of almost two million dollars. Its indirect influence on Tennessee's commitment to black education, however, is difficult to measure. Black schools merited little attention until the introduction of General Education Board agents and Rosenwald aid. Due to the new programs, admitted State Superintendent

Samuel E. Sherill, "There is a growing tendency among county and city boards to spend more money on Negro schools." Thanks to Julius Rosenwald, Sherill reported, blacks worked hard to obtain modern school buildings; county boards of education responded by providing more money for black schools.[40]

White observers such as Sherill were quick to congratulate the Rosenwald Fund, its building program director Samuel Smith, and the state black school agent. Certainly Tennessee public education in general benefited from the close relationship between Smith and the Department of Education. Smith used to good advantage his knowledge of the state's schools and his access to the state superintendent of education and the governor, as he personally supervised the distribution of aid across the state. As in other southern states, Tennessee's Department of Education made an annual request for Rosenwald aid, specifying the number and type (by number of teachers) of schools and related buildings it expected to build. The fund then made a general appropriation, from which it paid out funds as the black school agent certified that schools had been completed according to Rosenwald standards.

While state officials praised Smith, other reformers within Progressive philanthropies and those who labored at the community level knew that the Rosenwald agent and rural African Americans performed the real work of building a network of new black schools.[41] The Rosenwald agents, in particular Robert E. Clay, offer a unique opportunity for viewing reform efforts by African Americans who worked both with white Progressives and bureaucrats and within the rural South's African American communities. From both outsider and local perspectives, agents' reports document the process of reform, as well as the importance of rural activism.

Robert E. Clay was Tennessee's Rosenwald agent from 1918 to 1932, with a short hiatus from 1923 to 1925. As a self-described "original disciple of Dr. Booker T. Washington" and secretary of the state Inter-Racial League, Clay was ideally suited for this job.[42] By building new schools, he organized efforts to rebuild community identity as a bulwark against black migration; to rescue homes, farms, and families from moral and sanitary degradation; and to promote interracial harmony.

Clay toured the state constantly, speaking to black and white leaders and to local school officials about the Rosenwald program. All state officials working on reform issues recognized that their success hinged on the support of those who held the reins of power at the local level. Capturing the reformer's predicament, O. H. Bernard observed that "the State can do nothing more than co-operate in any movement that tends to make conditions better. It cannot very well initiate movements without the approval and support of the local authorities."[43]

As a black man working in the interests of black people, Clay had no choice but to be careful in his dealings with local white authorities. Often he faced initial hostility. For instance, Clay reported that the Tipton County school superintendent had told him to "get a hoe and chop cotton"—but then relented when Clay explained the nature of the Rosenwald Fund program. A more sympathetic Maury County superintendent asked Clay to come back to organize a Rosenwald campaign on another day, because "the white people were having a big meeting in this community" when Clay arrived.[44]

Time and time again, white racism and indifference hindered the construction of Rosenwald schools. Rosenwald agents noted counties where they encountered especially strong opposition: Bedford, Coffee, Dyer, and Lauderdale. Black citizens in a number of counties "were forced to the limit to make the building a reality."[45] In Haywood County, where African Americans were the majority, disfranchisement and racism meant that black citizens had little power to secure appropriations for their schools from the county government.[46] Across the state in Washington County, where African Americans were a tiny minority, numerical disadvantage and racism brought about the same result.[47]

Although the need for new black schools was most pressing, rural school agents and Rosenwald agents reported that most school boards preferred to build white schools first. Dyer County school board members expressed a common feeling that "the Rosenwald schools were too expensive for Negroes' use when white schools were so poor in many places."[48] Even if county officials lent their assent, white citizens raised objections. In several counties, whites living adjacent to the sites selected for Rosenwald schools objected to their construction.[49] State financial support for consolidated rural school construction eased the choice between funding white and black schools, but school officials continued to favor white education.[50]

Certainly this was the case in Hamilton County, where new black school construction got under way in 1922. The two frame schools constructed in 1922–23 may have been the one-teacher Rosenwald-assisted schools at Georgetown and Hixson. Hixson followed Community School Plan 1-A, being a narrow rectangle entered through a gable end. Booker T. Washington School, built in 1923–24, was a three-teacher brick structure. Summit School, built two years later with Rosenwald assistance, did not follow a community school plan. O. H. Bernard approved the building, along with a nonstandard white school, but he warned the superintendent against such future deviations.[51]

Bernard may have compromised to encourage J. E. Walker, the county superintendent, whom he described as expressing a "very friendly attitude toward the colored people." Both the superintendent and the county board of education favored improving black schools, as long as the white schools "come first."[52] This willingness to build black schools, however, suddenly came to a halt in the summer of 1927. Sensational newspaper articles tracked a spate of violence following a police raid on Chattanooga's Universal Negro

Improvement Association in August, and these developments may have impeded the progress of the Rosenwald program in Hamilton County. As a state officer of the Tennessee Inter-Racial League, Clay found himself in the middle of this Chattanooga controversy. In response, he organized African American leaders from the city and county for a meeting with leading whites to develop a program for improved housing and race relations that would avert further black protest and white backlash.[53] Hamilton County would not utilize the Rosenwald program for the next two years.

White racism made a policy of cooperation, rather than confrontation or criticism, less threatening and more productive, yet frustrating for African Americans. When county school boards expressed interest in Rosenwald aid, they generally demanded that blacks first raise their part of the cost—or more. In Tipton County, for instance, Clay won a promise to build a five-teacher school on a site already purchased by blacks for twelve hundred dollars—after they raised another thousand. This case, and many others across the state, set a pattern for black sacrifice, as hard-pressed tenant farm families raised thousands of dollars to leverage public investment in their schools.[54]

White attitudes meant that the Rosenwald agent had little choice but to adopt conciliatory tactics in dealing with local authorities. The agent and leading black citizens worked with the offices of local white community leaders and officials; they recruited influential white supporters to appear before the school board. After securing funding, the agent and his local allies pressured local officials to fulfill their promises. Occasionally, the Rosenwald agent intervened to keep discouraged blacks from refunding contributions when county officials delayed building projects.[55]

White inaction almost scuttled the first Rosenwald campaign in Obion County, although the county already had embarked on its extensive building program for white schools. Rosenwald agent H. N. Robinson conducted a fundraising rally there in March 1924, which generated $150 toward the construction of a two-teacher school at Rives. Blacks bought the land and provided the lumber. Even with black donations totaling $800 and the prospect of a $700 Rosenwald grant, white school officials "had about gotten out of the notion of erecting the building," and only Robinson's timely intervention rescued the project.[56]

The same indifference on the part of whites dogged other black school projects in Obion County. The county school board approved two new buildings as the black components of its 1925 school construction program; by January 1926, however, Robert Clay found only one under construction at Woodland Mills and repeated promises for the second school at South Fulton.[57]

Only when South Fulton African Americans increased their contributions did the school board move on construction. Black residents had been working toward a new school since May 1924, when they had promised donations as soon as the school board could estimate the cost of the six-teacher Rosenwald structure needed to replace two existing buildings. A year and a half later, the money had been raised and a six-acre site acquired, but school officials claimed that bad weather had delayed construction. At an assembly organized by Clay, black citizens pledged to perform all necessary hauling and labor. Squire McDade, a county magistrate involved in the negotiations, then gave assurances that construction would begin as soon as the weather improved. Construction finally got under way eight months later, much to Clay's relief.[58]

When completed in October 1926, South Fulton Consolidated Rosenwald School featured asbestos shingle sheathing, electric lighting, and a steam heating plant, all of which distinguished it from most rural black schools (fig. 17). O. H. Bernard judged that it was "a first class modern school building." The building followed Rosenwald Plan 6-A for an H-shaped, six-teacher school. It replaced a two-story, false-front, unpainted frame store building and a large, two-story, unpainted frame rectangle with a small bell tower, which probably had been a church or lodge hall (fig. 18).[59]

Another Rosenwald campaign in the town of Obion took almost eighteen months. In August 1926, black residents had $423 in the bank, a site had been purchased, and the school board promised that construction would begin in the fall. But by May 1927, discouraged local blacks told Clay that nothing had been accomplished. Clay met with the secretary of the board

Fig. 17. According to the state agent for black rural schools, the South Fulton Consolidated Rosenwald School, Obion County, was "a first-class modern school building." Photograph 1178, box 36, Tennessee Board of Education Records, Record Group 91, Tennessee State Library and Archives, Nashville. Used courtesy of the Tennessee State Library and Archives.

of education and received promises that construction would begin by July 1.[60] Work finally began in August, and Bernard made his final inspection for state consolidation and Rosenwald aid in November. Mrs. M. B. Lane happily informed Clay about the new building. She tempered her praise for the school and Obion whites with a jab at the building's size; Lane realized that something new was better than something shabby or nothing at all: "I cannot help from dropping you just a few lines to let you know just how we are rejoicing over our beautiful new building. They have it almost up, and the good white people are looking after it nicely for us. . . . The building is quite small, however, I think our people should be thankful."[61]

The new Rosenwald schools in Obion County were great sources of pride for blacks, but white officials consistently placed the program's burden squarely on the backs of local African Americans. In some communities, that burden proved too heavy. In January 1926, the school board's chairman and other board members told an assembly at the Troy Colored Methodist Episcopal Church that they would build a two-teacher school if blacks did all the hauling and labor. When Clay returned in September, he found that black patrons had been unable to purchase a site, and the building campaign soon disintegrated.[62]

As Obion's African Americans knew, building new black schools in Tennessee was no easy matter, even with the financial support of the Rosenwald

Fig. 18. Before Progressive building programs, many schools for black students met in buildings like this one in South Fulton, which probably had been a lodge hall or church. Photograph 1180, box 36, Tennessee Board of Education Records, Record Group 91, Tennessee State Library and Archives, Nashville. Used courtesy of the Tennessee State Library and Archives.

Fund. Blacks found their cooperative strategy discouraging when it yielded only white promises and demands for further contributions.

Shelby County was a notable exception to the general pattern of local white indifference to the Rosenwald program. Dynamic local leadership for reform among both races in Shelby County produced one of the South's most successful Rosenwald construction programs, as a succession of activist female county school superintendents and black educators focused attention on proper schools for African Americans.

Shelby's County's unique political climate doubtless helped. Former Memphis Mayor Edward H. Crump led a Democratic political machine that orchestrated black votes in spite of the state's prohibitive poll tax. African American Republican leader Robert R. Church, Jr., also organized black voters in the city and county. In return for their votes, blacks asked for, and often received, public facilities for black citizens. The Rosenwald philosophy of building new schools and promoting industrial education as ways of strengthening rural black communities and keeping people on the land also appealed to planters in a wealthy cotton county where over 90 percent of black farmers were tenants.[63]

In the spring of 1917, Shelby County kicked off a major school building initiative with a $200,000 bond issue, out of which $50,000 was earmarked for rural black schools. This amount funded twenty Rosenwald applications; Samuel Smith estimated that, with additional contributions from African American patrons, the county would spend $75,000 on new black school buildings over the following year. Each school would consolidate smaller ones and offer industrial education.[64] Smith and Charl Williams attributed voter approval of school bonds for both races to growing white appreciation of industrial education like that emphasized at the Woodstock County Training School.[65]

By 1922, Shelby County's twenty-five new buildings, each a consolidation of at least two smaller schools, led all southern counties in the number of Rosenwald schools constructed. Eight years later, the county's Rosenwald total, out of the eighty-six black schools operating in the county, had grown to fifty-nine schools, four teachers' homes, and three shop buildings. It was the largest Rosenwald-assisted building program for African American schools in Tennessee.[66]

Shelby County required little outside encouragement, assistance, or supervision in its Rosenwald program. Here the mere offer of assistance inspired county school officers and rural residents to implement reforms on their own. Sue M. Powers, Shelby's newest female superintendent, continued updating the county's black school facilities, with the construction of twenty-four schools and additions to five others between 1923 and 1926 (figs. 19 and 20).[67] H. N. Robinson found that, during his tenure as Rosenwald agent in 1923 and 1924, "but little work was necessary in Shelby as things have been so very well organized. Their buildings were all completed." When he returned as Rosenwald agent in 1925, Shelby County gave Robert E. Clay a welcome respite from his usual organizational and lobbying efforts; he "noted with pleasure the splendid work done in these schools by the teachers."[68]

For a decade, Shelby county officials planned and implemented their own school construction program. The Tennessee Department of Education, the General Education Board, and the Julius Rosenwald Fund provided funding, but minimal official intervention. Local people raised their contributions to match Rosenwald grants, from hundreds to thousands of dollars, without Clay's carefully orchestrated appeals to white politicians. Led by Jeanes supervisors and the black county agricultural agent, and assisted by reform-minded white county education officers, Shelby County African Americans needed little outside guidance.

Only when the county concluded its own school building program at the end of the 1925–26 school year did Clay swing into action. He and Superintendent Powers focused their efforts on expanding space in existing schools and adding new vocational programs and teachers' homes that would attract

Fig. 19. Augusta Rosenwald School (1925) was one of fifty-nine Rosenwald schools built in Shelby County between 1914 and 1926. Progressive local school officials and rural citizens directed Shelby's Rosenwald school campaign, the largest in Tennessee. Photograph in folder 7, box 559, Julius Rosenwald Fund Archives, Fisk University Special Collections, Nashville, Tennessee. Used courtesy of Fisk University Library.

better personnel and provide facilities for home economics instruction. Between the fall of 1926 and the summer of 1929, Shelby obtained Rosenwald assistance for two school additions, two teachers' homes, and the three shop buildings. But in the same period, the county cut back from three to two Jeanes workers.[69]

The reduction of the county's Jeanes staff created an opportunity for Robert Clay, who began organizational work in the county in the fall of 1927. He described Cora Taylor, the Manassas High School principal and a Jeanes supervisor, as "among the brainiest leaders of our race" and credited her with facilitating some "delicate" contacts for him. That December, Clay met with groups at the Lake Grove and Jones Chapel Colored Methodist Episcopal churches, but nothing came of their plans or of those for Capleville's intended three-room addition. In the 1929–30 school year, the Rosenwald Fund contributed to the two-room Black's School and to a six-room high school at Geeter, one of the largest black schools in the county, now incorporated within Memphis's city limits.[70]

As the Rosenwald agent, Clay depended on local African Americans like

Fig. 20. Unpainted, dilapidated, and dark buildings, like the school abandoned for the Oakville Rosenwald School, contrasted greatly with the county's new model schools. Photograph in folder 7, box 559, Julius Rosenwald Fund Archives, Fisk University Special Collections, Nashville. Used courtesy of Fisk University Library.

Cora Taylor to maintain the momentum of a building campaign. Clay's professional status secured him speaking engagements with such groups as the Memphis and Shelby County Social Leaders and Workers, the Tennessee Colored Women's Federation, and the Tennessee Inter-Racial League. He took the Rosenwald message to ministerial associations and all-black unions, whose members could provide local contacts and support. County school staff also were logical sources of leadership. Principals and teachers scheduled public meetings and drummed up a crowd in advance of the Rosenwald agent's visit.

Their shared faith in industrial or vocational education as the vehicle for rural African Americans' progress encouraged close cooperation between the Rosenwald agent and local Jeanes supervising teachers. Jeanes supervisors often accompanied Robert Clay on his visits to rural schools. Albura Fagala, Hamilton County Jeanes supervisor, addressed the 1928 summer school meeting of Jeanes teachers on "How I Secured Funds in Building Rosenwald Schools in My County."[71] African American extension agents and vocational teachers also provided leadership and assistance. Robert Clay visited their school classes and spoke to black farm men and women at their adult programs.[72]

Some rural residents did not wait for outside or local leadership, but took the initiative themselves. In 1924, H. N. Robinson coordinated a Rosenwald campaign in Decaturville, Decatur County. Robinson secured the support of the county superintendent, school board, and court. Mr. Crowder, a teacher, already had built local interest, so that citizens were ready when Robinson spoke at their meeting. They already had purchased the land and agreed to turn it over to the county, to supply and transport all rough materials, and provide labor.[73] In Haywood County, Jamestown African Americans sent a committee to see agent Robert Clay; they had already raised almost one hundred dollars for a new school and wanted Clay's assistance in getting approval from county officials. Later, Clay was "surprised," upon visiting the Cerrogordo School in Madison County, to find a school jammed with farm men and women who had come to demonstrate how overcrowded the school was and how willing they were to support a Rosenwald campaign.[74]

Although Robert Clay wrote as if he were the mastermind of every Rosenwald campaign, his own reports document that he depended on rural African Americans to act independently to bring a campaign to fruition. Local responsibility often meant that a handful of people had to meet with county officials and spearhead fundraising efforts, while many more participated in smaller ways. Indeed, as H. N. Robinson noted, "The patrons have more interest if given a prominent share of their own responsibility, yet in most places it is customary that the few do practically all the work."[75]

Robert Clay's visit to Barren Springs, in West Tennessee's Gibson County, was typical. He and the Gibson County supervisor met with farm families at the local Colored Methodist Episcopal (CME) church. Blacks wanted a new two-teacher school and voted to raise five hundred dollars; they collected almost half that amount in cash and subscriptions on the spot. Clay and the supervisor then met with a school board member and the mayor of Trenton, who agreed to the building if blacks contributed five hundred dollars, dug the basement, and graded the building site, conditions that black school patrons accepted.[76] Such public meetings, at which school patrons pledged themselves to a school campaign, organized their committees, and took up their first donations, were the catalysts for almost every Tennessee Rosenwald school.

A crucial task at the first public meeting was to select a committee that would, in Clay's words, make "the right approach to the white people in creating a favorable sentiment." The committee had to include individuals who could command the attention of local whites, men like John R. Bond, who owned hundreds of acres of land in Haywood County and agreed to lead its Rosenwald campaign. Madison County's committee included two ministers, the home demonstration agent, and a doctor. These men and women made appointments with school board members and the county supervisor, taking with them printed resolutions approved at the public meeting.[77] The committee also communicated with the school board about the pace of fundraising and the county's construction plans, and could call on prominent white citizens to exert political pressure on county officials if necessary.[78]

The next step was raising funds. Patrons attending public meetings contributed cash and pledged in-kind contributions, then discussed how best to reach their campaign goal. Clay monitored their progress; if dissatisfied, he readily intervened. In Shelbyville, county seat of Bedford County, where the effort to build a new school dragged on for years, he "rearranged their campaign committee by placing a number of good hussling women on it."[79] Clay suggested, and rural citizens adopted, several organizational strategies for their building campaigns. Shelbyville African Americans formed district Rosenwald Clubs. In Barren Springs and Alamo, school patrons formed a Parent-Teacher Association. Maury County residents divided their county into ten zones, each with its own fundraising captain and committee.[80]

Much of the work of collecting funds was divided by sex. For example, at a meeting for a shop building in the Right community of Hardin County, residents made plans to cut trees, haul them to the sawmill, and then haul the lumber to the site. Men probably performed this labor; women and girls joined a fundraising club organized by the Jeanes supervisor. Men also raised money by donating a day's wages or collecting donations at fraternal lodges.[81]

Robert Clay described several female fundraising committees that planned community entertainments and events. During a meeting in Carthage in October 1929, school patrons appointed a committee of five women to organize a chicken rally. They asked every black and white family in and near town for a chicken, and those collected were sold to benefit the school fund. Another committee of ten women was appointed to plan a series of suppers and entertainments. In 1932, community members used the same strategy of public entertainments to raise funds for a three-room vocational building and Rosenwald library.[82] Athens women hosted a Christmas dinner that featured donated "hams, chickens, cakes and other eatables." Williamson women sold refreshments at "an old time picnic."[83]

Farm families made cash contributions by designating crops for market sale to benefit the building campaign. Farm products, from eggs to cotton, raised the matching funds for the first Rosenwald school in Tennessee, the Reaves School in Fayette County.[84] Fayette African Americans, most of whom worked as tenants on some of the state's prime cotton land, regularly turned to the crop for cash contributions. Patrons of the Reaves Rosenwald School sold an acre of cotton to finance a building addition in 1929; farmers also had twelve acres of cotton set aside to sell for the construction of a teachers' home. Next year, the Tucker and Halls communities planted fourteen acres of cotton for a four-teacher school. They supplemented the crop profit with 22,000 board feet of lumber for the school building and the proceeds of a chicken rally.[85]

Some Rosenwald campaigns did not run so smoothly. Rural African Americans experienced the frustrations and animosities typical of small town and country communities. Black Tennesseans and their benefactors also confronted some of the same barriers that baffled other Progressives who crusaded for educational reform. As William Link has observed, the isolated rural school accurately reflected its community's independence from outside authority. Rural southerners of both races cherished their schools for precisely that reason and were unwilling to give control of schools and children over to self-proclaimed experts.[86]

Consolidation was the most common source of disagreement. In the spring of 1926, Clay received an "urgent request" for his presence from the principal and the president of the PTA of the Cookeville school for African Americans. He found community members "divided and fussing" about the location of the new consolidated school. Clay had little patience with such conflicts and generally treated the aggrieved parties to a "frank" and "plain" sermon on how "they would have to cut out their foolishness and selfishness." When the consolidation controversy was especially intense, he asked school patrons not to talk about the matter until their fundraising campaign was complete.[87]

Discord erupted any time that a Rosenwald campaign crossed the invisible lines separating community factions. In Covington, rivalry among religious denominations generated factions that threatened the Rosenwald campaign. In Martin, opposition to the school principal came from a civic club that had raised the money for repairs to the county training school.[88] At other times, the school campaign threatened the status of blacks who had allied themselves with white leaders for their own or their families' advancement.[89] The sources of other divisions are unclear. Unnamed factional divisions in Giles County delayed the Rosenwald campaign for five years. African Americans in Porter's Grove, Crockett County, raised $225 for an addition to their school, then disagreed about building it.[90]

Robert Clay decried such local conflicts; he did not hesitate to embarrass rural African Americans by his "frank" and "plain" critiques of what he perceived as their weaknesses in front of white officials.[91] Yet his frustrations tell us about the strength and the sources of community identity in the rural South. Black parents, like white parents, hated to see their children sent off to a distant consolidated school rather than attending one in their own community. If they supported consolidation, they wanted the prestige of hosting the new school. Identifying with their small neighborhoods, they saw them as the logical sites for new community-oriented buildings. Religious affiliation also was important for community identity. Many of the public meetings needed for a Rosenwald campaign were held in all-black churches, particularly Colored Methodist Episcopal and Baptist congregations. The Williamson County people who took up a Rosenwald collection during Sunday service surely were not the only ones to do so.[92]

Sacrifices made by blacks for the sake of new school buildings were legendary among southern reformers. In pursuit of their right to education, they complied with discriminatory requirements that, whether mandated by the Rosenwald Fund or the local school board, meant double taxation.[93] Tennessee's rural African Americans clearly understood that new school buildings, whether or not they possessed the potential for social regeneration ascribed to them by reformers, were essential to their struggle for a better life. Consolidation raised troublesome questions about community identity and control, but the standardized model schools pioneered on their behalf offered obvious, if repetitive, improvements.

In 1928, the Rosenwald Fund, in recognition of the difficulties faced by small black communities, introduced one last major initiative in school building. It offered a 50 percent increase in aid for "permanent" (generally brick) construction and for "backward" counties, defined as places with small African American populations who had no Rosenwald schools.[94] In Lewis County, one of the backward counties, the plan worked: Lewis constructed its first Rosenwald school that year in Hohenwald. Hohenwald Rosenwald School, a frame two-teacher structure, superseded Hohenwald Colored School and at least one other school. In place of an earlier rectangular block with a door and bell tower in its gable end now stood a boxy, functional school clad in neat, gleaming white clapboards.[95]

But the Rosenwald program to help "backward" counties was the only positive news in what otherwise was a year of unexpected setbacks for the cause of black education. The Tennessee legislature voted to discontinue its rural school construction program after the 1928–29 academic year, thus terminating a major new funding source for black education.[96] Simultaneously, the Rosenwald Fund reorganized itself and hired a new director, Edwin Embree, from the Rockefeller Foundation. Embree, whose own interests lay in race relations, questioned whether better school environments produced better learning. He soon pared down the school building program in order to broaden the scope of Rosenwald programs. Fund officers warned southern states that the construction program would end in the near future. In the meantime, in the summer of 1928, they eliminated aid for one- and two-teacher schools and additions.[97]

Tennessee agent O. H. Bernard agreed that such small schools were inefficient, in terms of both cost and quality of education—state policy already forbade them—but argued that they were a necessity in isolated areas with small black populations. State Superintendent Perry L. Harned noted that, without the carrot of Rosenwald money, Tennessee held no stick with which to force construction of black schools.[98] The Rosenwald Fund initially prevailed on this issue but backed down after it attempted to reduce, and then discontinue, its contribution to the Rosenwald agent's salary.[99]

The Great Depression accelerated the decline of the rural school program, as Rosenwald officials scrambled to conserve their resources, while states and counties lost school revenues. In 1932, the fund announced that the building program had accomplished its purpose and so would be closed. As the Depression deepened, rural blacks were thrown back on their own resources and their white neighbors' good will.

Tennessee's reforms in black schools reflect the collective efforts of state bureaucrats, local school administrators, county officials, and rural African Americans. The Rosenwald program seemed to validate the Progressive belief that reform could be effected simply by announcing a project and then providing the necessary administrative funding and machinery. Between 1920 and 1930, black school plant value jumped by $2,892,910, of which Rosenwald schools contributed $1,838,695 (63.6 percent). Per capita value of public school property for blacks increased by 135.4 percent, whereas for whites the rate of per capita growth was 167.5 percent. At the program's conclusion in 1932, Tennessee ranked eighth among fourteen southern states in the total number of Rosenwald schools erected: 354 schools (including 227 one- and two-teacher buildings), 9 teachers' homes, and 10 shops. Black Tennesseans contributed $296,388, whites gave $28,027, and the Rosenwald Fund donated $291,250. Public revenues supplied the bulk of the funds, $1,354,157. Thanks to public funding, Tennessee ranked fourth in Rosenwald school plant value.[100]

Along this path to progress, Tennessee's Progressive officials and private citizens had traveled territory familiar to reformers in southern states. As private philanthropies such as the General Education Board and the Rosenwald Fund moved in partnership with the state Department of Education, their staffs encountered the usual diversity of responses from county governments. Perceptions of the threat or opportunity posed by black education to the rural racial hierarchy influenced local reactions, which ran the gamut from intransigence to advocacy.

Local responses from both races, indeed, suggest important differences in Progressive reform when it concerned southern African Americans. Reforms for rural black education followed the same route from social idealism to business progressivism taken by other educational campaigns, but only at the higher echelons. When the Rosenwald Fund discontinued its building program in 1932, staff members contended that new schools had not materially improved the quality of education or the status of black Americans. Fund director Edwin Embree saw only that low instructional standards and racism endured even in progressive standardized facilities. Had he toured rural Tennessee with Rosenwald building agent Robert Clay, however, he would have found that the earlier dream of schools as agents of community advancement still motivated reformers who worked at the local level. As Clay campaigned in rural communities, his rhetoric and commitment remained unchanged. His audiences' responses, too, would have remained unchanged but for the economic hardship of the late 1920s and early 1930s.

Reform meant something different for rural African Americans than for rural whites. Progressives like Samuel Smith had envisioned that schools constructed through black self-help programs would bind rural African Americans more closely to each other, the countryside, and rural whites. That did not happen. For African American Tennesseans, self-help was not a choice but a necessity if they wanted their children to attend school in a decent building. They acted out of a preexisting sense of community identity, and that identity was strong enough to generate protests when offers of assistance threatened community pride.

Nor did interracial cooperation happen in the way that reformers planned, either. African Americans had to take a back seat while white schools forged ahead, and then dig deeper into their own pockets to pay when their turn came. Some white Tennesseans were interested and committed, and perhaps it was useful to identify white allies who were willing to live up to their part of the "separate but equal" bargain. Tennessee's Rosenwald school buildings, the material legacy of the rural African Americans who built them, suggest that, indeed, reformers and country people "built better than they knew."

• 4 •

Building a Bridge between School and Home Life: Home Economics for Rural Schools

Progressive reformers saw the school as a bridge to the rural home, the linch-pin of an improved country life. School buildings were object lessons, in which the teacher introduced Progressive values to pupils who, in turn, would share their knowledge with parents. The redesigned rural school provided a physical model of the ideal rural dwelling, a model that educators believed would spark imitation at home. The foundation for this bridge between home and school was home economics education, which assumed increasing importance in the curriculum of the reformed rural school. Home economics took advantage of the bonds between girls and their mothers to transmit from the school to the home new standards of domestic production and consumption.

When reformers targeted country schools and homes for reform, they highlighted the potential role of all rural women as agents of change. Progressives updated the traditional image of women as wives and mothers responsible for the family's moral values, by reaffirming its relevance and expanding its scope. Farm women, reformers asserted, bore the brunt of rural ignorance, isolation, and poverty. Such conditions prevented country women from properly safeguarding the health and morals of their families, from purchasing labor-saving technology for the home, and from taking a proper interest in the social welfare of their communities.[1] Thus, in her 1924 book, *The Woman on the Farm,* Mary Meek Atkeson advised rural women to join school boards and voluntary organizations, where they could apply their skills in housekeeping and decorating and create a homelike school more conducive to nurturing children.[2]

Reformers assured each other that rural life would not improve unless women changed the ways of their households and adopted a more expan-sive view of their influence over the home and community. Rural schools and home economics provided the means of teaching women these new lessons.

As Henrietta W. Calvin, home economics specialist for the U.S. Bureau of Education, reported to the 1920 National County Life Conference, "Thus far the rural school has contributed little to the rural home; yet if the rural home is to make its contribution as a social agency to the community and to the nation, it may rightfully claim help from all other social agencies and not least is its claim upon the one social agency which alone touches every family—the public school."[3]

Reformers saw a clear association between better schools and better home conditions. An environmental strategy, they believed, would enhance rural domestic uplift and make better rural communities. Consequently, reformers pursued school-based instruction in home economics as one promising channel for transmitting their message into rural homes.

During their pursuit of this end, however, many Progressives changed the goals of, and their professional attitudes about, home economics. Home economists during the 1920s began to seek their own professional identity as experts in the science of domesticity. They still argued that schools held the key to home life, yet they urged girls and women to make their individual homes more sanitary, efficient, and productive, rather than to use their homes as vehicles for social uplift.

In Tennessee during that decade, federal assistance and regulations supplanted philanthropic aid as inducements for state education officials to include home economics in the public school curriculum. Simultaneously, home economists at Tennessee's leading colleges responded to increased job opportunities for teachers at all educational levels by revamping curricula. Their programs followed the general trend toward business progressivism; yet, because of their gender-specific agenda, they would carve out professional niches that isolated them within academic and educational bureaucracies. And, contrary to reformers' expectations, home economics classes alone, even when taught by enthusiastic professionals and supported by benign administrators, could not guarantee an effective "entering wedge" into rural homes.

Vocational Education in Public Schools

Support for home economics as a solution to the problems of rural life grew out of the general Progressive faith in the transforming power of education. Vocational education in particular attracted support from both private philanthropies and the federal government after congressional passage of the Smith-Lever Act of 1914 and the 1917 Smith-Hughes Act.

The Smith-Lever Act created the federal and state extension services. As a result, county demonstration agents quickly organized girls' canning clubs in rural schools. Federal action encouraged other developments in rural vocational education as well. Tennessee's school officials introduced or enhanced home economics programs in elementary and secondary curricula as a strategy for correlating school lessons with rural life. They urged communities to build teachers' homes adjacent to rural schools, where household demonstrations could take place. Thus, white rural school agent John B. Brown described the teachers' home as "a model rural home, furnished with all of the conveniences that are within the reach of the farmer of average means. A modern heating plant, a lighting plant, water system septic tank, etc. It should also be provided with rooms for home economics for the school, for every rural school should have one teacher capable of teaching home economics."[4]

Samuel L. Smith, as state agent for black schools, quickly took advantage of the new federal program. Smith conferred with the director of Tennessee's agricultural extension service, Charles A. Keffer, on the distribution of Smith-Lever funds for black demonstration work. They agreed that white agents should work among blacks as well as whites, and that the extension service should provide black agents for areas with large black populations.

Home economics fit into Smith's larger vision for rural schools. In 1916, he directed all rural supervisors to "make the schools serve the most immediate needs of the homes," as the first step toward arousing parents' interest in better school buildings, equipment, and attendance. Besides overseeing teachers, organizing "vitalizing agencies," and turning the school into a community center, the supervisor should initiate vocational training in home economics. Smith suggested classes in foods, sewing, clothes selection, laundering, sanitary housekeeping, and household arrangement, supplemented by handicrafts.[5]

Like other white advocates of vocational education, Smith believed that African Americans had the most to gain from such programs. Vocational or industrial education would suit black abilities, provide employment opportunities, and instill better racial attitudes in both whites and blacks, without requiring whites or blacks to challenge segregation. During a tour of the state with other educational officials in the fall of 1914, Smith routinely addressed white and black audiences on the necessity of industrial education in black schools.[6]

In this decade, both the General Education Board and the John F. Slater Fund financed summer institutes for black teachers. Vacation offerings at white teachers' colleges, such as George Peabody College for Teachers and the University of Tennessee's Summer School of the South, trained rural teachers broadly; but black institutes limited their courses to simple manual training. The GEB also sent promising black teachers to summer schools at the Tennessee Agricultural and Industrial State Normal School (later Tennessee A&I College) and a select few to Hampton Institute or Tuskegee Institute.[7] These summer courses prepared teachers for work under the industrial supervising teachers sponsored by the Anna T. Jeanes Foundation. The number of Jeanes teachers rose from fourteen to twenty-four between 1915 and 1920.[8]

The Smith-Hughes Act of 1917 spurred further growth in vocational programs across the state. It appropriated federal funds for elementary, secondary, college, and adult training in the industrial arts, agriculture, and home economics. Women's organizations lobbied hard for the inclusion of vocational home economics in the Smith-Hughes Act as an optional state program eligible for 20 percent of federal vocational funds. State boards of vocational education distributed the funds, designated Smith-Hughes teacher training institutions, and interpreted federal guidelines for colleges and public schools.

Tennessee's vocational home economics programs began with less than five hundred students in 1917. The state's vocational education board named the University of Tennessee and Tennessee A&I State Normal School as approved vocational home economics teacher-training institutions and, as required, appropriated one-fifth of Smith-Hughes funds to programs for African Americans. In response to this incentive, Samuel Smith quickly revamped vocational programs at the black county training schools to qualify them for aid.[9]

Despite federal legislation and state initiatives, a 1920 survey found no home economics equipment or instruction in any of the one-room schools that constituted the majority of the state's rural schools, either black or white. But the federal acts and state programs promoted a remarkable expansion in home economics education over the next four years. By the 1924–25 school year, 10,457 of the 18,463 girls in Tennessee's county high schools were studying home economics. Part-time and evening classes reached girls and women outside schools; in rural areas, such classes often took place weekly for a full day of instruction.[10]

Why did home economics attract reformers and students? The new classes prepared adolescent girls and women for their "ultimate goal," the home. Students perceived this training as practical, useful, and focused on the household matters they addressed daily. Some home economists saw potential for rural uplift, if home economics extended beyond sewing and food preservation. Labor-saving devices, scientifically approved housekeeping methods, and art appreciation should receive equal weight, they argued, so that girls could balance technique with beauty. Others believed that aesthetic or social improvements were the results, not corollaries, of technical training. These differences about the curriculum, and about the value of individual courses, revealed tensions within the profession over the relative merits of technical, scientific, and social concerns, as well as over the role of women within rural households.[11]

In Tennessee, home economics educators usually emphasized technical training. Smith-Hughes programs at Tennessee's county and city high schools offered white girls either a two-year vocational program or the home economics instruction included in the requirements for a four-year high school degree. Students complemented daily ninety-minute home economics lessons with studies in biology or agriculture, physiology, sanitation, hygiene, and an art course in drawing and design. As class and home projects, white girls set up school rest rooms, refinished furniture, and renovated their home kitchens and bedrooms. African American girls spent two and a half hours daily in home economics classes covering sanitation, health and hygiene, child care, laundering, and home care, as well as cooking and sewing. They too conducted projects in home decoration.[12] Adult women could enroll in twelve vocational courses, including home management, house furnishings, health and sanitation, and labor-saving home conveniences.[13]

Home economics education for black girls already was entrenched in county training schools, where the Slater Fund and the Julius Rosenwald Fund required a vocational curriculum as a condition of construction grants. The General Education Board subsidized home economics, shop, and agricultural equipment in training schools, with home economics receiving as much as one-half of each school's total allotment. Equipment funds purchased sewing machines, stoves, cooking utensils, and laundry equipment, as well as water systems for the teachers' cottages in which most cooking classes were taught. Between 1921 and 1925, a loan fund of $150 for sewing materials circulated among the training schools, courtesy of the Slater Fund.[14]

Home economics had an additional vocational purpose for black females, as S. L. Smith indicated when he commended the Dyersburg Negro School, where white ladies aid societies from the local churches had furnished the school kitchen like "a well ordered kitchen of the city." "This will better prepare the girls to do cooking for the white people of the town," he noted approvingly.[15]

White home economics educators approached their black students with caution, assuming that they would encounter mistrust and resistance if they moved aggressively into black homes. White southern Smith-Hughes workers believed that they should plan an "appropriate" home economics curriculum based on a "diplomatic" investigation of home life among black girls. Marie White, Tennessee's supervisor of vocational home economics, reported in 1927 that she used the same course of study for adult women of both races, but that vocational programs for black homemakers had suffered for lack of good teachers. She recommended hiring Mabel Stinnett, who oversaw the state's Jeanes supervisors, as an itinerant trainer for black home economics teachers. White also worked with President William J. Hale of Tennessee A&I College in developing a vocational training program for black home economics teachers.[16]

Marie White noted that the greatest challenge faced by teachers of both races was bridging the gap between classroom instruction and home practices. She suggested that teachers decorate and arrange home economics classrooms as their students' "school home," and that they themselves take a summer course or practice household management lessons at home. Tennessee's vocational home economics programs did not require home projects before 1929, although some teachers assigned them. The impetus for change was the George-Reed Act of 1929, which increased federal aid and allowed greater flexibility in dividing instruction between home economics and related subjects in the sciences and arts. The Federal Board for Vocational Education's recommended course for rural schools under the George-Reed Act specified two years of a minimum of ninety minutes each day in home economics classes, supplemented by a daily period devoted to supervised home projects.[17]

Home economics made new demands on school building design and equipment. Smith-Hughes programs in Tennessee required sewing machines, work tables, wardrobes or lockers, mirrors, stoves, sinks, cupboards, garbage cans, cooking utensils, dishes, and laundry equipment. These requirements limited the number of rural schools that could afford to take on a Smith-Hughes program. Philanthropic aid for black schools ensured that they would have designated spaces and equipment for home economics education, although overcrowding or dislike of vocational subjects limited their use. White parents and demonstration clubs supported domestic education as well. Gertrude Folks's 1920 survey of rural schools found that parent-teacher associations and school patrons generally furnished a school's domestic science equipment. County agents and home demonstration clubs also raised funds and donated labor for domestic education rooms and equipment.[18]

Higher Education for Better Rural Homes

Two of the state's leading institutions of higher education, the University of Tennessee and George Peabody College for Teachers, initially featured home economics in curricula geared to the needs of rural life. As Country Life reformers across the nation adjusted their focus in the 1920s, however, these institutions reoriented their mission toward specialized academic training for the professions created by reform agencies.

In 1914, in a course entitled "Rural Education in Relation to Country Life," Harry Clark, secondary education professor at the University of Tennessee, taught about "the decline of rural life," tenancy, mortgages, farmers' organizations, demonstration work, and good roads, as well as school consolidation, supervision, and socialization. He also taught another course on rural economics and sociology in the economics department. In the 1920s, Clark and his successors in the education department turned over rural economics to the economists and redirected their education courses to correlating rural instruction with agricultural work and the administration of rural school systems.[19]

The Hatch and Smith-Lever acts placed agricultural experiment stations and divisions of extension under the aegis of state colleges of agriculture. The University of Tennessee's agricultural programs, like those at other land-grant institutions, emphasized scientific methods and experimental projects. Most of the university's agriculture courses concerned farm production. Its engineering program allowed the university to offer, as well, specialized courses that directed attention to rural living conditions, including the construction of farm buildings and domestic engineering.[20]

Home economics concerned itself directly with the standard of living inside rural homes. The state vocational education board designated the university's college of education to train white Smith-Hughes vocational home economics teachers. Between 1917 and 1921, the university's home economists broke out of the routine of cooking, sewing, and housekeeping courses. New courses in house planning and furnishing and home management promised instruction in the design, "organization[,] and scientific management of the household." Federal standards for vocational home economics teachers called for a four-year college course that included technical training, supervised practice teaching, experience in home management in a practice home or dormitory, and study in child development and family and community relationships.[21] The University of Tennessee added home economics education as a specialty for its bachelor of science degree in 1917 and in 1919 instituted a practice house requirement for vocational training.

For women interested in extension work, the home economics department suggested substituting agriculture for education courses. No doubt most chose the new "Country Life Course for Women," complementing the agricultural science curriculum for men. Agriculture, home economics, and science courses constituted the bulk of the Country Life curriculum, with the home economics requirements limited to elementary cooking and sewing and upper-level housewifery and food production. For women agents in service, home economists from the university and extension service instituted winter short courses in 1918.[22]

Although UT's home economists retained an interest in rural work, the Country Life course disappeared in 1921. Students could choose a special course of study in home economics as preparation for demonstration work or teaching the subject in rural schools. Their studies included required courses in home demonstration methods and practice; household mechanics, which covered basic household repairs; and house planning and furnishings, now an art course.[23] Rural issues retreated further in 1924, when home economics became an independent department. The department reformulated its mission, focusing on the vocational preparation of future home economics teachers and future homemakers. For a specialty in rural home economics, students could elect three courses in animal husbandry and horticulture. A new instructional building and a Tudor Revival practice house strengthened these curricula in 1926, followed in the next year by establishment of the first graduate work in home economics.[24]

Certainly these changes reflect a common trend in postwar social programs away from environmental solutions and toward specialized training for an individual's social and economic roles. Home economists emphasized the role of the homemaker as a manager of domestic consumption, rather than as the key figure in social progress. Hence, the UT home economics department defined family happiness as "the margin between income and expenditure" and claimed that, "since the home is no longer training girls to be homemakers[,] the state must assume the task." Yet it never completely dissociated itself from the university's rural mission. Faculty participated in the annual Farm Women's Week and on a home economics policy committee with extension staff. In 1927, the department announced a new "Rural Home Life Curriculum" for future demonstration agents, combining home economics with agriculture and rural sociology.[25]

At George Peabody College for Teachers, President Bruce R. Payne asserted his institution's preeminence in reforming rural homes and school buildings. The college's first announcement boldly proclaimed that it would "serve as an educational crown" for southern school systems.[26] A $250,000 contribution from the General Education Board in 1912 for the Seaman A. Knapp School of Country Life at Peabody underscored the commitment to rural uplift. By 1915, the college sported gardens and henhouses on campus and had acquired a demonstration farm on Elm Hill Pike.[27]

According to a writer in *Tennessee Agriculture*, the Knapp School promised more than the standard prescriptions of scientific agriculture; it would "show how it is possible to have proper sewerage systems, proper water supply, better home conveniences, so that living in the country will be even more pleasant than in the city." Peabody and its School of Country Life would pursue rural domestic reform by training home demonstration agents and home economics teachers for "more practical" rural schools. They would teach rural women how to increase earnings and then spend them "economically and scientifically," to the family's benefit.[28] Reflecting the importance of home economics to this agenda, the college built a $140,000 building for that department and in 1916 instituted the South's first graduate program in the subject.[29]

The Knapp School of Country Life added home economics to its courses on agriculture, rural economics, and rural education. During the summer of 1915, Peabody offered the South's first regular credit courses in canning club and home demonstration work.[30] These classes became standard summer and winter programs, providing working teachers and demonstration agents with necessary professional and practical training. According to a course announcement, the vocations of home demonstration agent and rural organizer held "special meaning" for Peabody, "in its whole-hearted attempt to serve the overwhelming majority of the rural population of the South, in the ways best suited to their own wishes and needs." Course offerings ran the gamut from "Canning Club Methods" to "Special English for Demonstration Agents." Instructors in fine arts, education, physical education, geography, and industrial arts joined those from the home economics and agriculture departments.[31]

By 1917, the home economics curriculum included a demonstration program; and, in the following year, Peabody created a bachelor of science degree in home demonstration. These years marked Peabody's high tide of rural reform. The college prepared women to teach farm wives "how to produce, conserve and utilize food to the most economical advantage." In 1918, the college consolidated its three vocational programs—agriculture, home economics, and industrial education—into a single division.[32]

The First World War placed a premium on women's domestic contributions to the war effort, which Peabody applied to its rural domestic programs.[33] Passage of the Smith-Hughes Act in 1917 also validated home economics' prominence in Peabody's reformist curriculum. Demand for white teachers in programs supported by the Smith-Hughes Act exceeded the numbers that the University of Tennessee, the designated vocational education institution, could supply. Peabody in 1920 attempted to meet the need by claiming that its graduates, too, were qualified vocational teachers. In 1925, the college offered home economics education as a specialty.[34]

Having secured a place in the academic curriculum, Peabody's home economists during the late 1920s followed other professionals in a general shift away from environmental reform and toward bureaucratic management by expert individuals. Rather than campaigning for better rural homes and homemakers in their course offerings, they emphasized women's managerial role as directors of household consumption.[35] At the same time, the college's programs became increasingly specialized and codified, in 1927 constituting twenty-nine separate curricula, including agriculture and home economics.[36]

As rural issues lost ground within the home economics department and the overall Peabody mission, management skills came to dominate other rural programs as well. The Knapp School distinguished its agricultural program from those of public colleges by emphasizing a primary mission of teacher training. At the same time, the Knapp School sought to make rural life "more humanly tolerable" and "more humanly interesting" by promoting rural sanitation, home demonstration, rural clubs, and art education.[37] Its future home demonstration agents supplemented home economics training in foods and clothing with studies of all aspects of the farm home and homemaking. The farm home received its due in fine arts courses on design, interior decoration, and "Home and Community Attractiveness," as well as courses on personal hygiene and rural sanitation. Future agents studied how to use school clubs and community organizations as conduits to transmute school lessons into home practices.[38]

Peabody's "human" concerns notwithstanding, the growth of state-funded agricultural education and experiment stations, as well as private agencies such as the American Farm Bureau Federation, superseded its offerings. Peabody terminated the School of Country Life in 1923, although it retained an agriculture department and continued to operate the demonstration farm on a reduced scale. Consequently, home demonstration lost its connection to an overall blueprint for rural uplift, which it once had shared with the Knapp School. It remained in the curriculum as a specialty within the home economics department until it also fell victim to growing state agricultural training programs in the 1928–29 academic year, just a year after the introduction of the new training course at the University of Tennessee.[39]

A new curriculum that redirected Peabody's reform energies into professional improvement soon ended the college's rural domestic programs. As attention shifted from the rehabilitation of country life to the preparation of teachers of future homemakers and their supervisors, and as the state extension service took over the rural domestic agenda, Peabody abandoned its commitment to rural homes. At the University of Tennessee, the presence of an agricultural college and the extension service headquarters permitted the survival of rural programs, albeit within the new context of professional specialization.

Teaching Home Economics in Rural Schools

Home economics teachers assumed a heavy burden of responsibility for the success or failure of rural reform at the local level. They expected that rural girls would embrace home economics as practical training for their futures as wives and mothers. White women then could be more productive themselves and improve their individual families' standards of living. Black women could do the same; in addition, they could, from their own viewpoint, advance their race and, from white administrators' viewpoint, provide a better domestic workforce for white households. None of this would happen, however, if the teacher failed in her duty. And even if she fulfilled her duty in the classroom, she might not be able to bridge the gap between the school and the home.

Hamilton County offers a particularly successful example of the implications of this reform for African American girls. Claudia P. Washington served as the county's first Jeanes supervisor and home makers' club organizer from 1915 to 1920. Washington made a total of eighty-five visits to seventeen black county schools in 1915 and raised $150 for school improvement. Girls in her home makers' clubs canned over two thousand quarts of vegetables and fruits that year and almost ten thousand the next year. In 1919–20, she visited only ten of the county's twenty-five black schools but raised an impressive $7,500 in school improvement funds.[40]

After succeeding Washington in 1920, Albura E. Henderson (later Fagala) focused on vocational classes and the schools housing them. She made almost two hundred visits to the county's twenty-two black schools in 1921 and 1922, and raised $522 for their improvement. Ollie H. Bernard, the state agent for rural black schools, credited Henderson with securing the three Rosenwald schools built in the county between 1922 and 1925. Albura Henderson Fagala probably worked with the county home demonstration agent in supervising home economics instruction in black schools. Extension officials reported successful "negro work" in the early 1920s, with school lessons following the white curriculum but "in simpler form." In 1927–28, the $313 raised by Fagala purchased pianos and cook stoves. The stoves probably served both for home economics classes and for heating lunches.[41]

Home economics, however, was a gender-defined field of study deemed essential for all women. White home economics teachers in rural schools, like the Jeanes supervisors, found that they succeeded best when they complemented classroom study with club work. Smith-Hughes vocational home economics teachers and programs could have conflicted with or duplicated the work of Smith-Lever extension agents and clubs. Charles Keffer, director of Tennessee's extension forces, reported that administrators of the two programs cooperated in order to avoid such situations. In some counties, demonstration agents supervised home economics instruction in schools. More commonly, agents established friendly relations with home economics teachers and school officials so that they could use school facilities for club activities.[42]

Hamilton County's experience once again offers a useful example. Home economics for white girls made its debut at Tyner High School in 1908. It became closely tied to the county's home demonstration program when collaborator Elizabeth Michael Bourges (Mrs. J. B.) Lauderbach initiated summer canning clubs in 1912. Lauderbach taught home economics at Soddy High School in 1911–12 and at Central High School the next year; she then turned to full-time home demonstration work. By this time, Hamilton provided vocational home economics classes at five high schools. In 1919, Hamilton County made home economics classes compulsory for all sixth, seventh, and eighth grades. Lauderbach considered this, along with providing equipment for seven white and two black school and community kitchens, her best achievement for the year.[43]

Two years later, Hamilton had "splendidly equipped [home economics] Depts with well trained teachers" for sixth through eighth grade white girls in twenty-one schools. Lauderbach supervised home economics instruction in all white county schools as part of her home agent responsibilities and cooperated with Hamilton's six Smith-Hughes vocational home economics teachers, who in turn assisted her with demonstration projects.[44]

Across the state in Shelby County, Superintendent Charl Ormond Williams was convinced that industrial education could build black and white support for the type of education which white reformers believed was best suited to black abilities and needs. Having three Jeanes supervisors already in the field, Williams sought to strengthen this curriculum with a white supervisor of rural black schools. With financial assistance from the General Education Board, she hired Lula H. Crim in the spring of 1919. Crim would ensure that black schools taught the vocational curriculum and simultaneously build bridges between the races.[45]

African American girls at larger elementary schools and the county training school already studied cooking and sewing, and now broom making and laundering joined the curriculum. Crim focused most of her effort on the county training school at Woodstock. Its female curriculum included vocational cooking and sewing courses, a course in health and sanitation, and a housework course covering practical matters of house cleaning and decorating, making household furnishings and conveniences, and personal hygiene.[46]

Nonetheless, interpersonal racial barriers threatened the cause. Crim could not bridge the gap between herself as a white supervisor and the African American educators she managed. The precise circumstances are unclear, but Williams found that Crim's insensitivity to African American wishes and needs created a deep antagonism that required Crim's resignation. Crim lacked "'that something'" essential for her work, according to Williams. Apparently Crim could not negotiate the boundaries between assistance and control, or between sympathy and condescension. As the Jeanes supervisors told Charl Williams, "Miss Crim just does not understand us."[47] From then on, African American teachers and Jeanes supervisors managed their home economics programs themselves.

Shelby's white home demonstration agents took credit for successful home economics programs among white girls. Cara L. Harris concentrated on girls' clubs and supervised home economics instruction. As a county school supervisor, Harris enjoyed the support of the home economics teachers' association; at monthly meetings with these teachers, she and women's club agent Mary MacGowan reviewed both class and club work.[48] In a 1921 article, Harris stressed the importance of organization and supervision, because turnover in many rural communities was high; a strong county organization depended on a county supervisor.[49]

Yet, when home demonstration club members surveyed conditions in twenty-seven white school lunchrooms in 1925 and 1926, they documented the difficulty in extending home economics methods beyond classroom instruction. These lunchrooms served hundreds of children daily. Twenty-one employed paid managers, six assistant managers, and seven hired white or black dishwashers; volunteers ran the other six programs. But only thirteen had running water, nineteen had sufficient stoves and storage space, and eleven had window screens.[50] Such conditions suggested that the home economics program, while established in individual classrooms, had not transformed other aspects of the schools.

Home economics also had a limited impact on rural education and uplift in Obion County, largely because Obion women accepted only half of the school-home equation. In 1917, the First World War's emergency food production drives brought Eva P. Luther to Obion County as home demonstration agent. Luther coordinated the establishment of eleven community kitchens, where white women's and girls' clubs met for demonstrations and shared equipment for preparing and preserving foods for home consumption. These kitchens provided the foundation for Luther's primary objective, the expansion of home economics instruction in the county's white public schools. One home economics teacher already was working at Kenton School in 1916, and another started at Troy in 1918. In the latter year, Luther proudly reported that she had convinced the superintendent of schools to hire an additional itinerant home economics teacher for girls' club work in community kitchens.[51] Part-time teachers worked at five locations with "well equipped class rooms," and Luther hoped for teachers at the remaining six community kitchens in the next year. In the meantime, Luther herself taught home economics at the county's white one-room schools and organized girls' clubs.[52]

After the wartime emergency ended, declining public interest and the resignation of the county agricultural agent threatened Luther's position. Luther added agricultural demonstration work to her workload but could not overcome community disinterest even after establishing a county Council of Agriculture. She felt awkward in dealing with male farmers, who did not send in their reports "simply because the ones in charge are not sufficiently interested to push," but she "hesitate[d] to take charge except to work with them." When the county terminated her services in 1920, only school-based home economics instruction remained to carry on Luther's energetic domestic agenda.[53]

Classroom instruction in home economics as an impetus for domestic reform had definite limits. As Tennessee's home economists discovered, it was one thing to introduce the subject to white rural middle-school and high-school girls and quite another to have any impact on their schools, let alone their homes. Home economics proved effective among whites only where school-based teachers joined efforts with effective home demonstration agents, although the latter depended upon local support for their jobs. African American home economists, interestingly, had more success in linking industrial education, school improvement, and domestic uplift. Jeanes supervisors made this possible, in part by following the same procedure of combining school lessons with home demonstration club work.

When reformers of the early 1920s compared their efforts to change country homes with similar efforts a decade earlier, the obstacles blocking entrance to country homes remained the same—simple indifference or outright opposition to outside intervention in rural communities, lack of resources, and variations in local leadership and personalities. Home economics education in schools did not create the transformation in values and behaviors the reformers desired. But they retained their faith in home economics. They had another promising solution for the problem of rural home life: the demonstration programs involving girls and adult women in club work that paralleled home economics education in rural schools. Home demonstration programs increased the incentives for home economists, the farm women who participated, and school girls to join forces in a common assault on the domestic environment.

• 5 •

Better Homes on Better Farms: Home Demonstration and Domestic Reform

"I am a country woman," Clara Boone Mason told her audience at the 1914 meeting of the Middle Tennessee Home-Makers' Association. "Women are largely responsible for the movement away from the farm, and I believe they are going to swing the pendulum back again. . . . The old farm-house will be inhabited again by a home-maker who sees its possibilities."[1]

Progressive Tennesseans such as Mason called on country people to reorder their homes as well as their schools. Education and country life reformers argued that domestic reform could hold families on their farms, revitalize rural communities, and enhance rural life. Homes kept traditional in appearance, furnishings, and purpose could never match their "possibilities," as Mason observed, and would prove to be a liability within a rapidly modernizing agricultural world. Better homes could produce better farms and an improved country life only if rural homemakers adopted new aesthetics and consumer goods.

Educational progressives looked to home economics training in new rural school buildings as an entering wedge of change. Here girls would learn new homemaking techniques and then work with their mothers to raise standards of living at home. Tennessee Commissioner of Agriculture Thomas F. Peck asserted that better-educated farm women "will make their homes so really homelike and inviting that the men and boys will be more content to remain in them."[2]

But rural schools proved to be erratic vehicles for domestic reform, especially during a period of rapidly accelerating change in all other aspects of Tennessee agriculture. By the mid-1920s, Tennessee's farm families were buying more gasoline-powered machinery, using new highways to move their crops to market, and producing greater quantities of the specialized agricultural commodities—such as dairy products, burley tobacco, and new breeds of livestock—associated with the term "progressive farming." Aggressive home demonstration work promised a similar modernizing process for rural homes. The creation of more "really homelike and inviting" abodes, to keep families farming and prosperous, became a long-term venture for Tennessee's rural reformers.

Was it realistic to think that better homes could create better farms and more contented farm families? Progressive reformers, architects, and interior designers of the early twentieth century thought so. They assumed that a satisfying home life was essential to personal and social well-being; few then or now would question that assumption. Recognizing that living conditions influenced people's lives, as well as reflecting their personal circumstances and preferences, reformers sought to change home environments in ways that would produce more desirable behaviors and values.

Their strategy now seems simplistic, naïve, riddled with class and gender bias, and based on assumptions rather than evidence of the power of the built environment to influence human behavior. The household appliances which were recommended by home demonstration agents could not by themselves strengthen family bonds, any more than consolidated school buildings could automatically improve education, but reformers believed that these material advances bespoke deeper changes for the better.

Like school building reforms, domestic reform through demonstration work enjoyed the support of private foundations and new federal, state, and local bureaucracies. After the 1914 Smith-Lever Act mandated home economics programs for the USDA Extension Service, both girls' canning and poultry clubs and women's home demonstration clubs were established across the state. From their inception, federal and state extension programs pursued a gendered division of labor, assigning male agricultural agents for work with farm men in crop production methods and female home agents for work with farm women on home economics projects. Few farm households organized their labor in such mutually exclusive gender categories; farm women across the nation rejected this aspect of reform. In the South, especially, extension officials and agents encouraged productive and income-earning work for farm women.[3]

In the 1920s, extension agents moved toward the business progressivism of their sister home economics professionals, forging public and private partnerships similar to those of professional educators. The rural South's entry into a national consumer economy in that decade also shaped domestic reform, and the extension service contributed to that development. As a joint federal-state government initiative, home demonstration reflected the tendency of Progressive reformers to mandate change from above. The standards against which county agents measured farm home hygiene, efficiency, comfort, and appearance embodied the principles taught in college home economics classes, discussed in popular national women's magazines, and promoted by the federal extension service. By stressing these standards, home agents introduced new domestic ideals into rural Tennessee.

Domestic reforms differed from other environmental reforms, however, in focusing on building interiors rather than exteriors. Although the extension service and private businesses stood ready with model farm home plans, few rural southern families could afford a new house. Demonstration agents focused on the domestic interior instead, as the locus of farm women's work and influence over family life.[4]

Rural domestic reformers also had no direct authority over rural women, lacking either the financial incentives or the curriculum requirements exercised by other educational progressives. Demonstration agents found rural women reluctant to accept their advice unless agents addressed local needs and interests. The interaction between professional agents and rural women thus shaped domestic reform in ways that limited its modernizing tendencies and preserved local traditions. Those women who did participate in home improvement projects adopted new standards of housework and home decoration, but on a sliding scale that ranged from a fireless cooker to a model farm home.

Regional concerns about race and segregation also shaped domestic improvement programs, coloring the perceptions of both white and black women concerning what was appropriate for their homes. Thus, projects for black women from the beginning included basket, rug, and mattress making—skills also taught in industrial classes. White women began this work later, and then with a market-oriented mindset fostered by the Appalachian handicrafts revival of the 1920s.

Country women of different races shared some common reform experiences. All club members participated in projects that reflected the changing priorities of federal and state programs. These projects had the potential, at least, of promoting standards of home life that transcended the barriers separating whites from blacks, southerners from northerners, and country folks from urban masses. Tennessee's rural women not only influenced how these projects were implemented locally but also determined their success. Country women pushed home agents to define their work in ways that would secure local support. Without that support, organized rural home improvement failed as a strategy for reconstructing country life.

Home improvement programs remained voluntary; agents could not require rural women to change. Yet some such women did change, and accepted the challenge of creating better homes to build better farms.

Productive Work and Home Conveniences

Women's demonstration work began in the summer of 1914 under the USDA Cooperative Extension Service, authorized by the Smith-Lever Act. In the southern states, where demonstration programs already operated, extension workers centralized their offices at land-grant universities. Tennessee's extension forces, financed by the federal government and the General Education Board since 1911, operated through the University of Tennessee's College of Agriculture. Virginia P. Moore, now assistant director for home demonstration, had eighteen agents in the field in July 1914 and twenty-six a year later.[5]

USDA programs shared the Country Life movement's general goal of rural uplift, in which communitarian ideals and scientific efficiency coexisted in an ill-defined vision of the rural future. Rural reformers and extension officials agreed that improved income and home life constituted the most effective means of keeping rural people on the land. The division between the male agricultural agent and the female home agent reflected their assumption that farm income correlated with a male sphere of production, while home life belonged to a female sphere of reproduction and consumption.

In theory, the home agent would extend home economics instruction to rural homes and introduce urban, middle-class standards through labor-saving equipment and mass-produced furnishings. As a result, farm women would be relieved of the drudgery of work in field and house, and would enjoy increased status with their exclusive domestic authority.[6] Historians have shown how the USDA, far from elevating farm women's status, advocated a new sexual division of labor that confined women to the home and threatened long-standing traditions of partnership and mutuality between husbands and wives—changes that rural women generally refused to make.[7]

Southern officials took a rather different approach. Seaman A. Knapp's demonstration programs to battle the boll weevil's threat to cotton cultivation preceded federal extension work in the South, whereas northern and western programs developed out of university extension. Southern agents emphasized local needs and voluntarism rather than the dissemination of professional expertise, and had already organized girls' and women's clubs. They identified cash-producing work as farm women's most urgent need; household technology was an auxiliary issue. As Bradford Knapp and Mary Cresswell of the Office of Extension Work in the South noted, "In many cases incomes must be increased before standards of living can be raised or progressive community enterprises fostered."[8]

According to J. A. Evans's *Recollections of Extension History,* home economists at colleges and extension divisions outside the South opposed the emphasis on productive work for income, as encouraged by southern demonstration agents. Southern agents also differed from their peers across the nation in structuring their programs along racial as well as gender lines for conformity with the region's practice of legal segregation. Consequently, the USDA's North and West Office and Southern Office operated independently until the merger of the regional offices in 1921.[9]

Between 1914 and 1921, southern home agents generally emphasized productive projects such as canning, poultry, and fruit production for market sales, which increased a woman's cash income. Women's incomes paid for the water systems, appliances, and furnishings deemed essential to the ideal rural dwelling, and often supported the farm family as well. Even as country women continued productive farm work, however, extension policy and rural people's own choices rearranged the gender division of labor on many farms. Rural women moved closer to the urban homemaker ideal, not by substituting housekeeping for productive work but by expanding their roles within the home.

If home agents were recruiting farm women for domestic reform, what did they want those women to do in their homes? In Tennessee's early demonstration program, not that much. Following the regional pattern, home improvement initially held a secondary place in Tennessee's demonstration program. From July 1914 through 1918, home agents focused on productive and organizational projects among white females, mostly girls' canning clubs. Virginia Moore appointed the first two district agents in 1915; two specialists in foods and clothing and in health, and a third district agent joined the extension division soon thereafter. Deferring to her state's racial segregation, Moore hired two African American district agents to coordinate a separate program for black women.[10]

Although few white reformers paid much attention, African American demonstration agents quickly developed useful and successful home improvement programs, suggesting that black women themselves possessed a broader plan for rural uplift. As district agents, Mabel Myers and Stella (Estelle) Richards supervised home makers club agents who organized women, girls, and some boys. Home makers clubs grew out of an experimental program funded by the General Education Board at Tuskegee Institute in 1914. Hoping to fill the gap in African American extension work left by the Smith-Lever Act, the GEB extended the program throughout the South in 1915. For four years, Tennessee extension administrators relied on GEB support, rather than ask white-controlled local governments to pay black agents.[11]

Home makers club agents usually were Jeanes industrial supervising teachers, who undertook club work during school vacation months. They reported to the state agent for black rural schools, Samuel L. Smith, as well as to the appropriate African American district agent. Ten club agents worked during the 1915 summer season; one year later, seventeen agents organized clubs in sixteen counties. Agents taught sewing to girls and women, organized fundraising activities for schools, and supervised whitewashing of houses, barns, fences, and school buildings. Given these agents' duties as Jeanes supervisors, the conjunction of home and school improvement is not surprising.[12]

Samuel Smith supported these initiatives in home improvement, as part of his effort to emphasize self-sufficiency in food production and home sanitation for blacks. Assuming that African Americans needed special training in these matters, Smith summarized the clubs' goals as "first, to induce [African Americans] to raise more vegetables . . . ; second, to allow nothing to be wasted; third, to improve and beautify the homes and make them more sanitary." He commented favorably on club supervisors' reports which "show[ed] how they have gone into the filthy homes and helped to clean them up and put things in orderly arrangement."[13]

As the home demonstration staff expanded in the decade after 1910, its members took a greater interest in white homes and adult females. Agents intended club experiences to socialize rural women for community uplift. In constructive yet agreeable group activities, rural women could learn about foods and nutrition, domestic hygiene, and family health. Having applied these lessons in their homes, rural women could extend them to schools, churches, and community clubs.[14] For these goals to be met, home demonstration workers needed access to rural women and their homes, which agents gained through girls' club projects. Girls' clubs devoted winter meetings to topics such as kitchen rules, table settings, and house cleaning that directly engaged each member in her mother's home domain.[15]

Whether agents or country women were more reluctant to engage in adult club work, the numbers of women involved in home demonstration programs grew slowly at first. Whereas 1,409 members joined sixty-five clubs in 1916, twelve months later their numbers had swelled almost fourfold. Specialist Geneva Conway described the greatest obstacle to the work of the demonstration agent:

> It is a well known fact that it is a difficult task to approach a woman who has been the queen of her castle for many years and have her change her methods of work, which may have been practical to her, but unscientific from the present day point of view, to have the daily dietary altered so as to meet dietetic standards instead of family custom, to install conveniences which to her are new, but which have proven their efficiency and last of all to get her to put her housekeeping on a business basis and have it run like a well oiled machine.

Hence, girls' clubs would serve as "our wedge to the home."[16]

Perhaps the best proof for Conway's assertion came from Hamilton County, where the dynamic Elizabeth Michael Bourges Lauderbach added girls' club work to the home economics instruction offered to white and black girls in county high schools. Lauderbach initiated summer canning clubs in 1912, a propitious moment of agricultural expansion. In that decade, Hamilton's predominantly white farm owners would more than double the value of their farm property.[17] At first Lauderbach found girls uninterested in joining her clubs: only twenty-six girls participated regularly in club activities. Among them, however, were three of the state's top ten club girls that year. Lauderbach enticed more girls with a canning party at the University of Chattanooga campus, where she selected a team that won a canning contest at the state fair.[18]

Lauderbach's own reports corroborate comments made by a "prominent business man in Chattanooga," quoted by Bradford Knapp and Mary Cresswell in a 1916 article on southern home demonstration work. Evidently Lauderbach's work had attracted the attention of the business elite in Chattanooga, the county's seat of government and its premier commercial center. As the Chattanooga businessman noted, the home agent had to convince her rural constituency of the value of her work, for "practically nothing had been done to arouse the interest of the young people in country life or home improvement. . . . Practically no demand for the work came from rural people." Lauderbach worked year-round as a "collaborator" in 1913, visiting communities and conducting demonstrations in vegetable and fruit gardening and preservation. After this intensive campaign, the Chattanooga businessman recounted, "For the first time the parents began to appreciate the advantages, both educational and economic, of having their girls and boys trained in club work."[19]

For the next two years, Hamilton club girls rated among the top canners in the state, and Lauderbach recruited more club members than any other home agent in 1915.[20] This resourceful home agent built club membership by emphasizing its social, as well as productive, purpose. Providing a "bountiful dinner spread, temptingly prepared and arranged," at day-long summer canning parties and picnics, she offered country girls welcome relief from their usual household chores during school vacation. Summer courses at the county high schools and the University of Chattanooga, where Canning Club Day had become an annual event with "many social features," also provided opportunities for socializing. Friendships and rivalries initiated in the summer program continued through the year in school clubs.[21]

A desire to reach mothers motivated Lauderbach's cultivation of girls' clubs. In one case, Lauderbach conducted demonstrations that taught girls proper canning methods "in the presence of their mothers" to convince the women to stop using commercial chemical preservatives. Visits to club girls' homes also served as a means of finding and instructing adult women in cooking, sanitation, making a fireless cooker, and proper selection of clothing and furniture. By 1916, one hundred women had joined ten clubs, each of which met every two weeks in the local school or a member's home. According to Bradford and Cresswell, "Women who formerly seldom left their homes now attend[ed] these meetings regularly." These women valued the social life of their clubs, which broadened their outlook beyond their individual homes to their shared community and county.[22]

Once inside farm homes, agents like Lauderbach preached the gospel of home conveniences. These ranged from an egg beater to a complete indoor water system. Reformers believed that such labor-saving devices could remedy what they saw as the primary problem in rural reform: the overworked farm wife. If her burdens could be lessened so that she might spend more time and effort on creating a homelike atmosphere in her own home and community, the quality of rural life would improve enough to keep her children in the country. Home economists had identified many instances of unnecessary domestic labor, such as the excessive steps women took in poorly arranged kitchens. Farm commentators noted that even the most progressive farmers, who outfitted their barns with the latest devices, turned miserly when it came to investing in domestic labor-saving equipment. "It is true that this may fairly be regarded as a private matter which each household must settle for itself," observed Tennessee's commissioner of agriculture, also dean of the University of Tennessee's College of Agriculture. "But in the large aspect of public welfare it is a question worthy of sympathetic and sensible consideration in every community."[23]

Tennessee women did consider it. Participants in the Round Table Love Feast at the Middle Tennessee Home-Makers' Association meeting in October 1914 exchanged housekeeping and cooking shortcuts; one of their featured speakers, Mrs. J. H. May of Pulaski, called for economies in time and labor through systematic household work. The East Tennessee Home-Makers' Association's 1915 annual meeting included an address on "The Practical Equipment of Our Country Homes," which recommended running water, a sink, a table and stool, and a fireless cooker in the kitchen, as well as a mangle and a clothes wringer.[24] Club members were no strangers to such devices. They installed one thousand home conveniences in 1916, ranging from homemade dustless mops to refrigerators, store-bought oil stoves, and gas irons.[25]

Home Demonstration as "War Work"

In retrospect, the early years of home demonstration work resemble a rural preparedness program for the First World War. Organized club activity promoting efficient domestic food production and conservation favorably disposed rural women to wartime food drives. Virginia Moore, who served as home economics director of the state Food Administration, reported that "there has been no dividing line between home demonstration work and the food administration work." Club membership expanded as both rural and urban women rallied behind Herbert Hoover's Food Administration.[26]

State extension staff and county agents held classes on food conservation, distributing recipes for weekly meatless and sugarless days and demonstrating preservation techniques. They trained food conservation volunteers at the University of Tennessee, the state normal schools, Tennessee Agricultural and Industrial State Normal School, and George Peabody College for Teachers. One thousand women earned certification as volunteer war workers. By June 1917, almost six thousand women, over seven thousand girls, and forty-seven white county agents were at work.

Wartime agricultural production required a massive expansion of the extension service. The Food Production Act authorized national emergency extension appropriations in August 1917; Tennessee used these funds to expand its home agents' numbers to ninety-four in 1918. While the number of club girls actually fell in 1918, almost two thousand more women joined home demonstration clubs.[27] Twenty-two black home makers club agents organized 12,744 girls and 5,536 women into 878 clubs in 1918. African American agents and demonstrators, like their white counterparts, canned and dried foodstuffs and organized drives for Liberty Loans, war stamps, and the Red Cross. "But few people really know the untiring efforts and the self-sacrifice of these agents in performing their duties this year," S. L. Smith told his superiors at the General Education Board.[28]

Agents and demonstrators believed that women's war contributions ennobled rural homemaking. The *Knoxville Sentinel* headlined an account of the East Tennessee Home-Makers' Association meeting with "Home Makers Now See the Dignity and Power in Their Great Labor." Ida McKay, president of the Middle Tennessee Home-Makers' Association, claimed, "Women used to think they were martyrs when subjected to such drudgery . . . but now they think they are recognized as heroines."[29]

Wartime production programs demanded administrative coordination and accurate record keeping. Consequently, federal and state extension service staff concluded that program planning, statistical records, and community organizations made their efforts among rural women more efficient. Virginia Moore's report for 1918 indicated her own growing interest in professional standards. For the first time, she and her agents made orderly statistical reports of club membership and project work. Job descriptions for specialists, district agents, and county agents, as well as outlines for each project area, defined home demonstration's goals and procedures. County agents' objectives included organizing extension work for women and girls, selecting projects appropriate to community needs, and doing "all possible to promote prosperity and contentment in the home." Under "Results Expected," their job description listed "Better farm homes in Tennessee."[30]

Demonstration clubs received a similar job analysis. Their objective was "to develop best methods in household management, so as to minimize time, strength and money and to increase the income of the home." Methods consisted of organizing clubs for all white women, regardless of class, selecting demonstrations suited to community needs, and meeting in homes whenever possible. "More vital and intelligent interest in the affairs of the home" would proceed from these techniques.[31]

Armed with records of unprecedented levels of productivity and organizational activity by rural women, Tennessee's home demonstration staff, like enthusiastic Progressives across the nation, assumed that victory abroad would pave the way for their agenda at home. Job descriptions and blueprints for community organizations developed during the war seemed to have won the allegiance of rural women. State home demonstration staff expected that rural community organizations, which the extension service had promoted since 1914, would become their next theater of action. Rural residents had expressed little interest in such organizations until their wartime experience with county Councils of Defense. The extension service sought to restructure the defense councils as permanent county Councils of Agriculture. Agricultural councils, extension officials hoped, would generate local leadership and support for planned farm and community modernization.[32]

Most home agents would be sorely disappointed by their county councils and by rural women. The war emergency may have galvanized home demonstration programs in other states and placed new power in the hands of state and local officials, but its effect on rural Tennessee women was limited.[33] By November 1920, only forty of ninety-five counties had even started agricultural councils. These groups focused primarily on farming and offered little support for farm women's issues, although women did join to further their own productive work and to support the councils' work in school improvement. Many councils converted themselves into county farm bureaus as that movement spread slowly into the South, but the American Farm Bureau Federation's structure and goals largely ignored women's concerns. As the redoubtable Elizabeth Lauderbach dryly observed, Hamilton County's farm bureau was "distinctly a man's affair" that attracted female members only when a separate Woman's Auxiliary was formed.[34]

What may have alarmed home demonstration staff even more was that rural women quickly lost interest in all organized activity. Rural women's enthusiasm for club work had been real but short-lived. Demand for food conservation and for the services of a home agent fell sharply with the armistice, revealing them to have been temporary responses to national crisis.

In some counties, World War I had been country women's first formal connection with the state extension service, and it would be their last. Lewis County took the same approach to domestic reform that it did to school reform, adopting an outside program only in extreme circumstances. Agent Harriette F. Parris organized five demonstration clubs in wartime Lewis County. Although membership was limited at only forty women, total attendance at club meetings reached 350, and girls' canning clubs attracted 130 members of their own.[35] But Parris's service was discontinued after seventeen months, and thenceforth Lewis County women closed their doors to domestic reform programs.[36] Even in more affluent Rutherford County, home of a state teacher's college and increasingly attuned to educational reforms, the war inspired only sixteen months of female demonstration work. Rural women there undertook no further organized home campaigns until 1935, except for a year's work among African American women in 1926.[37]

During the war, home agents had descended upon each Tennessee county whether local people wanted them or not. Rural women felt little commitment to a county agent or a home economics program once national food drives ended. Even with additional appropriations in November 1918, the number of home demonstration agents dropped to seventy-seven. Declining agricultural fortunes, which limited county governments' resources, pushed the number of agents down farther, from forty-one in 1920 to twenty-three in early 1922.[38]

Money was not the only problem. Three thousand women dropped out of demonstration clubs in 1919. Home agents found communities unsettled by the war and, according to Virginia Moore, tired of organized activity. Flora Melissa Byrd described Bradley County in 1919 as "rather disturbed after so much anxiety and war work." Public perceptions of the demonstration program as an emergency war project lingered. In 1922, district agent Mayme Parrott commented, "The people seem to have forgotten that it was home demonstration work, and speak of it as war work."[39]

Home Conveniences and Home Improvement

Women's marginal roles in county councils and farm bureaus, combined with the failure of home agents to engage the permanent interest of rural women, convinced reformers that an overhaul of Tennessee's female demonstration programs was imperative if they were to have any positive effect on farm women or rural life. Agents responded by expanding home convenience projects into a broader program of home improvement to better family life, a program endorsed by the federal extension service as the logical next step for southern demonstration work. Reviewing the work of southern home agents in 1920, O. B. Martin and Ola Powell described a linear progression from canning clubs to home convenience projects to home decoration. Now that female agents had gotten into farm homes, women wanted them to do more. Martin and Powell asserted that "practically every county home demonstration agent reported that home improvement is one of the things in which her club members are most interested and in which they are seeking help."[40]

At that time, however, Tennessee women had expressed only limited interest in home conveniences, let alone home decoration. Although county agents commonly reported interest in home improvement on their own part and on the part of local women in 1919, they spent little or no time on such projects; and few agents reported offering decorating assistance. The state home demonstration staff, now led by Margaret A. Ambrose, in 1920 decided that a renewed initiative for home conveniences once again would serve as a wedge for entering the homes and values of rural women.[41]

In a sense, Ambrose's decision returned home demonstration to the place where it had started in 1914: claiming to improve farm life simply by convincing women to improve conditions in the home. Announcing the "More Home Conveniences" slogan for 1920, a writer in the *Tennessee Agricultural Extension Review* observed that "more than a striking slogan is required to convince the average housewife of the great advantages of the many modern conveniences for the home." Demonstrations of those labor-saving devices most needed in the rural homes of a particular county, agents hoped, would achieve more than a slogan could.[42]

Home convenience projects picked up on suggestions made earlier by home economics specialist Mary Geneva Conway in her 1918 bulletin, *Make the Farm Kitchen Convenient*. In addition to urging farm women to obtain such standard equipment as a stool and drainboard, Conway stressed the necessity of sunlight, ventilation, heating, and room arrangement, for "the surroundings of the kitchen will influence the health, efficiency, and happiness of the worker."[43] In the 1920 home convenience campaign, agents especially urged homemakers to install kitchen sinks and washing machines, "relievers of the great back breaking jobs of the average housekeeper in the country."[44]

Maude Guthrie repeated, and elaborated upon, Conway's advice in *Home Economics Projects for Women's Home Demonstration Clubs in Tennessee* (1920). Guthrie outlined monthly programs in twelve areas of household management, clothing, food, and canning. A year of "Household Conveniences and Equipment" included sweepers, cookers, window screens, and home utilities. "Household Efficiency" demonstrators followed a parallel regimen that emphasized the planning, efficient methods, purchasing, and proper equipment that were necessary to make "housekeeping a profession."[45]

Still, home agents found that rural women would not, and sometimes could not, accept projects that promised to reduce their workloads. As the 1918 program outline for household equipment had warned, "Care must be taken in handling this subject not to antagonize housekeepers." Amid accounts of successful improvements and plans for more home projects in the next year, home agents across the state chronicled their frustration with rural women. Mary Lee Garrett from Lake County in northwestern Tennessee reported that she had difficulty interesting women in anything but canning, as "they think this is all there is for them to learn." Besides her new demonstrations of household conveniences, Myrtle Webb of McMinn County in southeastern Tennessee had to repeat almost all those given in the previous year. "Often the same demonstration must be given in the women's clubs a number of times before any impression is made," she complained.[46]

The primary reason most white farm women had little interest was that poor agricultural conditions between 1919 and 1922 severely limited farm income, making the purchase of home conveniences difficult. White home agents, such as Jeanette T. Ellis in Weakley County, had difficulty promoting the state home conveniences campaign when families purchased only essentials.[47]

Hard times hurt African American women particularly, for they had even less cash available for home purchases. The federal extension service had taken over black demonstration programs in 1918 from the General Education Board. In Tennessee, the burden of all county home demonstration work now fell on African American district agents, their salaries paid solely by the extension service. These women recorded little of their work, save for a 1919 bulletin, *Home-made Brooms, Rugs and Mattresses*. Prepared by district agents Mabel Myers, Stella Richards, and Lillian White, the bulletin emphasized industrial work and self-sufficiency.[48]

Paradoxically, the postwar agricultural depression increased the need for home improvement efforts even as it made them more difficult to achieve. Commissioner of Agriculture Dr. F. M. McRee told East Tennessee farmers in 1920 that the state had "scarcely any new farm homes, while the houses were sadly in the need of paint and repair, and . . . things generally had a run down appearance." Child labor investigator Charles E. Gibbons painted a similarly dismal picture of the state's housing stock, describing most homes he had visited as "deplorable." The disparity between owners' and tenants' homes appalled Gibbons, who described tenant houses as "tumble-down shacks," often worse than landlord's barns.[49]

With little interest in home improvement from most rural women, and little money to spend for those who were inclined to adopt home conveniences, home demonstration officials fought for their program. Tennessee's agricultural agents pushed farm modernization and coordinated crop planting and marketing to farm men as solutions to the unexpected economic crisis. Home demonstration agents reminded these same farmers that their homes deserved attention, too: "What is more important than a comfortable, joyous home life? Nothing in the world, and the equipment of it with modern labor-saving conveniences and comforts should have first consideration."[50]

The tide turned in the home agents' favor as agricultural fortunes began to revive in 1922. During the middle years of the decade, at the urging of extension agents, families turned to several new sources of income. Cash crops such as burley tobacco gained in popularity across the state. Production of hay, especially alfalfa, expanded, as farm families turned row-crop fields into pastures for increasing numbers of specially bred cattle. Some new breeds, such as Angus cattle, were designed for beef production; others, such as Jersey cows, were valued for their high yields of milk. Dairies multiplied throughout Tennessee during the 1920s, with trucks hauling the raw milk on such newly completed, hard-surfaced highways as the Dixie Highway, to centrally located milk plants which supplied the state's booming urban centers. Poultry products increased in number, with farmers using extension service plans to build modern chicken coops or larger chicken houses.

Better times boosted the number of white home demonstration agents from twenty-six to thirty-one between 1923 and 1926. But the number of black home agents actually fell, though one new black district agent joined the division in 1922. Without local government support for black demonstration work and unwilling to press the issue, the extension service allowed the number of African American agents to remain at prior levels, with each agent responsible for multiple counties and a staggering workload.[51]

Agricultural disaster then led to an expansion in the extension service's ranks. The 1927 Mississippi River flood prompted congressional relief to fund agricultural and home demonstration agents in affected counties. Increased federal extension appropriations under the 1928 Capper-Ketcham Act underwrote three additional flood-relief agents and three itinerant agents (one of whom was black), who joined five new county-supported home demonstration agents in 1928.[52]

Passage of the Agriculture and Home Economics Cooperative Extension Act by the Tennessee legislature in July 1929 proved a greater impetus to hiring. It halved the amount of matching funds a county needed to pay agents, quickly inspiring thirteen counties to add white home agents. The decade ended with the largest number of home agents since World War I: forty-six white county agents, five black agents, and four white itinerant agents.[53]

Over the course of the 1920s, the extension bureaucracy became increasingly specialized, standardizing its own products along with those of the state's farmers, who followed extension service advice. In the mid-1920s, home demonstration programs increased attention to domestic reform and home improvement. Beginning in 1922, a series of projects in household conveniences and equipment, household furnishings, the budget, and household efficiency constituted one of the four new core programs for home demonstration clubs.

The following year, Lillian L. Keller joined the Tennessee extension staff as a specialist in clothing and household management, adding professional expertise in domestic interiors. Keller's arrival reflected official support for home improvement. It coincided with a groundswell of local interest in household projects, as documented in a newly introduced "Annual Report of County Extension Workers." This standard federal reporting format detailed two household project categories, home management and home furnishings. Hattie L. Ross, an African American agent, defined these projects in familiar terms. Home management "stimulates interest in attractiveness of home and the elimination of unnecessary expenditure of money and to systematize house-work." Home furnishings "consists of all articles to improve the home" and "making a home attractive in the most economical manner."[54]

At the same time, agents began including copies of the annual project plans adopted by each of their clubs or farm bureaus with their narrative reports. In 1924, Margaret Ambrose reported that, as a result of her staff's emphasis on the topic, almost every community or club plan of work included some sort of home improvement project.[55] Even though foods and clothing projects still recorded greater participation, reports at the state and local levels trumpeted home improvement.[56]

Community efforts also boosted home improvement work, maintaining rural domestic reform's early connection with the Country Life movement. Wilson County agent Mary Stuart Henderson reported in 1921 on the first communitywide home improvement drive among white club members, who painted and whitewashed homes and fences, worked on their yards, and in some cases installed light and water systems in their homes.[57] Farm home improvement received an additional boost in 1923, when the state extension division began a "Name Your Home" campaign as an inducement to pride in farm ownership and appearance. Demonstration agents claimed that farmers cleaned up their property and repaired their houses before displaying their registered names, thus improving the general appearance of the countryside.[58]

African American agents already routinely linked the individual farm home with the rural community, crossing gender lines in the process. During spring clean-up campaigns, rural black Tennesseans whitewashed and painted their homes, put up window screens, repaired and remodeled houses, added wallpaper to their walls, and refinished furniture.[59]

Community clean-ups were not solely for club members, nor were they the exclusive province of home agents. African American agricultural agents also sponsored community improvement drives and took a greater interest than white male agents in the extension service's home construction, remodeling, and repair projects. Black agents' interest in homes perhaps derived from their awareness of the connections among tenancy, living conditions, and rural stability. R. T. Butler, agricultural agent in the cotton-producing counties of Madison and Haywood, counted "many good homes repaired, new houses built and a more contented people in the rurals" among his "successful undertakings" in 1922. "I am very much pleased with the prospect of a better and a more contented rural people. Altho there remain a sign of unrest," he concluded.[60]

Home Decoration and Domestic Consumption

By emphasizing home furnishings as well as conveniences, home improvement moved into the realm of interior decoration. According to Margaret Ambrose, a popular demonstration on making window shades of unbleached muslin provided a new "opening wedge" into the rural home interior. "Like the Easter lily in the dirty dingy home calling attention to the ugliness around it," remarked northeastern district agent Mayme Parrott, new shades stimulated complete interior renovations.[61]

Agents emphasized that it took only a little money to make real improvements in home decoration. Wilson County agent Mary Stuart Henderson showed how even the most financially strapped farm homemaker could join in a home improvement campaign. Cleaning up the lawn or sawing off the back of a baby's high chair to make a kitchen stool counted among her club members' projects. More prosperous women remodeled their kitchens, built cabinets, installed water and lighting, or put up new wallpaper "with better taste." Leah Parker recounted how she involved every Anderson County club in home improvement: "In each club one number of the program was given to home furnishings and house management. One woman rearranged her kitchen, another is keeping a budget for the first time this year. Following Home Improvement day at which time Specialists showed equipment needed in every kitchen, twenty one small articles such as measuring spoons, egg beaters, kitchen clocks, etc. were added. More convenient kitchens have been the topic of discussion in several community meetings."[62] Parker also listed a kitchen arrangement project. Rearranging a kitchen for fewer steps was easily understood and accomplished, making this project a favorite among efficiency-minded agents and cash-short demonstrators.

As Parker's account illustrates, local clubs and women translated the state home improvement directives into action, according to their own needs and resources. Parker's farm-family constituents generally owned their farms but had limited disposable income.[63] So club members tended to make items themselves or purchase inexpensive articles. While Parker worked in an Appalachian county, the trends she documented were found in many other rural counties. For instance, a mother and daughter in Giles County, in Middle Tennessee, made kitchen furniture out of scrap lumber (fig. 21).

Another way of making improvements without spending much money was to alter existing furniture or facilities to save expense and labor. Agents pointed out that raising a table surface or sink so that a woman did not bend over while working, or putting a wood box on casters to make it easier to move from the stove to the door for refilling, made domestic work a little less back-breaking. When Sallie I. Duvall wrote to her African American club members in 1924, "Let's have as our motto this year, 'My kitchen more convenient and comfortable,'" she set a goal that both home economists and rural women could accept and achieve.[64]

No matter what their cost, home improvement projects injected modern, urban-oriented standards of home economics into the rural home, reordering farm women's traditional domestic activities and spaces according to the principles of scientific management. In the mid-nineteenth century, urban, middle-class homemakers had assumed responsibility for the domestic environment. By the turn of the century, such women were redesigning their

Fig. 21. Kitchen furniture made from scrap lumber. Such projects allowed cash-poor farm women to modernize their homes. "Giles County Has First Kitchen Contest," *Tennessee Extension Review* 8 (Jan. 1925): 3. Used courtesy of the Archives and Special Collections, University of Tennessee Library, Knoxville.

households as models for community development.[65] Country Life reformers early in the twentieth century recruited rural women for the same sort of domestic reform. In the 1920s, demonstration projects in home furnishings added an entirely new role, that of interior decorator, to rural women's duties. Fanny Liggett described the impact on older women in Marshall County, remarking that "when these old country grandmothers asked to know how, at this late year, to make their homes more beautiful, it proved that ignorance and not indolence is the cause of their homes being so bare and plain."[66]

House furnishings demonstrations sought, at the very least, to introduce the contemporary aesthetic of simplicity and order to a rural home's appearance. Agents told farm women that their jumbled and cluttered rooms were unattractive as well as unsanitary. Instead, furniture and decorations should be kept to a minimum and arranged neatly around the walls. Agents detested the ubiquitous "callenders and Bricabracs" in farm homes. As with kitchen rearrangement, agents and club members recommended disposing of such items as an inexpensive yet valuable home furnishings project. Northeastern district agent Lizzie Reagan reported in 1923 that "club members have been taught to first rid their houses of the unnecessary and the 'unbeautiful' things that cluttered up. A surprising amount of junk has been discarded."[67]

County agents illustrated proper room decoration with photographs sent out by the state office or magazine pictures. They favored standard design principles of selecting "warm" or "cool" tones according to the lighting and function of a room, as well as shading colors from dark to light from the floor to ceiling. White dominated in the kitchen, but elsewhere agents recommended decorative schemes in the Colonial Revival palette, combining shades of blue, off-white, and brown in floor and window coverings.[68]

In keeping with the popular interest in antiques, inspired by the Colonial Revival and promulgated by national women's magazines, agents commented favorably on the "old," probably handmade, furniture country women showed them. Refinishing demonstrations encouraged them to use and value family pieces. Blending traditional furnishings with the Progressive aesthetic of simplicity produced unified interiors like those described by Lizzie Reagan: "Some homes have been papered, soft colors being selected. Old furniture and old floors have been treated, and rag rugs have become very popular." Kate B. Gresham took credit for better harmonized colors in walls and rugs and reconditioned furniture in four hundred African American homes in East Tennessee. Only one agent proved completely unsympathetic to traditional decorations. Bama Finger, the new Davidson County agent in 1929, asserted that her home furnishings demonstrations inspired women to throw out "many heirlooms, which were entirely out of harmony but kept for sentiment" and to replace pieced quilts with wool comforters.[69]

Still finding it difficult, as well as rude, to criticize women in their own homes, agents once again targeted daughters. They introduced bedroom improvement projects that encouraged girl club members to follow their decorating suggestions. In addition, agents recruited one girl from each community for an "Own Your Own Room" project. While she sewed bed coverings and curtains, club members discussed the room's decoration. As Mayme Parrott explained, "We insist on simplicity."[70]

One of the state's most successful club girls, Ellen Latting of Shelby County, demonstrated how such projects could blossom. Latting began converting a small storage room into her bedroom in 1923 and continued the project during her years at West Tennessee Normal College. The thrifty club member reused many items, turning the floor matting over, painting blemished furniture, and decorating with painted bottle vases and framed magazine pictures. As every agent hoped, this project led to a complete renovation of the home. Latting, her mother, and her sister proceeded to redecorate two other bedrooms, replace drapes in the living and dining rooms, and repaint the dining room and kitchen.[71]

In 1930, the state extension service promoted homemaking among girls with an enlarged "Own Your Own Room" campaign. Five hundred and sixty-one white girls and forty-five black girls practiced their interior decoration skills on their own rooms. They refinished walls, woodwork, and furniture, and made rugs, curtains, and (sometimes with their brothers' help) new furniture.

Lillian Keller had prepared a model girl's bedroom for the 1929 Mid-South Fair in Memphis and Knox County Better Homes demonstration house (fig. 22). Her prototype featured remade and refinished pieces that home agents commonly suggested as substitutes for commercially produced, but expensive, furnishings: "An old iron bed painted a soft green, a dressing table made of two paint boxes with a dyed feed bag curtain around it, a bedside table made of scrap lumber, covered with green fabricord, a home made book shelf, a waste basket made of an old tin bucket painted, and a picture pasted on it, a hooked rug and dyed flour sack curtains." Refurbished existing furniture, homemade pieces, and such recycled cast-off items as buckets and sacks enabled girls on limited budgets to create the equivalent of any scheme found in a mail-order catalogue or country town emporium. The desire to imitate "modern" standards must have been strong: after visiting the fifteen bed-

Fig. 22. Girl's bedroom exhibit prepared in 1929 by Lillian Keller, specialist in clothing and household management with the Tennessee Division of Extension. Everything in the room was renovated or refurbished. *Tennessee Extension Review* 13 (Jan. 1930): 3. Used courtesy of the Archives and Special Collections, University of Tennessee Library, Knoxville.

rooms improved by Knox County club girls, Keller found that twelve had used the same green-and-yellow color scheme as her model room.[72]

Later in the 1920s, two new aspects of home decoration, handicrafts and picture study, gained in popularity among club women. Craft work supplemented ongoing projects in sewing, basketry, and rug making. Rather unexpectedly, home agents and rural women found that they could make money by combining the skills developed in home furnishings projects with traditional female crafts. In the 1920s, Colonial Revival taste for old-fashioned or handmade furnishings created an expanding market for traditional Appalachian handicrafts and hand-produced textiles. Responding to this demand, some Tennessee women found new ways of increasing their cash income through productive work in home decorations, rather than foodstuffs. One of the most popular crafts produced for market sale was basketry. Proceeds from these endeavors increased the disposable income women had available for modern home improvements.[73]

Hamilton County, befitting its position as a leader in women's demonstration work and the early recognition of that work by Chattanooga business interests, profited most handsomely. White club girls had sold crocheted items, along with canned and baked goods, at the Chattanooga market house since 1916. They also took orders for handmade rugs, which became the mainstay of home furnishings sales organized by white home demonstrators, not merely the self-sufficiency project advocated for black club women. By 1922, district agent Lizzie Reagan could report that "rug making has become a profession in this county."[74]

Reagan mentioned that women from one community worked cooperatively on their rugs. Probably she referred to Apison, Tennessee's most successful example of the rug, basket, and handicraft associations that flourished in other southern communities by the mid-1920s. About one hundred women participated in rug production, using standardized sizes, patterns, and colors for their products. After contracting with a Chattanooga department store, home demonstrators sold rugs valued at $1,500 in 1923. Two years later, Apison women sold $4,000.00 worth of handmade rugs, wall hangings, table linens, dresser scarves, and draperies. Most of their goods went to out-of-state purchasers, thanks in part to a favorable article describing their products in *The Farmer's Wife,* a national farm periodical.[75]

Location on a key transportation route also benefited Hamilton County's handicraft industry. The Dixie Highway, the nation's premier north-south automobile route, brought potential customers through the county and the city of Chattanooga, a significant marketing advantage. Similarly, women in the Asbury community of Knox County sold rugs at their 4-H shop in Knoxville. Women in other counties not as well known for club work also profited. Union County home demonstration women set up a club shop in Maynardsville in 1929 that also catered to travelers on the Dixie Highway.

Here they sold baskets, vases, pottery, linens, and quilts. Agent Lillie F. Oakley noted, "Many sales have been made to people of the Northern states."[76]

The Colonial Revival and the attendant fad for Appalachian crafts hopelessly entangled tradition and modernity for the producers and consumers of Tennessee crafts. Hamilton women and girls blended traditional skills with modern standards of taste when they made rugs, mats, and draperies for market sale and for the "old fashioned" bedroom exhibited at the Chattanooga fair in 1927. They now had the cash to improve their own homes. These, their demonstration agent hoped, would combine modern utilities and conveniences with contemporary interpretations of traditional decorative schemes. Like the electric light concealed in an oil lamp beneath a cretonne shade in Lillian Keller's model bedroom, Apison rug makers reinterpreted their heritage for contemporary consumer tastes in a manner that unified their customers' homes with their own.[77]

Handicrafts became a major enterprise in only a few rural communities; most club members made crafts for domestic consumption. Home agents across the nation found handicrafts a drawing card useful among otherwise indifferent women. Earline Brown, the new African American agent for southeastern counties, commented, "There are so many little things that can be takend up aside from the main line of work that will create interest in the routine of club work. Some of these things are lamp shades, Aurora Velors painting, [tie] dying, door stops, pin trays made from beaverboard, this also taking in oil painting, and rose painting, that is, taking pickle or mustard jars and making roses from them."[78]

As Brown's comments indicate, not all handicrafts employed traditional materials or techniques. A number of rural homemakers employed club crafts projects as an inexpensive means of participating in the wave of domestic consumption at the end of the decade. Elizabeth L. Fowler, working in Sumner County in 1929, noted that "basketry, the use of lacquer, making of lamp shades, and modernistic odds and ends has interested the women and girls very much and has assisted in putting over other projects."[79]

Some agents chafed at the seeming triviality of craft work, which contradicted their prescriptions for simple living. Rhoda Hawes, Marshall County agent, cautioned that "on the whole[,] country women do not need to be encouraged to clutter up their homes." Williamson County agent Virginia E. Carson dutifully reported the popularity of such projects, although "many useless articles have been fixed simply for ornaments having little value either before or after." Typically, demonstration clubs added crafts to their programs, and agents followed their lead: three years after her first disparaging comment, Virginia Carson announced that Williamson County club women dedicated the month of July 1930 to handicrafts.[80]

While agents debated the place of farm women's crafts in proper home decoration schemes, their picture study programs created no such dilemma.

At the same time, these programs produced neither income nor much interest in fine art among rural women. Picture study assumed that art exercised the same environmental influence as other elements of the domestic interior; reformers championed the use of fine arts reproductions in the home. In Montgomery County, members brought pictures from their homes so they could discuss them with "a real authority in the study of good pictures." "In most instances, the owner knew very little about her own picture, which was influencing the lives of her family to the extent that pictures can," agent Ruth McClure related. In similar demonstrations across the state, agents or guest speakers recommended traditional images that were deemed appropriate for country homes: images of motherhood and family life, such as the Madonna and the child Jesus, or rural scenes, such as landscapes or *The Gleaners*. They also advised the rural home decorator to hang only one picture on a wall, and to place it at eye level, lower than was common practice.[81]

Home improvement and decoration projects were intended to transform farm homes into places of orderly yet relaxing contentment for family members. Mrs. A. E. McLaughlin humorously suggested what that might look like in her poem, "When My Wife Went to College," describing what she learned at the University of Tennessee's Farm Women's Short Course:

> No more catacornered tables—
> The lines don't harmonize at all;
> All the folding beds and sofas
> Must parallel the walls.
>
> Then there was Grandpa's picture
> That always hung so high;
> She has it down now
> On the level with the eye.
>   . . . .
> A hooked rug now she's making
> Of the family's worn-out hose;
> What she'll tackle next
> I'm sure nobody knows.[82]

Demonstration agents preached that home improvements would create better homes on better farms. They used home conveniences and interior decoration lessons to buttress their own work within the extension service, whether as a vital element of war work or as a means of redressing the sorry state of rural affairs in the postwar years. When conditions seemed brighter, home agents structured their work into annual plans and specialized projects that further accentuated the distinctive place of home improvement in the extension service's agenda for rural women. Demonstration programs expanded the range of duties for farm women, increasing their responsibilities in the home while productive work continued. By drawing attention to a woman's place in her home, demonstration programs weakened but did not sever the connection between domestic and community reform, especially among African American participants.

At all times, a home agent depended upon a responsive group of rural women. To recruit their support, an agent had to include women in program planning, even entice them with special projects. Agents also learned to adapt their projects when they were impractical and unaffordable. Ellen Latting, who had won acclaim as a club girl for her bedroom decorating project, became a home agent after graduating from West Tennessee Normal College. As she worked in Decatur County in 1929, she adjusted the state extension program and her own working methods to local interests. "The work being new and my being a little young I have to watch my step to keep the idea that I am just coming to tell them that the way they have been canning, cooking etc. always is all wrong, from developing," she confided. Consequently, she did what the women wanted to do—which in this county meant projects on food preservation and preparation and clothing.[83] Meanwhile, Earline Brown had found handicrafts just the thing to keep women interested in their club work.

Ultimately, even the least costly home improvement projects encouraged interested rural women to model their homes after the standards of the consumer culture of 1920s America. Some Tennessee women produced the very goods that were part of that consumer culture. Others found home improvement attractive when the extension service explicitly linked its projects to domestic consumption in special events and campaigns. In so doing, they redefined both their roles as farm women and the image of the farm home.

· 6 ·

Domestic Consumption and Competition: A New Ethic for Rural Homes

As home improvement campaigns attracted the attention of rural women during the 1920s, their success hinged on changing women's ideas about their roles in rural life and expanding their consumer ethic. Domestic reformers in the Tennessee extension service magnified home improvement projects, transforming them from an auxiliary to female farm production into a vital exercise of women's domestic skills. Home improvement's place on the rural reform agenda owed much to circumstances in the growth of the extension service as a joint federal-state agency; but the place of home improvement in the life and daily routines of rural women depended on whether and how their interests and circumstances meshed with those of a home agent.

Rural women and home agents modified the relationship between domestic production and consumption as they worked together on projects for better living in the farm home. This process, which went beyond following instructions from the agent or copying a model room design, depended upon women's willingness to take on new responsibilities and to involve themselves in new relationships with merchants and merchandisers. As with any demonstration project, many rural women ignored or rejected the concept of themselves as domestic consumers. Those who considered it did so on their own terms, tackling what they could and wanted to change about country life.

Rural women who wanted something different could choose from many sources of advice, as well as a number of projects. Special events and contests in home improvement, sponsored by the state extension service, encouraged rural women to compare their homes with the tempting array of goods available at their local emporia and to rate themselves against their neighbors. Regional and national organizations also recruited rural southern women. The Better Homes movement dovetailed nicely with demonstration projects in house furnishings. Farm journals sponsored their own competitions, designed to find women who excelled at home improvement or who were outstanding farm homemakers.

When country women in Tennessee responded to these initiatives, they took on more work as managers of both productive work and domestic consumption. They demonstrated how the commercial products of the twentieth century could transform the farm home. Domestic reformers in the extension service claimed victory, but their success was limited to more affluent farm women and owed more to the appeal of consumer goods than to rural uplift.

Home Improvement Days

Agents who attempted to implement the 1920 "More Home Conveniences" slogan faced the obstacles of female disinterest and rural poverty. Even so, a few enterprising home agents identified new allies in town merchants and bankers. They hit upon a winning method with countywide home improvement events. Agents and business leaders, both eager to guide farm wives in exercising their purchasing power, provided special programs and displays of household equipment for clubwomen's inspection. County home agents seem to have initiated the relationship, partly as an expression of their programmatic goal of educating women about home improvement. Agents also acted out of self-interest, for local leaders might be more disposed to support county agents who promoted their businesses.

Home agents in five East Tennessee counties organized the state's first "Home Convenience," or "Home Improvement," days in 1921. These events typically brought interested rural women to the county courthouse for a morning program of speeches and demonstrations by county and district agents, as well as club leaders. After a picnic lunch, women toured commercial establishments, most of which featured special displays of home equipment and furnishings and offered promotional gifts and prizes. Local banks provided rural women with explanations of their savings and checking accounts.[1]

Demonstration agents believed that the special Home Improvement days educated farm women about products and services for rationalized homemaking, while storekeepers and bankers believed the promotional events reached new customers; participating country women were exposed to the broader range of consumer goods and services in town. By 1924, fourteen towns hosted Home Improvement days, and the events remained popular thereafter, each attracting as many as five hundred women to town.[2]

As home improvement projects gathered momentum, the alliance between home agents and business leaders strengthened. The evolution of Home Convenience Day in Greene County is a good example of this statewide trend. Home agent Mabel Moore began work in the county in 1915, at a time when the extension service stressed productive work in girls' clubs and

the county had shown its aptitude for reform by instituting a school building program. Moore initially concentrated on schoolgirls: by 1919, she had
organized almost two thousand in sixteen clubs. Two hundred women met
in five adult home demonstration clubs, but only fourteen engaged in home
improvement work. In 1920, when the state slogan called for "More Home
Conveniences," Greene demonstrators added only fifteen such devices.
Those paltry numbers did not prevent Moore from claiming success for the
campaign; she listed "home conveniences and home furnishings and flowers
at home" after poultry as her most effective projects.[3]

In 1921, Mabel Moore discovered an effective promotional tool for home
improvement, in her first "Home Convenience Day." After a program at the
courthouse in Greeneville, clubwomen ate a picnic lunch, then viewed displays at various mercantile establishments and the local bank. In 1923,
Moore retitled the event "Greene County Women's Day." During a morning program at the courthouse, country women observed demonstrations of
meat canning and clothes selection, and listened to a panel discussion of the
farm housewife's duty to provide social activities for her family and a speech
on the ideal living room.[4]

Local merchants realized the event's potential. In advance of the 1924
women's day, newspaper advertisements touted "Thousands of Useful
Things . . . That will greatly aid in making Better Homes for Greene County."
Ads exhorted, "Throw Away Your Mail Order Catalogues/Thousands of
People are Making Arrangements to attend/IMPROVEMENT DAY/. . . /SPEND
YOUR MONEY AT HOME AN[D] BE PROSPEROUS."[5] Reinforcing that message, Lillian
Keller, extension specialist in clothing and household management, spoke
on convenient kitchens, displaying "useful articles" of "reasonable cost."
District agent Oma Worley demonstrated steam pressure cooking and
"urged that the women of the county secure these cookers before another
year." State home demonstration director Margaret Ambrose concluded the
program with a lecture on "Buying for the Home," in which she exhorted
women to patronize local stores before buying "out of town."[6]

Promenading through those local stores, women collected souvenirs and
viewed model rooms; inspected hardware, utensils, and ready-to-wear clothing; and watched demonstrations of dish washing, table setting, and baking.
Mabel Moore recorded little impact on club members' homes, counting only
twenty kitchen cabinets and two sinks added, and seven kitchens, ten living
rooms, and eight bedrooms improved in her 1924 statistical review. Yet this
one-day event had enticed a larger number of women to consider increasing
home consumption with the mass-produced bounty filling nearby shops, bringing images from magazines and catalogues closer to home.[7]

Moore and her superiors in the state extension office did not measure the
event's success by enrollment in home improvement projects. Home Improvement days served a larger purpose: to foster the commercial relationship

between rural homemakers and local businesses. Promoting the rural housewife's consumer consciousness ostensibly ran counter to the extension service's claim to increase her productivity, but this contradiction ran throughout extension work. Agricultural extension programs promoted diversification for self-sufficiency, yet increased farmers' expenditures on commercial fertilizer, seed, feed, and equipment. Similarly, home improvement projects emphasized how a thrifty housewife could make her house a home by making her own draperies, doing her own painting and refinishing, reusing discarded furnishings, and transforming magazine illustrations into framed artwork. But home agents encouraged women to buy household gadgets, install expensive utilities, and invest their poultry and butter profits into the fabrics, wallpapers, and furniture depicted in mass-circulation women's magazines.[8]

Home Improvement days explicitly connected domestic and commercial interests. Margaret Ambrose noted that they gave "an excellent opportunity for the linking of the interests of country and town and the presenting to the merchants and bankers the home demonstration program. They generally realize before the day is over that a program of improvement in the country home means an opportunity for the town merchant if he is ready with the material the country woman wants to buy."[9] Franklin County home agent Lemma P. Boles promoted her event for eight months to skeptical Winchester businessmen. Afterward, they asked why she had not organized one sooner: "Said it was one of the greatest ways of advertising they had ever had." These events promoted the extension service to local business interests, who could influence county courts to appropriate funds for agents' salaries. Lillian Keller declared that the Home Improvement days "probably [did] more than any other phase of Extension work to convince merchants and business men of the worth of the Division of Extension and the ability and value of its workers."[10]

Home Improvement days also document a shift in domestic reform in the 1920s. Agents still suggested the same types of equipment, furnishings, color schemes, and arrangements. They still described projects in the language of home economics: efficiency, hygiene, simplicity, good taste. At the same time, they cloaked domestic and community uplift in commercialism and consumerism. Only those country women with disposable income needed to attend a Home Improvement Day, so this aspect of domestic reform was limited to more prosperous farm families. Demonstration agents now pursued the same alliance between affluent farm families and commercial interests that was fostered by agricultural agents and the American Farm Bureau Federation.[11]

Simultaneously, home demonstration agents and businesses encouraged country women to join the consumer mainstream of the 1920s. They promoted the image of the farm homemaker, although the real farm woman probably performed productive farm work and earned her own income for her purchases. As historians of rural women have shown, such efforts prescribed more restrictive roles for farm women. They also brought country women into the public eye by bringing them off the farm and into town, where their patronage was courted. Home Improvement days identified women as the arbiters of farm homes and set a precedent for public campaigns showcasing women who transformed their country homes.

Kitchen and Living Room Campaigns

In 1923, Greene County agent Mabel Moore adopted contests as another novel method of demonstration work. Contests helped to propel home improvement to the top of the demonstration agenda in the mid-1920s. Kitchen and living room competitions, in which peer pressure and rivalry motivated domestic improvement, added new incentives for participants to buy massproduced furnishings for kitchens, living rooms, and bedrooms. The contests directly rewarded women who transformed farm homes into rural versions of contemporary middle-class interior design.

The kitchen, as the key female space within the reformed rural home, had top priority for improvement. It was the focal point of women's domestic work and the room that best combined efficiency, sanitation, and decoration. Kitchen improvement projects, like the Home Improvement Day, transmitted mixed signals to country women about domestic production and consumption. Mabel Moore's kitchen contest offered prizes to the women who made the most improvements for the least amount of money.[12] By promoting thrift as well as efficiency, the contest encouraged women to invest large amounts of their own and their families' labor in kitchen renovations and their cash in new equipment. Perhaps for that reason, only five women registered for the contest and only three submitted final reports.

First prize went to Ruth Ann Doty. She and her husband William performed most of the labor, which she valued at $6, and she hired another worker for $3. Doty described the improvements that this labor and cash expenditures of $45.65 produced:

> We having built an addition to our house it enabled us to enclose a small
> back porch for a pantry. Giving 5'× 7' which we plastered and painted white.
> By moving the cabinet in pantry gave room in kitchen for a cook table, which
> I obtained from one of my neighbors which she had thrown away. I painted
> my table and cabinet white and put new white oil cloth on each. We installed
> a range boiler and enameled iron sink with drain board, and have both hot
> and cold water. We painted walls and ceilings of kitchen white, varnished doors
> and casings, put glass door opening from pantry to platform of cistern, and
> put curtain and shade at window.[13]

Not only had Ruth Ann Doty reduced the time that she spent cleaning a tiresome drainboard and heating water, but also she had turned an average farm kitchen into a modern, antiseptic workshop.

Apparently the Greene County contest's limited appeal allowed it to be forgotten by state officials. Instead, Margaret Ambrose hailed the 1924 Giles County kitchen contest as the first in the state. Agent Emma Re Lewis organized an elaborate contest with overall prizes, community prizes, and prizes for model kitchens. Of the forty women who entered the contest, Lewis asserted that thirty-seven did "excellent" work. One of these women was a tenant farmer who spent $1.70; she and her husband painted and wallpapered their house with supplies provided by their landlord. Lewis claimed that the contest elicited a greater response than any other project and piqued local interest in home improvement work.[14]

Following the lead of agent Lewis and other rural states across the country, Tennessee's home demonstration staff made kitchen improvement its first statewide project in 1925. In 1921 and again in 1923, the USDA had issued Ruth Van Deman's *The Well-Planned Kitchen,* which contained a one-page scorecard, perfect for contests. More than eighteen states from Massachusetts to Montana held kitchen improvement campaigns in 1925.[15]

"Plan for a contest or campaign this year and help change your tired, overworked and discouraged house-keepers into happy, efficient home-makers," urged the *Tennessee Extension Review* in 1925. In thirty-four counties across the state, 5,191 women, including 514 African Americans, enrolled in the project. The kitchen campaign was officially noncompetitive; these women enrolled in the kitchen improvement project and worked on it like any other club activity. In practice, however, the project encouraged a competitive spirit by using scorecards to measure women's progress. Lillian Keller prepared written materials for local agents that set the procedures and standards for all to follow, including scorecards and questionnaires. To inspect kitchens and make out reports, county agents appointed club leaders as kitchen campaign chairwomen, although it was not always easy to find willing leaders. District agents and specialists organized contests in counties lacking home agents.[16]

Some agents openly converted the project into a contest with prizes donated by local businesses and Farm Bureaus.[17] Inspection teams graded kitchens according to a standard scorecard before and after the owner made her improvements. Each participant submitted an itemized list of her improvements and their cost, and the woman who most improved her kitchen score for the least cost won the contest. Essay and jingle writing contests for women and girls and model kitchen exhibits supplemented the work done inside rural homes.[18]

Home demonstration agents claimed that the kitchen campaign was the leading project of the year—not surprisingly, since it was the officially sanctioned state project. The agents' own comments, and others repeated by them, suggest that the project indeed excited clubwomen and encouraged them to take steps they otherwise would not have taken.[19] Men supported the project as well, whether out of their own interest in farm efficiency or, in Weakley County homemaker Kate Radford's words, as "Mr. Handy Man" assisting with the renovations. Sallie Duvall credited the campaign with involving the entire family in home improvement.[20]

Questionnaires completed by county agents indicated that agents and some rural women accepted modern housekeeping standards of efficiency, sanitation, and beauty. In keeping with the standard home management project, agents recorded new labor-saving devices and the number of kitchens rearranged for convenience. Project guidelines emphasized raising working surfaces to proper height, placing wood boxes on casters, construction or purchase of kitchen cabinets and wheel trays (to carry dishes and food between kitchen and table), and installation of water systems and sinks. Participants enumerated every new window, door, and screen installed to improve light, ventilation, and sanitation.[21]

Kitchen decoration received its due as well. White demonstration agents in Davidson and McMinn counties noted with approval that women commonly began their projects by painting kitchen walls in light colors such as yellow, cream, gray, and tan, thus making noteworthy improvements in appearance and lighting. One clubwoman, Mrs. W. H. Phillips of Oglesby, Davidson County, created the unified decorative scheme advocated by home agents in her "most enviable kitchen," using the pattern of her new linoleum to harmonize the yellow walls, white woodwork and cabinets, and curtains.[22]

Families who renovated their kitchens absorbed the generally accepted images of the 1920s homemaker as both an efficient household manager and a fashion-conscious, contented domestic worker. The *Tennessee Extension Review* featured the kitchen of Mrs. Bert Erwin, a Maury County clubwoman, which she had transformed into a modern workplace (fig. 23):

> From an ill arranged, badly lighted room with its only conveniences being a range and a cabinet, this kitchen . . . was raised from a score of 40 at the beginning of the kitchen contest to a score of 91 at the close at a cost of $48.50. Two new windows were added, a modern table replaced an old door balanced on a flour barrel, water works were installed, floor covering laid and many other things added and changes made that turned the place into one of the most pleasant rooms in the house, one in which it is now a "real joy to work in," to quote Mrs. Erwin.[23]

Another "Enthusiastic Contestant" vindicated domestic reformers' claims that physical improvements lessened drudgery, creating a positive atmosphere that improved rural attitudes. She reported that she had "heard several ladies

Fig. 23. Mrs. Bert Erwin of Maury County improved her kitchen score from 40 to 91 points, spending almost $50 to create a modern domestic workshop. *Tennessee Extension Review* 9 (Dec. 1925): 3. Used courtesy of the Archives and Special Collections, University of Tennessee Library, Knoxville.

say that they never slighted their kitchens any more when it came to cleaning them. And that it was a joy to go into them to cook and the cleaning after meals was a pleasant task since they could make them look so nice." "The women appreciate the fact that if the kitchens especially are conveniently arranged," concluded Hallie Mary Prather, Sullivan County agent, "more steps are saved, less time spent in the kitchen—more for other home duties, and a better disposition to offer the other members of the family."[24]

In Greene County, Mabel Moore successfully incorporated the state kitchen campaign into women's activities there. Mrs. W. N. Roberts, who chaired the county campaign, recounted the personal significance of kitchen improvement. Of course, she observed, a cleaner, better arranged, and better equipped kitchen allowed a housewife to prepare healthier food more efficiently. Having eliminated some drudgery, the farm woman could summon "renewed courage" for her continual round of preserving, cooking, and washing.[25]

The true significance of these improvements, however, lay in Roberts' "changed attitude of mind" toward her work, herself, and her family. Labor-saving devices in the kitchen freed this country woman to read magazines, play music, visit a friend, or drive into town with her husband. Her kitchen's blue ceiling, yellow walls, white woodwork, and blue and white checked curtains and linoleum looked so pretty that it seemed a shame to dress dowdily, so she wore a matching checked housedress or complementary apron. She kept a powder puff handy by the white-framed mirror, too. "And when we see the look of admiration in his eyes," she gushed, "we are more than repaid for any trouble or time spent in making ourselves as attractive looking as our kitchens." Kitchen improvement had "done more than any one thing in our county to change 'housekeepers' into 'homemakers,'" Roberts asserted. The farm wife performed her work better, with a "broader outlook" and "more even temper," because she spent more time in recreation and personal cultivation. She also provided a better home for her children and a more appealing companion for her husband.[26]

As Roberts' account suggests, the kitchen campaign moved farm wives closer to the roles of the urban homemaker of the 1920s: home consumption manager, attractive wife, affectionate mother.[27] Many more women sought such "cheerful, well-lighted, convenient workshops" and new roles in them. Mabel Moore recorded that 319 women had rearranged their kitchens, although only 182 club members actually had enrolled in home management projects. Besides purchasing cabinets, stoves, sinks, tables, and cooking utensils, they had covered floors and tables, installed water pumps, and screened porches. Moore photographed two improved kitchens equipped with gleaming white cabinets (both built-in and free-standing "Hoosier" units), stools, and tables, that blended renovated or homemade pieces with store-bought items.[28]

Buoyed by the success of their first statewide campaign, Tennessee's home demonstration staff undertook a second project—this time, living room improvement—in 1926. This campaign attracted over three thousand adult participants in thirty-one counties, more than the kitchen campaign. Teams of club girls gave lecture demonstrations on living room furnishings. Lillian Keller's 1925 bulletin, *The Living Room That Is Livable,* outlined the project by providing decorating principles proper for rural homes.[29]

Keller assumed that farm women, like Country Life advocates and interior designers, preferred a living room to a pretentious formal parlor. The living room required special attention as the center of farm family life. As "the room which every one visualizes as the place for ease, comfort and relaxation—pleasing to the eye and restful to the body," this room's furnishings should express the family's individuality, informality, and good taste. Keller's principle for selecting those furnishings paraphrased William Morris's aesthetic dictum: "To be really beautiful an article must be useful."[30]

In her bulletin, Keller combined Morris's earlier Arts and Crafts precepts with the rational Progressive aesthetic. Furnishings, wall and window treatments, floor coverings, and ornaments should be simple, light, uncluttered, and well balanced. "The keynote of the attractively furnished living room is simplicity in the selection and placement of articles going into it," Keller declared. Rather needlessly, she warned housewives that "a gilt chair of the Louis XIV style has no place in the farm home living room."[31]

Agents and club leaders scored living rooms according to Keller's criteria. As spelled out in the bulletin's scorecard, these ranged from fairly objective categories of hygiene and ease of cleaning to more subjective issues of comfort, beauty, and restfulness. Narrative and statistical reports indicated that living room improvement often consisted of furniture refinishing and rearrangement, with secondary attention to room surfaces and window treatments. Home demonstration staff singled out Mrs. P. E. King of Dyer County's Hurricane Hill community for praise:

> Her living room has a library table in the center, a divan in one corner, set straight with the wall, the radio in another corner and chairs grouped for convenience about the room facing the grate. The room has been newly papered with paper that lightens the room considerably. A matting rug covers most of the floor, and her window hangings will be cream marquisette. The library table and seat by the radio were made by one of her boys in a manual training class, the radio sets on an old fashioned desk which makes a very good radio table.[32]

Simplicity, as always, was the keynote of decoration. Identifying order with beauty and gentility, agents insisted that women clear out excess items and adorn their walls with appropriate artwork. African American club members in southern Middle Tennessee found "much more satisfaction" in their orderly living rooms and bedrooms. In Dyer County, white home agent Neta McFee was "glad to say that some 'Cupie' dolls and hideous calendars have been removed." An exhibit at the East Tennessee Fair contrasted a typical farm living room, "overcrowded, ill-arranged, calinders and unnecessary bric-a-brac in evidence," with a proper one that featured refinished furniture in a "neat, simple and attractive" setting (fig. 24).[33]

The living room campaign succeeded from a statistical standpoint, but agents' reports hinted that it never caught the imagination of club members. District agents did not trumpet their sections' contributions, and county agents reported room improvements without mentioning the campaign. The project itself was more diffuse. Women could elect to improve dining rooms or bedrooms as well, which made it harder to distinguish the living room initiative from regular home furnishings projects.[34]

No doubt the extensive kitchen campaign already had exhausted the energy, interest, and resources of many agents and club members. Giles County's new agent, Maude Gentry, found that to be the case. Having inaugurated the kitchen campaign in 1924, county women two years later expressed little interest in the living room project—only twelve entered the county contest. Neta McFee made no apologies for Dyer County club members, who did more work on their kitchens than living rooms, "as the kitchen work was very much needed dispite the kitchen campaign last year." To agents like McFee, this apparent failure actually proved the staying power of home

Fig. 24. This exhibit, prepared for a living room improvement project in 1926, contrasted a "typical" cluttered farm living room with one furnished and arranged properly. *Tennessee Extension Review* 10 (Oct. 1926): 3. Used courtesy of the Archives and Special Collections, University of Tennessee Library, Knoxville.

demonstration, which had a cumulative effect on rural homes. Farm wives dependent on good crops or flocks for improvement funds might take years to complete their projects and could not afford additional decoration work.[35]

Having shown how to modernize the kitchen and living room, state extension staff moved on to annual campaigns in home gardens, horticulture, and waterworks, leaving kitchen improvement and home furnishings work to proceed at a steady pace.[36] At the end of the decade, state staff collapsed home management and furnishings into a single home improvement project, in which women could add home conveniences, rearrange furniture, and "eliminate useless bric-a-brac."[37] The shift away from extension service home decoration campaigns did not reflect declining interest. Rather, home agents and clubwomen had begun directing their home improvement work into regional and national competitions.

Better Homes and Master Homemakers

Home improvement campaigns led by private organizations celebrated country women who excelled as homemakers. The Better Homes movement and farm home improvement contests sponsored by rural magazines appealed to national audiences but utilized demonstration agents' expertise and organizational experience with country women. The merger of state and county extension work with these national campaigns offers another example of the recruitment of farm women into a mainstream culture of domestic consumption.

Better Homes in America, a national domestic reform organization, flourished between 1922 and 1935, under the leadership of Herbert Hoover, *Delineator* editor Marie Meloney, and Harvard University professor James Ford. The Better Homes movement pursued two goals: improving the quality of housing and promoting the homemaker's role as an educated consumer. Local Better Homes committees, which operated with a great deal of autonomy in the mid-1920s, cooperated with other voluntary groups on public programs and demonstration houses.[38]

In some Tennessee communities, Better Homes chairwomen relied on home demonstration agents for organizational and furnishing advice. In others, county agents and clubs accepted responsibility for the campaign. Bertha Corbitt of Madison County was the first Tennessee home agent to organize a Better Homes Week, complete with a model "colonial bungalow" open to the public in Jackson.[39] Home demonstrators in six counties planned their kitchen campaign events in conjunction with the 1925 Better Homes in America Week; the 1926 living room state project officially closed during Better Homes Week.[40]

Tennessee performed well in national Better Homes contests. Montgomery County won second place in 1926, with two demonstration homes; Madison and Williamson counties also earned honorable mentions. Madison had two demonstration homes, one for whites, organized by Corbitt, and one for blacks, directed by Rebecca Davis. In the 1927 contest, one of Knox County's three demonstration homes merited fourth place. The state made its best showing in 1928, when a Gatlinburg cabin won second place, and eight communities, including two African American demonstrations in Hamilton and Blount counties, garnered honorable mentions. In 1929, Knox County maintained its competitive status with an honorable mention.[41]

Rural clubwomen channeled their interest in home improvement into Better Homes programs. Hamblen County women "worked out their own house problems" while studying the demonstration house, according to agent Lucy Filler.[42] Interested women placed better homes discussions on their annual club plans.[43] More active clubs renovated and furnished rooms of demonstration houses and served as hostesses for public tours.[44]

Better Homes projects capitalized on the same partnership between reformers and commercial interests that produced county Home Improvement Days. Local committees often borrowed demonstration houses from building contractors. Working from a supposedly typical family budget, club members made the furnishings and decorations, or bought or borrowed them from local merchants.

Vigorously promoted by the federal and state extension services, Better Homes campaigns identified country women with the urban mainstream of women's domestic experience. Better Homes in America took the improvement of urban and suburban housing as its primary mission, with little or no consideration of rural conditions. Rural clubwomen who were involved in the movement created ideal room settings in demonstration homes like those illustrated in photographs and advertisements seen in contemporary women's magazines (fig. 25). Most of their model houses stood in country

Fig. 25. Interiors of the Williamson County Better Homes demonstration house, which won an honorable mention in the national contest. Few rural families could have afforded such decorative schemes. *Tennessee Extension Review* 10 (Jan. 1927): 3. Used courtesy of the Archives and Special Collections, University of Tennessee Library, Knoxville.

towns, suburbs, and mill villages, not on farms. Judging from available photographs and descriptions, the houses tended to be small bungalows or cottages with faintly colonial styling. These typified suburban architecture rather than utilizing traditional rural vernacular forms such as the wing-and-gable house.[45]

The furnishing schemes of Better Homes model houses assumed cash incomes and housing standards far beyond the general experience of rural families. As with Home Improvement Days, these model homes made no allowances for women who were content with rearranging furniture while they saved for future home improvements. Indeed, some clubs found demonstration houses too labor-intensive or too far removed from rural experience. Agent Glenn McClellan persuaded Columbia merchants to allow her clubs to set up model rooms in their stores, which rural women toured on a combined Home Improvement and Better Homes Day.[46] Shelby and Williamson county agents arranged farm tours, supplemented by Better Homes programs at county seats.[47]

Better Homes sent a distinctly ambivalent message to rural black Tennesseans. Beginning in 1924, Better Homes in America organized "Negro Better Homes Campaigns" in southern states. Black home demonstrators in Madison, Knox, and Blount counties responded enthusiastically and won national attention for their efforts. District agent Oma Worley recorded the potential benefits to the extension service itself, observing that "not only did the [Alcoa, Blount County] demonstration prove helpful to the negro men and women in showing how their homes may be made attractive though inexpensive, but also served as an eye-opener to some of the business people that the negro people are getting a real service from the home demonstration agent and that Blount county should have a home demonstration agent for the white people too."[48] Doubtless the eyes of Alcoa's white business leaders opened even wider when they realized that black citizens were potential customers for their products.

Within competing communities, African Americans transferred their enduring goals of communal uplift into Better Homes demonstrations and programs. In an interracial context, however, the demonstrations bolstered segregation and racism. Black agents like Rebecca Davis recorded white approval of their Better Homes work with mixed pride and deference. Meanwhile, white observers assumed that blacks had greater need of such projects and used stories of their improvements to spur whites' interest in such projects.

Better Homes still meant homes beyond the reach of most rural families, black or white. Mrs. Robert T. Burt of Montgomery County insisted that the 1930 Better Homes week, sponsored by the African American Crocus Art Club of Clarksville, intended "to meet the needs of the masses of our people." But her description of the demonstration house suggests otherwise. The dwelling had four rooms, was valued at $1,192, and was temporarily furnished with goods selected from Montgomery Ward & Co., which cost $336.88. Its eight-piece walnut dining room set and Congoleum rugs would have been beyond the means of most rural black Tennesseans; despite Burt's claim that "we can have a comfortable and attractive home on a small income," most aspiring black farm women would have had to follow their home agents' advice to rearrange and refurbish what they already owned.[49]

Better Homes in America at least attempted inclusive programs. Two contests sponsored by major farm journals, the *Southern Ruralist* and the

Farmer's Wife, recruited select white farm women. The monthly *Southern Ruralist,* based in Atlanta, sponsored home improvement contests in 1928–29 and 1929–30. Lillian Keller served as one of five judges who reviewed scorecards, photographs, and written narratives. Contestants rated a maximum total of one thousand points for location and sanitation, convenience and comfort, appearance, cost, and documentation of improvements. *Southern Ruralist* home editor Lois P. Dowdle described contestants' homes as demonstrations for their communities, claiming that "the most valuable prize obtainable is the elevated standard of living made possible through improved material conditions in the home."[50]

Fifty-five women from seventeen Tennessee counties were among 386 entrants in 1928; in the next year, Tennesseans sent in 45 of 154 entries. Mabel Worley of Shepherd, Hamilton County, won the first contest. Worley sold flowers, vegetables, and poultry; kept boarders; and worked as a stenographer to earn improvement funds. She altered Worley Manor (Worleyanna), a "rather unattractive" two-story folk vernacular "I" house with a central gable, into a "beautiful southern colonial" home replete with gleaming white columns (fig. 26). Worley rejoiced in this endorsement of her "struggles and hardships in making a 'real home'" and credited the contest for "a great awakening in Home Improvement."[51]

Fig. 26. Worley Manor. Mabel Worley's "beautiful southern colonial" home in Shepherd, Hamilton County, won the *Southern Ruralist's* 1928 home improvement contest. *Improved Country Homes in Tennessee* (Nashville: Tennessee Department of Agriculture, 1928), 4.

The home improvement contest looked to both the history and the future of the rural South. The contest, and Worley Manor itself, echoed the traditional values of affluent white rural southerners. An engraving of Henry W. Grady's home headed the *Southern Ruralist*'s home section, evoking "the strength and glory of the Old South [as] found in those ideals and traditions which were so beautifully cherished in the colonial homes of which Grady's is typical." Like Grady, the *Southern Ruralist* recast Old South values for the New South's economic success, championing "colonial" columns and refinished antique furniture, as well as modern appliances and housekeeping methods. The magazine embraced the Colonial Revival movement in domestic architecture and decorative arts, which powerfully influenced southern attitudes and images of rural life, often grafting onto the most modern farm home the symmetry and classical overtones of the manor houses of one hundred years earlier.[52]

The *Southern Ruralist* took this link between Old South values and New South success one step further by using the contest as a way to introduce the potential market of southern female consumers to the nation's manufacturers. Editors wooed potential advertisers by boasting that they had "Disclose[d] Untapped Reservoirs of Undreamed Spending Power." Home and community uplift thus boosted the region's commercial opportunities:

> The results of this first contest show that money for home improvements was available; the desire for better things was there just waiting a constructive selling campaign to produce action; the plan developed and carried out by *Southern Ruralist* provided the incentive for undertaking the improvements.
>
> Such a campaign of house and landscape improvement over a period of years is certain to yield far-reaching and incalculably large results of obvious interest and value to national advertisers as well as to the great rural South.[53]

A second national contest emphasized rationalized housework, rather than domestic consumption, for better farm living. In 1928, the *Farmer's Wife,* a farm monthly published in St. Paul, Minnesota, honored the first Master Farm Homemakers. Based on Master Farmer campaigns begun in 1925, the *Farmer's Wife* program advertised itself as a noncompetitive recognition of outstanding farm women. Five neighbors nominated a woman from their county for the honor, with a home demonstration agent certifying her eligibility and achievements. Lillian Keller reviewed seventeen nominations in 1927, from which the journal selected five women as Master Farm Homemakers for 1928; another five women received the honor in 1929.[54]

Each nominee completed an eighty-four page questionnaire about her home and activities. Questions covered five categories, for a total of one thousand points: the farm home plant, home management, health and living conditions, family recreation, and community service. Judges meted out a maximum of one hundred points for the home plant, which they rated according to its condition in relation to financial resources and efficient use of facilities. Master farm homemakers organized their work and homes for minimal housekeeping and maximum homemaking and community work. As 1928 Master Farm Homemaker Mrs. James G. Yarbrough of Jackson, Madison County, stated, "We are all working together to make the living side of our farm better. We try to use our home as a background against which we may enjoy and get the best possible from life, rather than have the home be a burden to the homemaker."[55]

The *Farmer's Wife* claimed that women could be master homemakers, whether or not their families owned their farms or could afford home conveniences. Master homemakers of every economic status had planned work spaces and housekeeping routines; they beautified their homes in some way. Tennessee's master homemakers represented the most ambitious of the organized, efficiency-conscious middle-class farm women cultivated by home agents. They generally resided on large farms (between 160 and 260 acres, compared to the state average of 73 acres in 1930). Among them, they had installed electricity in a historic family farmhouse, kept home accounts for ten years, planned meals days in advance, and managed community food and rug markets. They participated in Parent-Teacher Associations and the Farm Bureau, and presided over the West Tennessee Home-Makers' Association; their children were 4-H club prizewinners. Master Farm Homemakers also were income earners, who made tidy profits from the sale of their poultry, garden, and crafts products. Their roles as agricultural producers spoke to enduring differences between farm women's lives and the urban homemaker ideal.[56]

Only a relatively few farm families had the resources to participate in national competitions like the Master Farm Homemaker program. But Tennessee's home agents had a vested interest in promoting those rural homemakers who transformed their homes with modern equipment, rationalized housework, and genteel decorative schemes, despite their small numbers. Demonstration workers accorded women a pivotal role in rural progress. At the same time, rural home economics teachers and home agents promoted housekeeping standards that implicitly rejected traditional ways for the methods and images of urban and suburban homes. Kitchen and living room campaigns, along with the Better Homes movement, deliberately held up suburban and urban models from mass-circulation women's magazines and contemporary urban tastes as yardsticks for rural homes. The *Southern Ruralist* blatantly sold its home improvement campaign to companies eager to develop markets in the rural South. Despite claims from farm women's magazines that their domestic improvement campaigns upheld a rural ideal, their standards reflected the precepts of an urban-oriented home economics profession that idealized domestic consumption.

In 1928, the Tennessee Division of Extension published *Improved Country Homes in Tennessee,* tangible evidence of its new slogan, "Better Homes on Better Farms." *Improved Country Homes* listed the white owners of farms with registered names. African American agents had reported their constituents' farm names since 1923, yet only a page of photographs of "Improved Negro Homes" represented their efforts.[57] Illustrations of white-owned farm homes included views of improved interiors and Better Homes demonstration houses. In her introductory essay, "Five Years of Home Improvement Work in Tennessee," Lillian Keller aptly summarized for readers how demonstration work introduced country women to national domestic standards:

> Until comparatively recent times most women measured their own homes by the homes of their neighbors, or the homes of their mothers and grandmothers, rather than by any abstract standards of convenience and beauty. Women in rural communities are not so isolated now, and through county tours, home improvement days at the county seat, home demonstration club meetings, parent-teacher associations and in other educational ways they have been led to realize that their homes must be modern, convenient and comfortable if their boys and girls . . . are to be kept satisfied on the farm.[58]

Keller's goal, keeping boys and girls on the farm, echoed the thoughts of Clara Boone Mason and Thomas Peck on women's club work a decade and half earlier. Hopes that women would initiate widespread rural environmental uplift endured from 1910 through the 1920s, whether expressed by an idealistic Country Life reformer such as Virginia Moore, a professional home economist such as Lillian Keller, the editors of a commercial farm journal such as the *Southern Ruralist,* or the designers of Tennessee's new rural schools.

How much did home improvement programs change rural homes? Certainly, home improvement campaigns infused urban values and material goods into country life. Rural revitalization through home improvement increasingly meant absorption into a national consumer culture, rather than community building, especially for white women. At the same time, domestic reform programs succeeded best when adapted to the resources and ambitions of local women; farm women modernized their homes in ways that preserved tradition. For those involved in kitchen improvement or Better Homes campaigns, their work yielded personal results for their homes and families and provided an avenue for building community pride. Their vision was neither what Country Life reformers had dreamed of in 1914, nor the model "better home" of the 1920s. A vision uniquely their own, it reflected rural women's own blend of tradition and modernity.

• 7 •

Legacies of Rural Reform

Progressive reformers assembled an impressive array of people, institutions, and programs to rebuild rural Tennessee. Believing that social and economic conditions in the countryside had degenerated, propelling whites and blacks into cities, reformers planned to stabilize rural communities by improving the quality of life in the southern countryside. In typically Progressive fashion, they started with education, so that farm families could learn how to become more productive, prosperous, and contented.

Educational crusades and legislation created new organizations and financial sources for an expanded rural public school system. Aid from the General Education Board and related foundations, the Julius Rosenwald Fund, and the federal government's vocational education program swelled the staff and budget of Tennessee's Department of Education. A corps of white state school agents, as well as African Americans who served as the Jeanes industrial supervising teachers and Rosenwald building agent, tackled the countryside's schools. Tennessee's two land-grant colleges for whites and blacks, three new white normal colleges, and the George Peabody College for Teachers also promised to supply teachers and administrators trained in the latest concepts and methods in rural education. Simultaneously, the state extension service sent out agricultural and home demonstration agents to organize and educate farm men, women, and children. By acting in concert, these Progressive forces would galvanize country folk into action and lift them out of ignorance and backwardness.

On the surface, the Progressive call for rural uplift seemed reasonable and possible to achieve. Behind the rhetoric, however, was a nebulous vision for rejuvenating country life that proved difficult to translate into effective programs for skeptical rural southerners. Between 1900 and 1930, Progressive educators and state officials moved in two directions: instituting reform vertically from the top down, reaching from the regional and state levels into the county and community, and then moving horizontally from the school outward into the home and the community.

Both strategies relied on new material environments to reach their goals.

Farms, homes, and schools appeared to share a general state of dilapidation and squalor. Reformers prescribed new rural schools, expertly designed and standardized, as models for clean, attractive, and productive homes and communities. Model rural homes, reformers claimed, could anchor white farm families and the black labor force in a more contented, comfortable rural South.

Rural women of both races held primary responsibility for the positive or negative conditions inside schools and homes that reformers felt encouraged or hindered community progress. Recruiting their support would be essential. African Americans might be socially marginal members of rural communities, but economically they were indispensable. African Americans would have to be educated to achieve better living and working standards; convincing white Tennesseans that this was so would be essential as well.

By the early 1920s, Tennessee's Progressive school officials and extension workers, and their philanthropic backers, had achieved impressive legislative and bureaucratic gains. They had anticipated immediate success from their efforts but experienced instead the frustration of slow and inconsistent change in rural life. In their own Progressive agencies, what had seemed visionary and innovative endeavors became routine statistics in the reports of professionally staffed bureaucrats. Those statistics measured the success of one reform goal: setting minimum standards of living in rural communities, homes, and schools. Still searching for rural uplift, rural reformers and their allies began reevaluating their goals and strategies.

Some did so in light of their own professional and organizational development. Progressive concern for efficiency and scientific research refocused the education profession's attention away from community uplift and toward the psychology of individual learning and standardization of programs. Comprehensive Country Life training programs for rural teachers and extension agents splintered into narrow professional training programs for country teachers, vocational workers, administrators, school and sanitary engineers, and demonstration specialists. Rural school agents narrowed their work from general community campaigns that built support for new schools to inspection tours during which agents met with administrators and educators, their local bureaucratic counterparts, rather than with school patrons.

In other cases, reformers reappraised programs in light of shifting social trends. Home economics, once in the vanguard of social reform, retreated to a marginal position in the educational hierarchy. As the female component of the vocational education that would revitalize country schools, and as the program that would forge the strongest link between schools and country homes, home economics had promised that rural girls and women would lead their families and communities to a better life.

Yet home economics declined in the 1920s, when educators redefined it as a gender-specific vocational study. Consequently, ideal homemakers narrowed their goals from extending improved family living conditions into their communities, to the search for individual and family fulfillment within their own households. The results pushed Tennessee women in different directions. In an academic setting, this shift weakened the home economics program at George Peabody College for Teachers. When combined with the lure of domestic consumerism, it actually boosted home demonstration work among farm women.

By the time of the Great Depression, reform advocates were terminating programs that apparently had failed to live up to their promise. The Julius Rosenwald Fund curtailed its school building program for southern African Americans in 1928 and discontinued it in 1932. Fund director Edwin Embree contended that, contrary to earlier expectations, new material environments in Rosenwald schools had not improved the quality of education or the status of black southerners. In rural communities across Tennessee, however, black school patrons valued those new buildings as tangible evidence of their success in pressuring white officials to improve the education of black children.

Had the original vision of uplift completely faded by 1930? Environments for living and learning still attracted professional bureaucrats' attention as promising means of pushing Tennessee and the South toward modernity. In 1928, the state's Department of Agriculture published *Improved Country Homes in Tennessee*, a registry of progressive family farms, documenting the department's commitment to the quality of life on Tennessee farms. That same year, the Tennessee Department of Education temporarily realized its dream of financing the complete overhaul of rural public education through the rural school building fund. A new Division of Schoolhouse Planning, funded by the General Education Board in 1929, and the Rosenwald-funded Interstate School Building Service assured continuing advances in educational facilities.

Yet the reform vision had cracked at a fundamental level. Those who administered reform programs aimed at the same targets: material conditions in rural schools and homes, farm women, rural African Americans. They increasingly pursued a strategy of imposing reform from above, deciding on goals and methods at the top in their own bureaucracies and then enforcing their implementation. What had weakened—indeed, largely disappeared—was the second strategy, moving from schools out into homes and then into the community at large. This strategy had been a crucial component of the original reform vision, for it blended the efforts of various agencies in a common mission to revitalize rural communities. When reform managers stopped equating their programs with community progress and began seeing them as ends in themselves, they renounced the very goal for which their own agencies had been created. The irony of their situation was lost on reformers in the 1920s, who saw only that professional, bureaucratic, and societal trends sanctioned their actions.

Fifteen years of dealing with rural communities and their residents played an equally important role in that shift, however. While overestimating the power of model schools and homes as inexorable environmental agents of change, reformers had underestimated the power of traditional rural community values embodied in prevailing standards of home and school construction and appearance. As rural southerners sifted through the reform agenda for the changes that promised most in terms of their own needs, southern Progressives focused on more limited and attainable objectives.

The complexity and strength of rural life complicated the reform process for all concerned. Community uplift elicited a range of local responses, from emphatic refusal to indifference, from ambivalence to eager participation. Studying Progressive rural reform through material evidence underscores the changing meanings of reform over time and the complexity of rural responses. Country schools and homes expressed in physical terms what reformers and rural Tennesseans wanted and what was feasible.

Strong local leadership supported by a majority of residents could, as in Shelby County, undertake rural uplift on its own initiative and require little management from outsiders. It could just as effectively block reform, as in Lewis County, where local people and their leaders strongly supported tradition. If local leaders interested in Progressive measures lacked popular support, as they did in Obion County, outside assistance and supervision provided them with standardized school buildings. Some rural people kept their options open. Greene County's scheme of parallel small, often vernacular school buildings and larger, style-conscious consolidated schools blended a modern educational system with community identity and tradition.

Rural programs aimed at African American Tennesseans faced problems stemming both from the reluctance of white officials and taxpayers to support improvements for blacks and from the limited resources of most black families. Rural whites and their local governments demanded additional inducements for African American schools before they took action. The Julius Rosenwald Fund's rural school building program provided one such financial stimulus; contributions from black school patrons added another. White local officials still responded cautiously, a measure of the challenge to the existing social order posed by these structures.

By the 1920s, modern school buildings for blacks and whites served as physical models for homes only in the most abstract sense. Large consolidated schools were sharply differentiated from the rural landscape. Their functional floor plans and unilateral lighting, as well as the design of their façades, whether embodying rational simplicity or references to classical architecture, identified them as public, formal spaces. They obviously invited comparison with their ramshackle, nonstandard predecessors and with their patrons' homes. What that comparison meant—an improvement, an alternative, an imposition—depended on the community.

Bungalow and Colonial Revival elements that were incorporated into smaller Rosenwald school plans and state school architect designs suggested that modernized schools and homes still might share a common visual and material structure. Here the successes and limitations of rural home improvement campaigns underline the problematical relationships between rural values, tradition, and reform. Annual Home Improvement Days and competitive projects in the 1920s, like those pioneered in Greene County, suggested that white country housekeepers increase their household consumption. The county agent, speakers brought in from the state extension service, and local merchants encouraged buying new appliances and utensils for greater efficiency and furnishings in contemporary taste.

Agents who recruited rural women for home improvement projects assumed that farm homemakers controlled some disposable cash income for new purchases, even as they showed club members how to make their own household furnishings and recycle old ones. In Hamilton County, the home agent and local demonstrators diversified their income-earning activities by producing goods for other women's domestic consumption. Apison rug makers hit upon a remunerative project based upon their skills as homemakers rather than as farm producers. By stitching household linens and hooking rugs for market sale to outsiders intrigued by the neocolonial style and the handicraft revival of the 1920s, they generated the cash needed to modernize their own homes.

Women of both races who participated in extension service campaigns and the Better Homes movement, and those singled out by the *Southern Ruralist*'s home contest and the Master Farm Homemaker program, sought modern methods of reducing traditional female burdens. The Colonial Revival style seen in so many demonstration living rooms and bedrooms, as well as in Mabel Worley's plantation-style "manor," blended tradition with modern utilities, comfort, and convenience. The style accurately reflected home economists' and agents' intention: to promote efficiency and better taste. In the process, interested country women were given an acceptable means of balancing their traditional female and farm roles with the standards of contemporary urban society.

Rural reform left a legacy of uplift, but one that touched a minority of country people. Many rural Tennesseans watched with indifference as home demonstrators, Jeanes supervisors, school agents, and other activists at the local and state levels experimented with environmental uplift. Their stolidity frustrated and restricted reform initiatives, which passed by many country schools and homes and, thus, ultimately failed at rebuilding rural communities. Reform failed because rural communities had not deteriorated, as the Progressives charged, but in fact had sustained strong identities. Rural people were not, however, uniformly resistant to change. They chose if, when, and how they would participate in outsiders' programs, according to their own needs and aspirations. Rebuilding schools, homes, and communities in rural Tennessee began and ended with the people inside them.

Notes

Abbreviations

ARCEW Annual Reports of County Extension Workers

ESART *Extension Service Annual Reports: Tennessee,* Records of the Federal Extension Service, Record Group 33, National Archives, Microfilm T-889

GEB General Education Board

GEBA General Education Board Archives, Rockefeller Foundation Archives, Rockefeller Archive Center, Sleepy Hollow, New York

GPO United States Government Printing Office, Washington, D.C.

JRF Julius Rosenwald Fund

JRFA Julius Rosenwald Fund Archives, Fisk Univ., Special Collections, Fisk Univ. Library, Nashville, Tennessee

PA Peabody Archives, Special Collections and Archives, Jean and Alexander Heard Library, Vanderbilt Univ., Nashville, Tennessee

RAC Rockefeller Archive Center, Sleepy Hollow, New York

RSC Rockefeller Sanitary Commission

RSCA Rockefeller Sanitary Commission Archives, Rockefeller Foundation Archives, Rockefeller Archive Center, Sleepy Hollow, New York

SSPIT State Superintendent of Public Instruction of Tennessee

TAER *Tennessee (Agricultural) Extension Review*

TBE Tennessee Board of Education Records, Record Group 91, Tennessee State Library and Archives, Nashville, Tennessee

TCE Tennessee Commissioner of Education Records, Record Group 92, Tennessee State Library and Archives, Nashville, Tennessee

TDE [Tennessee] Dept. of Education

Introduction

1. Carlton, David L., and Peter A. Coclanis, eds., *Confronting Southern*

Poverty in the Great Depression: The Report on Economic Conditions of the South (Boston: Bedford Books, 1996), 42–44 (quotation on 42).

2. Tennessee's nineteenth-century rural communities are ably depicted in Stephen V. Ash, *Middle Tennessee Society Transformed, 1860–1870: War and Peace in the Upper South* (Baton Rouge: Louisiana State Univ. Press, 1988); Robert Tracy McKenzie, *One South or Many? Plantation Belt and Upcountry in Civil War–Era Tennessee* (Cambridge, England: Cambridge Univ. Press, 1994); and Donald L. Winters, *Tennessee Farming, Tennessee Farmers: Antebellum Agriculture in the Upper South* (Knoxville: Univ. of Tennessee Press, 1994).

3. Bureau of the Census, *14th Census of the U.S. Taken in the Year 1920,* vol. 6: *Agriculture* (Washington, D.C.: GPO, 1922), tables 2–5, p. 437; Bureau of the Census, *Statistical Atlas of the U.S.* (Washington, D.C.: GPO, 1925), plate 249, p. 283; McKenzie, *One South or Many,* 102–20, 194.

4. *14th Census of the U.S.,* vol. 6: *Agriculture,* tables 10–11, pp. 438–39; McKenzie, *One South or Many,* 121–49, 194–95.

5. Joseph H. Cartwright, *The Triumph of Jim Crow: Tennessee Race Relations in the 1880s* (Knoxville: Univ. of Tennessee Press, 1976); Lester Lamon, *Blacks in Tennessee, 1791–1970* (Knoxville: Univ. of Tennessee Press, 1981), 26–84; Paula Giddings, *When and Where I Enter: The Impact of Black Women on Race and Sex in America* (New York: Bantam Books, 1984), 17–31.

6. William R. Majors, *Change and Continuity: Tennessee Politics Since the Civil War* (Macon, Ga.: Mercer Univ. Press, 1986); Roger L. Hart, *Redeemers, Bourbons, and Populists: Tennessee, 1870–1896* (Baton Rouge: Louisiana State Univ. Press, 1975); Robert E. Corlew, *Tennessee: A Short History* (Knoxville: Univ. of Tennessee Press, 1981), 347–64, 372–91.

7. Paul E. Isaac, *Prohibition and Politics: Turbulent Decades in Tennessee, 1885–1920* (Knoxville: Univ. of Tennessee Press, 1965); William D. Miller, *Memphis During the Progressive Era, 1900–1917* (Memphis: Memphis State Univ. Press, 1957); Don H. Doyle, *Nashville in the New South, 1880–1930* (Knoxville: Univ. of Tennessee Press, 1985); A. Elizabeth Taylor, *The Woman Suffrage Movement in Tennessee* (New York: Bookman Associates, 1957); Marjorie Spruill Wheeler, ed., *Votes for Women! The Woman Suffrage Movement in Tennessee, the South, and the Nation* (Knoxville: Univ. of Tennessee Press, 1995); Corlew, *Tennessee,* 415–46.

8. Tennessee Highway Planning Survey Division, *History of the Tennessee Highway Department* (Nashville: n.p., 1959), 17–24, 30–38.

9. *Tennessee—A Guide to the State: The WPA Guide to Tennessee* (New York: Viking Press, 1939; reprint, Knoxville: Univ. of Tennessee Press, 1986), 77–79.

10. Bureau of the Census, *13th Census of the U.S. Taken in the Year 1910,* vol. 7: *Agriculture* (Washington, D.C.: GPO, 1913), 570; *14th Census*

of the U.S., Agriculture, tables 1, 3–5, 11, on pp. 435, 437, 439; Bureau
of the Census, *Negroes in the U.S., 1920–1932* (Washington, D.C.: GPO,
1935), 220, 583.

11. Austin P. Foster, *Counties of Tennessee* (Nashville: TDE, 1923; reprint,
Greenville, S.C.: Southern Historical Press, 1990), 14–15, 19.

12. Ibid., 67, 83.

13. Ibid., 119, 121–22. For more detailed accounts of reform projects in these
six counties, see Mary S. Hoffschwelle, "Rebuilding the Rural Southern Community: Reformers, Schools, and Homes in Tennessee, 1914–
1929" (Ph.D. diss., Vanderbilt Univ., 1993).

1. The Progressive Impulse and Southern Rural Education

1. Historical studies of the Progressive era owe a great debt to Robert H.
Wiebe, *The Search for Order, 1877–1920* (New York: Hill and Wang,
1967). Among many other studies that also have contributed to my
understanding of Progressive reformers are Jean B. Quandt, *From the
Small Town to the Great Community: The Social Thought of Progressive Intellectuals* (New Brunswick, N.J.: Rutgers Univ. Press, 1970), 20,
41–49, 133; Richard L. McCormick, "The Discovery That Business
Corrupts Politics: A Reappraisal of the Origins of Progressivism," *American Historical Review* 86 (Apr. 1981): 247–74; and David Glassberg,
*American Historical Pageantry: The Uses of Tradition in the Early Twen-
tieth Century* (Chapel Hill: Univ. of North Carolina Press, 1990).

2. See Grant McConnell, *The Decline of Agrarian Democracy* (Berkeley:
Univ. of California Press, 1953), 19–35, 44–54; Roy V. Scott, *The Re-
luctant Farmer: The Rise of Agricultural Extension to 1914* (Urbana:
Univ. of Illinois Press, 1970); William L. Bowers, *The Country Life
Movement in America, 1900–1920* (Port Washington, N.Y.: Kennikat
Press, 1974); David B. Danbom, *The Resisted Revolution: Urban
America and the Industrialization of Agriculture, 1900–1930* (Ames:
Iowa State Univ. Press, 1979); David B. Danbom, *Born in the Country:
A History of Rural America* (Baltimore, Md.: Johns Hopkins Univ. Press,
1995), 161–84. Deborah Fink, *Agrarian Women: Wives and Mothers
in Rural Nebraska, 1800–1940* (Chapel Hill: Univ. of North Carolina
Press, 1992), exposes the agrarian myth's consequences for rural Americans, especially how it has obscured rural women's subordination within
the farm household. Mary Neth, *Preserving the Family Farm: Women,
Community, and the Foundations of Agribusiness in the Midwest, 1900–
1940* (Baltimore, Md.: Johns Hopkins Univ. Press, 1995), demonstrates
the implicit and explicit connections between the Country Life movement and the interests of commercial farmers and agricultural businesses.

3. Arthur S. Link, "The Progressive Movement in the South, 1870–1914,"

North Carolina Historical Review 23 (Apr. 1946): 172–95; Dewey W. Grantham, "The Contours of Southern Progressivism," *American Historical Review* 86 (Dec. 1981): 1035–59; Dewey W. Grantham, *Southern Progressivism: The Reconciliation of Progress and Tradition* (Knoxville: Univ. of Tennessee Press, 1983), 7; William A. Link, "The Social Context of Southern Progressivism," in *The Wilson Era: Essays in Honor of Arthur S. Link,* ed. John Milton Cooper, Jr., and Charles E. Neu (Arlington Heights, Ill.: Harlan Davidson, 1991), 55–82; William A. Link, *The Paradox of Southern Progressivism, 1880–1930* (Chapel Hill: Univ. of North Carolina Press, 1992).

4. For Progressive concerns about the rural South, see C. Vann Woodward, *Origins of the New South, 1877–1913* (Baton Rouge: Louisiana State Univ. Press, 1951), 406–16; Grantham, *Southern Progressivism,* 320–48; William A. Link, *Paradox*; and Jeanette Keith, *Country People in the New South: Tennessee's Upper Cumberland* (Chapel Hill: Univ. of North Carolina Press, 1995).

5. Lawrence A. Cremin, *The Transformation of the School: Progressivism in American Education, 1876–1957* (New York: Knopf, 1964), 26–89.

6. William A. Link, *A Hard Country and a Lonely Place: Schooling, Society, and Reform in Rural Virginia, 1870–1920* (Chapel Hill: Univ. of North Carolina Press, 1986); Thomas W. Hanchett, "The Rosenwald Schools and Black Education in North Carolina," *North Carolina Historical Review* 65 (Oct. 1988): 387–444. James D. Anderson's *The Education of Blacks in the South, 1865–1935* (Chapel Hill: Univ. of North Carolina Press, 1988) offers a regional overview against which to measure African American education in Tennessee. The historical literature on urban southern education is more extensive; a useful overview is David N. Plank and Rick Ginsberg, eds., *Southern Cities, Southern Schools: Public Education in the Urban South* (New York: Greenwood Press, 1990).

7. Grantham, *Southern Progressivism,* xv–xix, 3–12, 320–48 (quotation on xviii); William A. Link, *Paradox*; Jack Temple Kirby, *Darkness at the Dawning: Race and Reform in the Progressive South* (Philadelphia: J. B. Lippincott, 1972), 1–25. For comparison with southern Progressives' urban economic and social concerns, see Don H. Doyle, *New Men, New Cities, New South: Atlanta, Nashville, Charleston, Mobile, 1860–1910* (Chapel Hill: Univ. of North Carolina Press, 1990).

8. For approving and critical interpretations of Progressive educational initiatives, compare Charles William Dabney, *Universal Education in the South,* vol. 2: *The Southern Education Movement* (Chapel Hill: Univ. of North Carolina Press, 1936); with William A. Link, *Hard Country*; and James L. Leloudis, *Schooling the New South: Pedagogy, Self, and Society in North Carolina, 1880–1920* (Chapel Hill: Univ. of North Carolina Press, 1996).

9. Wayne E. Fuller, *One-Room Schools of the Middle West: An Illustrated History* (Lawrence: Univ. Press of Kansas, 1994), 76–77.

10. Cremin, *Transformation*, 59–89; William L. Bowers, "Country Life Reform, 1900–1920: A Neglected Aspect of Progressive Era History," *Agricultural History* 45 (July 1971): 216, 221; William A. Link, "Making the Inarticulate Speak: A Reassessment of Public Education in the Rural South, 1870–1920," in *History of Education in the South*, ed. Clinton B. Allison and Chipman B. Stuart, 63–75 (Norman: Univ. of Oklahoma Press, 1983).

11. George M. Fredrickson, *The Black Image in the White Mind: The Debate on Afro-American Character and Destiny, 1817–1914* (New York: Harper and Row, 1971), 256–319; Woodward, *Origins of the New South,* 369–95; Hugh C. Bailey, *Liberalism in the New South: Southern Social Reformers and the Progressive Movement* (Coral Gables, Fla.: Univ. of Miami Press, 1969); Kirby, *Darkness at the Dawning*; J. Morgan Kousser, *The Shaping of Southern Politics: Suffrage Restriction and the Establishment of the One-Party South, 1880–1910* (New Haven, Conn.: Yale Univ. Press, 1974); Dewey W. Grantham, *The Regional Imagination: The South and Recent American History* (Nashville, Tenn.: Vanderbilt Univ. Press, 1979), 77–106; Dewey W. Grantham, *Southern Progressivism,* 230–45; William A. Link, *Paradox,* 58–75.

12. John Dittmer, *Black Georgia in the Progressive Era, 1900–1920* (Urbana: Univ. of Illinois Press, 1977); Cynthia Neverdon-Morton, *Afro-American Women of the South and the Advancement of the Race, 1895–1925* (Knoxville: Univ. of Tennessee Press, 1989); Jacqueline Anne Rouse, *Lugenia Burns Hope: Black Southern Reformer* (Athens: Univ. of Georgia Press, 1989); Anne Firor Scott, "Most Invisible of All: Black Women's Voluntary Associations," *Journal of Southern History* 56 (Feb. 1990): 3–22; Darlene Clark Hine, "'We Specialize in the Wholly Impossible': The Philanthropic Work of Black Women," in *Lady Bountiful Revisited: Women, Philanthropy, and Power,* ed. Kathleen D. McCarthy (New Brunswick, N.J.: Rutgers Univ. Press, 1990), 70–93; Dorothy C. Salem, *To Better Our World: Black Women in Organized Reform, 1890–1920* (Brooklyn, N.Y.: Carlson Publishers, 1990), 65–100, 103–44, 181–253.

13. Dabney, *Universal Education,* 2:3–18, 2:32–73, 2:89–104, and passim; *The General Education Board: An Account of Its Activities, 1902–1914* (New York: GEB, 1915), 11–12, 179–80, and passim; Raymond B. Fosdick, *Adventure in Giving: The Story of the GEB* (New York: Harper and Row, 1962), 17–22. Grantham, *Southern Progressivism*; William A. Link, *Paradox*; and Leloudis, *Schooling the New South,* also discuss these meetings and institutions.

14. James D. Anderson dissects the racial ideologies of educational reformers working in the South in his "Northern Philanthropy and the Shap-

ing of Southern Black Rural Education, 1902–1935," *History of Education Quarterly* 18 (Winter 1978): 371–96, and in his *Education of Blacks,* 33–109. So does William A. Link, *Paradox,* 58–75. Theodore R. Mitchell, "From Black to White: The Transformation of Educational Reform in the New South, 1890–1910," *Educational Theory* 39 (Fall 1989): 337–50, argues that reformers subsequently applied their experience with black industrial education to poor whites.

15. Dabney, "The Public School Problem in the South," in *Proceedings of the 4th Conference for Education in the South, 1901* (Harrisburg, Pa.: Mount Pleasant Press, 1901), 62; Dabney, *Universal Education,* 2:39.

16. Edgar Gardner Murphy, "Within the Year," 1902, folder B, box 17, MS 278, Philander P. Claxton Papers, Univ. of Tennessee Special Collections, Hoskins Library, Knoxville (hereafter cited as Claxton Papers), 11.

17. Anderson, *Education of Blacks,* 79–109, and passim.

18. As Fuller explains in *One Room Schools,* Progressive educators also denounced midwestern rural schools and called for consolidation under professional administrators. Fuller demonstrates that rural people's insistence on controlling their schools defended a successful public education system in the Midwest. But, as his statistics on literacy, school attendance, and expenditures show (76–77), public education in the South lagged far behind.

19. Edward J. Ward, "The Schoolhouse as the Civic and Social Center of the Community," in *Journal of Proceedings and Addresses of the 50th Annual Meeting of the National Education Association* (Chicago: Univ. of Chicago Press, 1912), 250–57; Herbert Quick, "The Social Center and the Rural Community," in *Journal of Proceedings and Addresses of the 50th Annual Meeting of the National Education Association* (Chicago: Univ. of Chicago Press, 1912), 436–49; Wayne E. Fuller, "Changing Concepts of the Country School as a Community Center in the Midwest," *Agricultural History* 58 (July 1984): 423–41.

20. Louis R. Harlan, *Separate and Unequal: Public School Campaigns and Racism in the Southern Seaboard States, 1901–1915* (Chapel Hill: Univ. of North Carolina Press, 1958), 20.

21. William D. Jenkins, "Housewifery and Motherhood: The Question of Role Change in the Progressive Era," in *Woman's Being, Woman's Place: Female Identity and Vocation in American History,* ed. Mary Kelley, 142–53 (Boston: G. K. Hall, 1979); Dolores Hayden, *The Grand Domestic Revolution: A History of Feminist Designs for American Homes, Neighborhoods, and Cities* (Cambridge, Mass.: MIT Press, 1981); Martha Elizabeth May, "Home Life: Progressive Social Reformers' Prescriptions for Social Stability, 1890–1920" (Ph.D. diss., State Univ. of New York at Binghamton, 1984); Glenna Matthews, *"Just a Housewife": The Rise and Fall of Domesticity in America* (New York: Oxford Univ. Press,

1987), 145–66; Suzanne M. Spencer-Wood, "Diversity and Nineteenth-Century Domestic Reform: Relationships Among Classes and Ethnic Groups," in *Those of Little Note: Gender, Race, and Class in Historical Archaeology,* ed. Elizabeth M. Scott, 175–208 (Tucson: Univ. of Arizona Press, 1994).

22. Allen F. Davis, *Spearheads of Reform: The Social Settlements and the Progressive Movement, 1890–1914* (New York: Oxford Univ. Press, 1967); Judith Ann Trolander, *Professionalism and Social Change: From the Settlement House Movement to Neighborhood Centers, 1886 to the Present* (New York: Columbia Univ. Press, 1987), 7–24; Ellen Fitzpatrick, *Endless Crusade: Women Social Scientists and Progressive Reform* (New York: Oxford Univ. Press, 1990); Robyn Muncy, *Creating a Female Dominion in American Reform, 1890–1935* (New York: Oxford Univ. Press, 1991); Anne Firor Scott, *Natural Allies: Women's Associations in American History* (Urbana: Univ. of Illinois Press, 1991).

23. Anne Firor Scott, *The Southern Lady: From Pedestal to Politics, 1830–1930* (Chicago: Univ. of Chicago Press, 1970), 150–98; Nancy Forderhase, "'Limited Only by Earth and Sky': The Louisville Women's Club and Progressive Reform, 1900–1910," *Filson Club History Quarterly* 59 (July 1985): 327–43; Anastatia Sims, *The Power of Femininity in the New South: Women's Organizations and Politics in North Carolina, 1880–1930* (Columbia: Univ. of South Carolina Press, 1997); Marjorie Spruill Wheeler, *New Women of the New South: The Leaders of the Woman Suffrage Movement in the Southern States* (New York: Oxford Univ. Press, 1993); Margaret Ripley Wolfe, *Daughters of Canaan: A Saga of Southern Women* (Lexington: Univ. Press of Kentucky, 1995), 110–44.

24. *Report of the Commission on Country Life* (New York: Sturgis and Walton, 1911; reprint, Chapel Hill: Univ. of North Carolina Press, 1944), 106, 124; John M. Gillette, "Conditions and Needs of Country Life," *Annals of the American Academy of Political and Social Science* 40 (Mar. 1912): 7. The Commission on Country Life held one of its public meetings in Knoxville, Tenn., on 13 Nov. 1908.

25. Helen Campbell, *Household Economics* (1897), quoted in Glenna Matthews, *Just a Housewife,* 145–66 (quotation on 155); Jenkins, "Housewifery and Motherhood"; Jane Bernard Powers, "The 'Girl Question' in Education: Vocational Training for Young Women in the Progressive Era" (Ph.D. diss., Stanford Univ., 1987), 21–57; David Tyack and Elisabeth Hansot, *Learning Together: A History of Coeducation in American Schools* (New Haven, Conn.: Yale Univ. Press, 1990), 215–20; John L. Rury, *Education and Women's Work: Female Schooling and the Division of Labor in Urban America, 1870–1930* (Albany: State Univ. of New York Press, 1991), 135–47.

26. J. L. Whitfield, "An Indictment of the Rural School," in *Education in the South*, U.S. Bureau of Education Bulletin No. 30 (Washington, D.C.: GPO, 1913), 43–44.

27. Bailey Meador Wade, "The Development of Secondary Education in Tennessee" (Ph.D. diss., George Peabody College for Teachers, 1938), 63–66; and Andrew David Holt, *The Struggle for a State System of Public Education in Tennessee 1903–1936* (New York: Teachers College, Columbia Univ. Bureau of Publications, 1938), 16–18, 34–43, trace the history of Tennessee public schools in the late nineteenth and early twentieth centuries.

28. Holt, *Struggle for a State System*, 71–74; Dabney, *Universal Education*, 2:74–88, 2:110–14; Charles Lea Lewis, *Philander Priestley Claxton: Crusader for Public Education* (Knoxville: Univ. of Tennessee Press, 1948), 112–17; Joe Michael Shahan, "Reform and Politics in Tennessee, 1906–1914" (Ph.D. diss., Vanderbilt Univ., 1981), 34–37. For the key role played by graded schools and their administrators in North Carolina reform, see Leloudis, *Schooling the New South*.

29. Tennessee Dept. of Public Instruction, *Rural School Situation in Tennessee* (Nashville: McQuiddy Printing Co., 1911), 7.

30. Dabney, *Universal Education in the South*, 2:361–68; Holt, *Struggle for a State System*, 91–264; Robert Hiram White, *Development of the Tennessee State Educational Organization, 1796–1929* (Kingsport, Tenn.: Southern Publishers, Inc., 1929), 148–54; Shahan, "Reform and Politics," 38–42, 108–27, 198–202, 341–43.

31. The 1903 rural school course promised instruction in "how to overcome obstructions from parents and friends of children"; prominent rural educator and author Mabel Carney taught the course in 1914. *University of Tennessee Record* (hereafter *UT Record*) 6 (Mar. 1903): 20; 17 (Mar. 1914): 30; and vols. 7–21, passim; William B. Eigelsbach, "The Rise and Fall of a Summer School," in *Library Development Review 1987–88* (Knoxville: Univ. of Tennessee, 1987), 16–19. The records of the Summer School of the South, 1902–15, are in AR-249, Univ. of Tennessee Archives, Hoskins Library, Knoxville.

32. *UT Record* 6 (Feb. 1903): 73 (quotation), 92–93.

33. Lester Lamon, "The Tennessee Agricultural and Industrial Normal School: Public Higher Education for Black Tennesseans," *Tennessee Historical Quarterly* 32 (Spring 1973): 42–58; Samuel H. Shannon, "Agricultural and Industrial Education at Tennessee State University During the Normal School Phase, 1912–1922: A Case Study" (Ph.D. diss., George Peabody College for Teachers, 1974), 66–121, 174–80.

34. Rose declined an offer of the presidency of George Peabody College for Teachers. Holt, *Struggle for a State System*, 241–42; *GEB: An Account*, 9, 157. See also Charles E. Little, comp., "George Peabody College for

Teachers: Its Evolution and Present Status," *George Peabody College for Teachers Bulletin* (hereafter *Peabody Bulletin*) 1 (Sept. 1912): 1–160; Edward Neely Cullum, "George Peabody College for Teachers, 1914–1937" (Ed.D. diss., George Peabody College for Teachers, 1963).

35. Wallace Buttrick to Wickliffe Rose, 8 May 1912; Rose to Buttrick, 9 May 1912; Rose to Buttrick, 18 May 1912; and [Rose?], "The Task of the Seaman A. Knapp School of Country Life," typescript, 6; all in folder 1355, box 146, series 1, subseries 1, GEBA); and [Bruce R. Payne], "Report of the President for the Year Ending July 2, 1912," box 9, PA, n.p. "The Seaman A. Knapp School and Farm," *Peabody Bulletin* 1 (Jan. 1913): 1–11, incorporates much material from the "Task" typescript.

36. Dabney, *Universal Education in the South,* 2:114, 2:221.

37. *Biennial Report of the State Superintendent of Public Instruction of Tennessee for the Scholastic Years Ending June 30, 1911–1912* (Nashville: Brandon Printing Co., 1912), 45; Tennessee Dept. of Public Instruction, *Rural School Situation,* 68–69; John W. Brister, "The Rural School Situation," *East Tennessee Farmers' Convention Program and Proceedings,* 21–23 May 1912.

38. Tennessee Dept. of Public Instruction, *Rural School Situation,* 57, 59. Interesting evidence of how reformers distributed such propaganda and then rewarded its use can be found in a prize-winning essay by Nell E. Griswold, a student from Morrison, who quoted this pamphlet's description of a model rural school building in "The Ideal School" in 1912. See folder 12, box 3, MS 1546, in Virginia P. Moore Papers (hereafter Moore Papers), Univ. of Tennessee Special Collections, Hoskins Library, Knoxville.

39. Robert H. White, *Development of the Tennessee State Educational Organization,* table 4.

40. Wade, "Development of Secondary Education," 175–83; Harry Clark, map of Tennessee high schools, in folder 1321, box 142, series 1, subseries 1, GEBA; "Progress in County High Schools," *Tennessee Educational Bulletin* 1 (Oct.–Nov. 1922): 6.

41. Moore, a Sumner County native, took her training in art education at Peabody Normal College, where Wickliffe Rose was one of her professors. She also took education courses for ten summers at Chautauqua Lake, New York. She rejected a college position to answer a "call" to rural work in her home county. Virginia P. Moore, "A Review of a Few Steps in Home Demonstration Work, 1908 to 1939," folder 8, box 1, Moore Papers, [1]; Holt, *Struggle for a State System,* 171–77 (quotation on 171–72). James L. Leloudis II, "The Woman's Association for the Betterment of Public School Houses in North Carolina, 1902–1919," *Journal of American History* 69 (Mar. 1983): 886–909, analyzes the school improvement organizations of North Carolina, which provided

the model for Tennessee's movement. See also William A. Link, *Paradox,* 134–39; Scott, *Natural Allies,* 149–50, 155.

42. Virginia P. Moore, "School Improvement Associations of Tennessee," 1909, folder 13, box 1, Moore Papers, cover (quotations), 5, 9–14. In her first year of work, Moore convinced 1,200 teachers to pledge that they would begin improvement work at their schools and organized 14 countywide associations, as well as local associations in 35 counties. Attachment to circular letter by Philander P. Claxton, 21 Jan. 1910, folder E, box 16, Claxton Papers.

43. Photographs 5, 7 (Sumner County); 10 (Lauderdale County); 12–14 (Bradley County), box 4, Moore Papers; Mrs. Everett Bryan Roberts, comp., *Tennessee Congress of Parents and Teachers History: 31 Years in Retrospect, 1911–1942* (Memphis, Tenn.: Murdock-Johnston Printing Co., [1942]), 8–14; Holt, *Struggle for a State System,* 175, 177.

44. Philander P. Claxton, "Brief Summary of the Progress of Education within the Last Year and the Present Educational Situation," 28 Nov. 1907, folder H, box 14, Claxton Papers; Adams and Alsup, *Plans and Specifications for Public School Buildings* (Nashville: Tennessee Dept. of Public Instruction, 1907), 3.

45. Adams and Alsup, *Plans and Specifications,* 3–8, 14–17, and passim; photographs 12–13, box 4, Moore Papers.

46. Fletcher B. Dresslar, "How Can Country Schools Be Made More Helpful to Country Life," manuscript, [1907?], in box 1, Fletcher B. Dresslar Papers (hereafter Dresslar Papers), Vanderbilt Univ. Special Collections and Archives, Jean and Alexander Heard Library, Nashville, Tenn., p. 5. See also "Suggestions with Reference to New School Buildings" [1913], in *Biennial Report of the State Superintendent of Public Instruction of Tennessee for the Scholastic Years Ending June 30, 1913–1914* (Nashville: Brandon Printing Co., 1915), 410. On rural architecture, see Jan Cohn, *The Palace or the Poorhouse: The American House as a Cultural Symbol* (East Lansing: Michigan State Univ. Press, 1979), 70–83, 145, 228; on Progressive aesthetics, see Gwendolyn Wright, *Building the Dream: A Social History of Housing in America* (Cambridge, Mass.: MIT Press, 1981), 160–64.

47. Fletcher B. Dresslar, *American Schoolhouses,* U.S. Bureau of Education Bulletin No. 5, 1910 (Washington, D.C.: GPO, 1911), 100–106 (quotation on 103). See also Edward R. Shaw, *School Hygiene* (New York: Macmillan, 1911); Dwight H. Perkins, "The Relation of Schoolhouse Architecture to the Social Center Movement," in *Journal of Proceedings of the 50th Annual Meeting of the National Education Association* (Chicago: Univ. of Chicago Press, 1912), 234–39; Fletcher B. Dresslar, "The Hygiene of Rural Schools," in *Journal of Proceedings of the 50th Annual Meeting of the National Education Association* (Chicago: Univ. of

Chicago Press, 1912), 1103–11; Luther L. Wright, "The Rural School Plant," abstracted by Frederick K. Noyes in *Current Educational Topics No. 2*, U.S. Bureau of Education Bulletin No. 15 (Washington, D.C.: GPO, 1912), 23–24; Ellwood P. Cubberly, *Rural Life and Education: A Study of the Rural-School Problem as a Phase of the Rural-Life Problem* (Boston: Houghton Mifflin Co., 1914), 208–18; William W. Cutler, III, "Cathedral of Culture: The Schoolhouse in American Educational Thought and Practice Since 1820," *History of Education Quarterly* 29 (Spring 1989): 17, 23, 25–27, 30, 32–33.

48. Fletcher B. Dresslar, *Rural Schoolhouses and Grounds*, U.S. Bureau of Education Bulletin No. 12 (Washington, D.C.: GPO, 1914).

49. *UT Record* 12 (Mar. 1909): 36; *UT Record* 13 (Mar. 1910): 38; *UT Record* 14 (Mar. 1911): 38; *UT Record* 16 (Mar. 1913): 27. The quotation is from an untitled and undated newspaper clipping in folder 1327, box 143, series 1, subseries 1, GEBA.

50. "Education in General Hygiene and Sanitation," *Peabody Bulletin* 1 (Jan. 1913): 15.

51. The GEB served as a model for the Rockefeller Sanitation Commission. John Ettling, *The Germ of Laziness: Rockefeller Philanthropy and Public Health in the New South* (Cambridge, Mass.: Harvard Univ. Press, 1981), 86, 97–177, 213–23; William A. Link, "Privies, Progressivism, and Public Schools: Health Reform and Education in the Rural South, 1909–1920," *Journal of Southern History* 54 (Nov. 1988): 623–42; William A. Link, "'The Harvest Is Ripe, but the Laborers Are Few': The Hookworm Crusade in North Carolina, 1909–1915," *North Carolina Historical Review* 67 (Jan. 1990): 1–27. See also J[ohn] A. Ferrell, *The Rural School and Hookworm Disease*, U.S. Bureau of Education Bulletin No. 20 (Washington, D.C.: GPO, 1914).

52. Ferrell's bulletin included photographs of a dispensary day at a Tennessee school and of a public demonstration at a dispensary. See his *Rural School and Hookworm Disease*, plates 2B and 5A. On Tennessee dispensaries, see correspondence between Olin West and Wickliffe Rose, folders 147–51, box 8, series 2, RSCA. On infection, see West to Dr. J[ohn] Ferrell, 9 Aug. 1913, folder 150, box 8, series 2, RSCA.

53. State agriculture departments and railroad corporations across the country jointly promoted scientific agriculture through annual tours by special train car exhibits and on demonstration farms. Wickliffe Rose to Olin West, 3 Oct. 1910, folder 145; and West to Rose, 15 Nov. 1911, folder 145 (quotation); both in box 8, series 2, RSCA.

54. Olin West, "Campaign Against Hookworm Disease: Summary of Methods, Activities, and Results up to Jan. 1, 1911," folder 152, pp. 6 (quotation), 10; and West to Rose, 30 Apr. 1913, folder 149; both in box 8, series 2, RSCA. On agents' work with local school authorities, see cor-

respondence between West and Rose, folders 146–50, box 8, series 2, RSCA.

55. Darlene L. Hutson, "The Jeanes Supervisory Program in Tennessee" (Ed.D. diss., Univ. of Tennessee, 1964), tables 25 and 37, pp. 205–12; Lance G. E. Jones, *The Jeanes Teacher in the United States, 1908–1933* (Chapel Hill: Univ. of North Carolina Press, 1937), 48–55, 65; Mildred M. Williams, Kara Vaughn Jackson, Madie A. Kiney, Susie W. Wheeler, Rebecca Davis, Rebecca A. Crawford, Maggie Forte, and Ethel Bell, *The Jeanes Story: A Chapter in the History of American Education, 1908–1968* (Jackson, Miss.: Southern Education Foundation, 1979), 160–63.

56. Edward E. Redcay, *County Training Schools and Public Secondary Education for Negroes in the South* (Washington, D.C.: John F. Slater Fund, 1935), 30–31.

57. Morris R. Werner, *Julius Rosenwald: The Life of a Practical Humanitarian* (New York: Harper and Row, 1939), 127–31.

58. Claxton quoted in D. B. Johnson, "The Conference on Education of Women in the Country," in *Education in the South,* U.S. Bureau of Education Bulletin No. 30 (Washington, D.C.: GPO, 1913), 42.

59. *UT Record* 6 (Feb. 1903): 93, 209–10; *UT Record* 9 (Mar. 1906): 34–35 (quotation on 34), 83; and *UT Record* 10 (Mar. 1907): 84. Of course, teachers in training still took home economics in preparation for future work. See also Evelyn Shipe Simpson, "The Development of Home Economics at the University of Tennessee" (Ed.D. diss., Univ. of Tennessee, 1961); and, for a national perspective, Matthews, *Just a Housewife,* 145–71.

60. *UT Record* 6 (Mar. 1903) through 21 (Mar. 1918): passim; Catharine A. Mulligan, *A Brief Course in Domestic Science for State Institutes of Tennessee* (Nashville: Superintendent of Public Instruction, 1913); Simpson, "Development of Home Economics," 71.

61. Mrs. L[izzie] Crozier French, *Home-Making Efficiency* (Nashville: n.p., 1912), 3–7. On French, see Anastatia Sims, "'Powers that Pray' and 'Powers that Prey': Tennessee and the Fight for Woman Suffrage," *Tennessee Historical Quarterly* 50 (Winter 1991): 205–6; and Lucille Rogers, *Light from Many Candles: A History of Pioneer Women in Education in Tennessee* (Nashville: Xi State, Delta Kappa Gamma, 1960), 94–95.

62. Mrs. James C. Bradford, "The Decoration of the Home," *Tennessee Agriculture* 2 (1 Feb. 1913): 33–35 (quotation on 33).

63. Ibid., 35. For a similar discussion focused on country dwellings, see William A. McKeever, *Farm Boys and Girls* (New York: Macmillan, 1913), 56–64.

64. Virginia P. Moore, "Tennessee's Early Tomato Club and Home Demonstration Work from 1911–1919," folder 8, box 1, Moore Papers, p. 1;

Moore, "Review of a Few Steps," 3; Ada Cooke Settle, "The Home-Makers of Tennessee," *Tennessee Agriculture* 2 (1 Apr. 1913): 108–9.

65. Settle, "Home-Makers of Tennessee," 109; "Proceedings of the Middle Tennessee Home-Makers Association," *Tennessee Agriculture* 2 (1 Dec. 1913): 529–30. For examples of Home-Makers' Association activities, see "Proceedings of the Middle Tennessee Home-Makers' Association," *Tennessee Agriculture* 2 (1 Dec. 1913): 520–35, and 3 (1 Nov. 1914): 461–79.

66. Mrs. James A. Reagan, "The Farm Woman at the Institute," *East Tennessee Farmers' Convention Program and Proceedings,* 21–23 May 1912, n.p.

67. Virginia P. Moore, "The Girls Industrial Club Work," *East Tennessee Farmers' Convention,* 1912, n.p.; Seaman A. Knapp, quoted in Wallace Buttrick, "Seaman Asahel Knapp," *Proceedings of the 4th Annual Convention of the Southern Commercial Congress* (Nashville, Tenn.: n.p., 1912; reprint, Washington, D.C.: GPO, 1914), 9, in folder "Knapp Farm," PA. See also Joseph Cannon Bailey, *Seaman A. Knapp: Schoolmaster of American Agriculture* (New York: Columbia Univ. Press, 1945), 187–243.

68. Otis W. Caldwell, "Home Economics and Rural Extension," *Journal of Home Economics* 6 (Apr. 1914): 105 (quotations), 107–8. See also Marie Willoughby, "What Is the Best Method of Getting Home Making in the Public Schools and Rural Communities?" *Tennessee Agriculture* 2 (1 Aug. 1913): 271–78.

69. *GEB: An Account,* 36–37; J. A. Evans, *Recollections of Extension History,* Extension Circular No. 224 (Raleigh: North Carolina State College of Agriculture and Engineering, 1938), 25; Almon J. Sims, *A History of Extension Work in Tennessee: 25 Years of Service to Rural Life, 1914–1939,* Publication 223 ([Knoxville]: Univ. of Tennessee, 1939), 11; H. D. Tate to Bradford Knapp, 15 Nov. 1911, and "Boys Demonstration Work in Tennessee," 1911, both in *ESART,* roll 1. Theodore R. Mitchell and Robert Lowe argue that the GEB also sought rural political stability through agricultural improvement, in their "To Sow Contentment: Philanthropy, Scientific Agriculture and the Making of the New South: 1906–1920," *Journal of Social History* 24 (Winter 1990): 317–40.

70. [H. D. Tate,] "State of Tennessee Annual Report of Progress," 1 Nov. 1911, *ESART,* roll 1, p. 11; Almon J. Sims, *History of Extension Work,* 14–16; Moore, "Tennessee's Early Tomato Club," 2–6. Moore hired Lizzie Reagan as collaborator in McMinn County in 1913. Moore recalled that female club workers received the title "volunteer collaborator" because "men in authority in Washington held up their hands in 'Holy horror' over having women agents of the Government"; Moore,

"Tennessee's Early Tomato Club," 5. USDA policy toward female agents followed the precedent set in 1906 with the first black agent, Thomas Monroe Campbell, who also received the title of collaborator and a token one-dollar salary. See Campbell, *The Movable School Goes to the Negro Farmer* (Tuskegee, Ala.: Tuskegee Institute Press, 1936; reprint, New York: Arno Press, 1969), 76, 93, 161. James Leloudis, *Schooling the New South*, 162–69, documents similar personnel and organizational connections among school improvement, demonstration work, and programs for the farm home.

71. [Virginia P. Moore,] "Report of Girls' Canning Clubs of Tennessee up to Dec. 10, 1912," *ESART,* roll 1, p. 2 (emphasis in original); Almon J. Sims, *History of Extension Work*, 16; Virginia P. Moore, comp., "Canning Club Work in Tennessee," *Tennessee Tomato Club Bulletin* 1 (1913): 9–10; Moore, "Tennessee's Early Tomato Club," 13; Martha Foote Crow, *The American Country Girl* (New York: Frederick A. Stokes Co., 1915), 190–91. Local references to the organization of county canning clubs can be found in Tennessee Home Economics Association, *Home Economics Heritage in Tennessee, 1909–1959* ([Nashville]: n.p., 1959). Collaborators did no work among black girls before 1914. Although Moore claimed that agents promoted home conveniences for black cooks in Bluegrass counties, her comments indicate that these conveniences were provided for black women's use in white employers' kitchens. Moore, "Review of a Few Steps," 10.

72. [Virginia P. Moore,] "Summary of the Canning Club Work in Tennessee," 1913, *ESART,* roll 1; Moore, "Canning Club Work in Tennessee," 5; Moore, "Tennessee's Early Tomato Club," 10.

73. Moore, "Tennessee's Early Tomato Club," 6–7, 10.

74. [Moore,] "Summary of the Canning Club Work"; Moore, "Review of a Few Steps," 5; Moore, quoted in Almon J. Sims, *History of Extension Work,* 16.

75. Moore, "Tennessee's Early Tomato Club," 5, 7, 11.

76. Ibid., 13. Presumably Page asked for Moore's lobbying assistance during early deliberations on this legislation in 1913, before his appointment as ambassador to Great Britain.

77. For a concise discussion of the passage of the Smith-Lever Act, see Dewey W. Grantham, Jr., *Hoke Smith and the Politics of the New South* (Baton Rouge: Louisiana State Univ. Press, 1967), 254–67.

2. Consolidation and New School Buildings

1. George B. Tindall, *The Emergence of the New South, 1913–1945* (Baton Rouge: Louisiana State Univ. Press, 1967), 224, 259–64; Grantham, *Southern Progressivism*, 412–13, 416–17.

2. Cremin, *Transformation of the School*, 184–85, 197–99; David B. Tyack, *The One Best System: A History of American Urban Education* (Cambridge, Mass.: Harvard Univ. Press, 1974), 13–27; Tindall, *Emergence of the New South*, 497–99; William A. Link, *Hard Country*, 124–42.

3. Walter Burr, *Small Towns: An Estimate of Their Trade and Culture* (New York: Macmillan, 1929), 105–6; Bowers, *Country Life Movement*, 102–8.

4. William A. Link, *Paradox*; Keith, *Country People*, 118–42; Joseph F. Kett, "Women and the Progressive Impulse in Southern Education," in *The Web of Southern Social Relations: Women, Family, and Education*, ed. Walter J. Fraser, Jr.; R. Frank Saunders, Jr.; and Jon L. Wakelyn (Athens: Univ. of Georgia Press, 1985), 171–76.

5. Abraham Flexner to S. H. Thompson, 1 July 1914, folder 1463, box 157, series 1, subseries 1, GEBA.

6. Thompson to Flexner, 18 July 1914, folder 1463, box 157, series 1, subseries 1, GEBA.

7. *Biennial Report, SSPIT, for 1913–14*, 36–37, 243–51 (quotations on 247 and 249).

8. "Brief Statement of Progress in Rural Schools of Tennessee, 1915–16," attached to Brown to Flexner, 20 Sept. 1916, and [J. B. Brown,] "Consolidation and Transportation," [1916,] both in folder 1463, box 157, series 1, subseries 1, GEBA, pp. 1–3 (quotation on 3); *Outline on Rural School Supervision*, Bulletin No. 1 (Nashville, Tenn.: State Dept. of Public Instruction, 1916).

9. Photomontage of consolidated schools in Anderson County, in *Biennial Report of the State Superintendent of Public Instruction of Tennessee for the Scholastic Years Ending June 30, 1915–1916* (Nashville: Baird-Ward Printing Co., 1916).

10. "Lewis County," *Biennial Report, SSPIT, for 1913–14*, 382.

11. "Lewis County," *Biennial Report, SSPIT, for 1915–16*, 257.

12. "Lewis County," *Biennial Report, SSPIT, for 1913–14*, 381; "Lewis County," *Biennial Report, SSPIT, for 1915–16*, 258.

13. See *Lewis County Herald*, 22 Apr. 1920, 12 Aug. 1920, 22 June 1922, 13 Dec. 1923, 10 Jan. 1924 (quotations), 9 July 1925, 17 Sept. 1925, 12 Mar. 1928, 5 Apr. 1928.

14. Author's photographs of Napier School (date of construction unknown); photographs 909 (Garrett), 912 (Lawson), 913 (Springer), 914 (Loveless), all in box 34, TBE.

15. Times indeed were hard for Lewis County's small corn- and hay-producing farmers and iron miners. Between 1900 and 1925, the number of farms in Lewis County increased 12 percent, while average farm size fell from 115 to 74 acres. Farm tenancy rose from 30 percent to 40 percent between 1910 and 1925. By the mid-1920s, Lewis County ranked 90th

out of Tennessee's 95 counties in population density (20 per square mile), 92nd in gross farm income, and 94th in farm property value. C. E. Allred, S. W. Watkins, and G. H. Hatfield, *Tennessee, Economic and Social,* pt. 2: *The Counties* (Knoxville: Univ. of Tennessee, 1929), 25, 52–55, 59, 82, 135.

16. The high school continuously maintained a nine-month term. *Lewis County Herald,* 21 May 1915, 24 June 1920, 3 Feb. 1921, 21 Feb. 1924; "Cost of Teaching One Pupil One Day," *Tennessee Educational Bulletin* 1 (Oct.–Nov. 1922): 2; Allred, Watkins, and Hatfield, *Tennessee: Economic and Social,* pt. 2, p. 156; James A. Roberts to P. L. Harned, 10 Oct. 1925, in folder 2, box 14, TCE.

17. "Thinks School Costs Too Much," *Lewis County Herald,* 30 July 1925 (quotation); "To the Voters of Lewis County," *Lewis County Herald,* 10 Dec. 1925.

18. "Greene County," *Biennial Report, SSPIT, for 1913–14,* 374. As in Lewis County, the number of farms in Greene County was increasing—by 21 percent between 1910 and 1925, with average farm size decreasing to 58 acres and tenancy increasing from 25 percent to 32 percent. But in 1925 Greene County's farms ranked 3rd in overall value and 12th in gross farm income from corn, hay, and wheat production. Allred, Watkins, and Hatfield, *Tennessee: Economic and Social,* pt. 2, pp. 52–55, 59, 82, 135.

19. All statistical information about schools is derived from the successive *Biennial Reports, SSPIT,* 1913–22, and from *Annual Reports of the TDE for the Scholastic Year Ending June 30,* 1923–30.

20. Greene raised $7,810 in additional building funds in 1928, qualifying the county for $9,850 in matching funds. See P. L. Harned to Edgar Graham, 28 Dec. 1927, folder 13, box 25, and "State Rural School Building and Repair Fund," folder 9, box 184, both TCE; "Rural School Building and Repair Fund," *Tennessee Educational Bulletin* 7 (June 1928): 4.

21. Cedar Creek School, photograph 500, box 30, TBE; author's fieldwork, 1991.

22. Harry Clark to Brown Ayres, 10 Oct. 1913 and 1 Feb. 1914, folder 1324, box 143, series 1, subseries 1, GEBA; "County High Schools Arranged by Counties and the Class of Each, 1915–16," *Biennial Report, SSPIT, for 1915–16,* 110.

23. "Report of Joe Jennings, State Agent for Secondary Education for Tennessee, Mar. 1924," folder 1329, box 143, series 1, subseries 1, GEBA, p. 1.

24. Shelby County ranked first in total farm property value in 1910 and 1920 and second in both property value and gross farm income from cotton and corn in 1925. Tenancy declined somewhat, from 78 percent to 72

percent between 1910 and 1925; in 1925, 35 percent of farmers were white. Allred, Watkins, and Hatfield, *Tennessee: Economic and Social,* pt. 2, pp. 29, 54, 82, 135.

25. The Williams sisters were from Arlington, Shelby County. After leaving the superintendency at her marriage, Mabel Williams Hughes rose through the ranks of Parent-Teacher Associations, serving as national president in 1946. Charl Ormond Williams later became a leader and staff member in the National Education Association, serving as its president in 1921 and then as director of field services until 1949. She was one of Tennessee's woman suffrage activists and a member of the Democratic National Committee, being its first Tennessee woman member and first female vice-president. Rogers, *Light from Many Candles,* 123–26, 231–33; Grace Elizabeth Prescott, "The Woman Suffrage Movement in Memphis: Its Place in the State, Sectional, and National Movements," *West Tennessee Historical Society Papers* 18 (1964): 100, 105.

26. M. H. Furbringer, *Domestic Architecture* (Memphis: W. C. Jones, M. H. Furbringer, 1916), 78. The Cordova school still stands, in what is now a suburb.

27. Photographs of schools in newspaper clipping following p. 7 of "Narrative Report of Agricultural Extension Work in Shelby County for the Year 1926," *ESART,* roll 18; and photograph of Whitehaven School in TDE, *Report of the Tennessee Educational Commission,* pt. 1: *Facts Regarding Public Education and Resulting Problems* (Nashville: Ambrose, 1934).

28. "Report of Work of the County Agent," Shelby County, 1916, *ESART,* roll 2; "State-Aided Consolidated Schools, 1919–1920," *Biennial Report of the State Superintendent of Public Instruction of Tennessee for the Scholastic Years Ending June 30, 1919–1920* (Nashville: Ambrose, 1921), 161; "Consolidation," *Biennial Report of the State Superintendent of Public Instruction of Tennessee for the Scholastic Years ending June 30, 1921–1922* (Nashville: Baird-Ward, 1922), 270.

29. "Annual Report of the State High School Inspector," *Biennial Report, SSPIT, for 1913–14,* 137–38; "County High Schools Arranged by Counties and the Class of Each, 1915–1916," *Biennial Report, SSPIT, for 1915–16,* 113; "Report of Harry Clark, Professor of Secondary Education for Tennessee, Oct. 1915" (quotation) and "High School Report, Sept. 1916," both in folder 1325, box 143, series 1, subseries 1, GEBA.

30. "Progress in County High Schools," *Tennessee Educational Bulletin* 1 (Oct.–Nov. 1922): 6.

31. Gertrude Folks, "Schools," in *Child Welfare in Tennessee: An Inquiry by the National Child Labor Committee for the Tennessee Child Welfare Commission* (Nashville: Tennessee Child Welfare Commission,

[1920]), 95, 98, 103, 178, 180–81; *Annual Report, TDE, for Scholastic Year Ending June 30, 1922* (Nashville, 1923), 20.

32. Martin Leander Hardin, "A Study of Rural School Buildings and Grounds, with Special Reference to Union County, Tennessee" (M.A. thesis, Univ. of Tennessee, 1923), 34, 36, 41–48, 107 (quotation). Hardin himself was a former county superintendent for Hardeman County in southwestern Tennessee.

33. *Biennial Report, SSPIT, for 1919–20,* 21; *Biennial Report, SSPIT, for 1921–22,* 26. No published 1921 plans have been located.

34. "Report of S. L. Smith, State Rural School Supervisor for Tennessee, Nov. 1919," in folder 1469, box 158, series 1, subseries 1, GEBA. Smith may have borrowed his title from Gustav Stickley's "Craftsman Rural Community Schoolhouse," which was illustrated in Arthur D. Cromwell, *Agriculture and Life: A Text-book for Normal Schools and Teachers' Reading Circles* (Philadelphia: J. B. Lippincott, 1915), figs. 130 and 131.

35. Dresslar, *American Schoolhouses*; Dresslar, *School Hygiene* (New York: Macmillan, 1925); "In Memoriam," *Peabody Reflector* 3 (Apr. 1930): 7–8. Examples of similar contemporary thinking about school and classroom design are Lewis M. Terman, *The Hygiene of the School Child* (Boston: Houghton Mifflin, 1914); May Ayres, Jesse F. Williams, and Thomas D. Wood, *Healthful Schools: How to Build, Equip, and Maintain Them* (Boston: Houghton Mifflin, 1918).

36. *Biennial Report, SSPIT, for 1919–20,* 156; *Biennial Report, SSPIT, for 1921–22,* 269–71; "Consolidation," *Tennessee Educational Bulletin,* supp., 1 (Mar. 1922): 11–12.

37. "Report of Committee on Standardization of Elementary Schools," 16–19; "Objectives for County Federation of Parent-Teacher Associations or Community Leagues," 20–23; "Report of Committee on Community Organization," 23–24; all in *Tennessee Educational Bulletin* 1 (Mar. 1922).

38. Like Shelby, Obion County could afford this construction program, standing 8th in gross farm income and 9th in total farm value in 1925, though prosperity was skewed toward white landowners. Increasing numbers of farms (46 percent in 1910, 52 percent in 1925) relied on tenant labor in corn, hay, and cotton fields, but only 6 percent of farmers were black. Allred, Watkins, and Hatfield, *Tennessee: Economic and Social,* pt. 2, pp. 54, 82, 84, 135.

39. "Report, J. W. Brister, Associate State High School Inspector for Tennessee," Oct. 1920, p. 2, folder 1329, box 143, series 1, subseries 1, GEBA; *Obion County History* (Union City, Tenn.: Obion County Historical Society, 1981), 1:488, 1:490.

40. Photograph 1166, box 36, TBE.

41. "Counties Which Received State Aid on Consolidated School Buildings,

July 1, 1924–May 5, 1925," folder 7, box 270, TCE; photograph 1169, TBE. The three outbuildings probably were outhouses for boys, girls, and the teacher.

42. "Report of O. H. Bernard, State Rural School Agent for Tennessee," Dec. 1925, folder 1, box 14, pp. 1–2, and May 1926, folder 7, box 270, pp. 2–3 (quotation on 3), both in TCE; "Obion County Building Program," *Tennessee Educational Bulletin* 5 (Jan.–Mar. 1926): 1.

43. "Obion County Building Program"; "Report of O. H. Bernard," Dec. 1925, p. 2 (quotation).

44. Photographs 1181 and 1193–95, all in box 36, TBE.

45. "Report of O. H. Bernard," Dec. 1925, p. 2; photographs 1172 and 1175, box 36, TBE.

46. P. L. Harned to Edgar Graham, 28 Dec. 1927; T. C. Callicott to P. L. Harned, 16 May 1928 (quotation); Harned to Callicott, 21 May 1928, all in folder 13, box 25, TCE.

47. J. S. Glover to P. L. Harned [Jan. 1928], folder 12, box 34, TCE.

48. P. L. Harned to C. F. Fowler, 21 Jan. 1928 (quotation); Fowler to Harned, 23 Jan. 1928; Harned to Fowler, 1 Feb. 1928, all in folder 12, box 34, TCE.

49. Allred, Watkins, and Hatfield, *Tennessee: Economic and Social,* pt. 2, pp. 168–69; *Obion County History,* 1:488.

50. For examples, see letters to the state superintendent from Cannon, Perry, Putnam, Stewart, and Wayne counties, in folder 13, box 25, TCE.

51. *Annual Report, TDE, for Scholastic Year Ending June 30, 1926* (Nashville: Ambrose, 1927), 24; *Annual Report, TDE, for Scholastic Year Ending June 30, 1927* (Nashville: Baird-Ward, 1928), 17–18; *Annual Report, TDE, for Scholastic Year Ending June 30, 1928* (Nashville: Baird-Ward, 1929), 20; "Rural School Buildings," *Tennessee Educational Bulletin* 7 (June 1928): 11–12.

52. *Building Plans for Rural School Houses* (Nashville: State Dept. of Education, 1928), 3 (quotation) and passim.

53. Thanks to its affinity with Progressive aesthetics, the Colonial Revival (or Modern Colonial) style became a "popular and pervasive" expression of middle-class taste in the early twentieth century. See Bridget A. May, "Progressivism and the Colonial Revival: The Modern Colonial House, 1900–1920," *Winterthur Portfolio* 26 (Summer/Autumn 1991): 107–22 (quotation on 107).

54. Interestingly, Mahan's plans made no provisions for agricultural work, a school garden, or a workshop to supplement work done in the industrial room. Earlier Country Life reformers had recommended them as "vitalizing" factors in rural education.

55. "Rural School Building and Repair Fund," *Tennessee Educational Bulletin* 7 (June): 4.

56. J. Dallas Jacobs, *Report, 1915–1916,* quoted in Louise Houck Wiser, comp., *A History of Rutherford County Schools to 1972* (Murfreesboro, Tenn.: Rutherford County Historical Society, 1986), 2:293–94; J. B. Brown to Samuel H. Thompson, 15 Feb. 1915, folder 1463, box 157, series 1, subseries 1, GEBA.

57. "Rutherford County," *Biennial Report, SSPIT, for 1915–16,* 272, 273.

58. William F. Walker, "A Study of Public Health Activities in Rutherford County, Tennessee, for the Year 1926," 19–24 Feb. 1927, folder 46, box 3, Commonwealth Fund Archives, Child Health Demonstration Series, RAC.

59. "Report of Joe Jennings, State Agent for Secondary Education for Tennessee," Feb. 1924, folder 1329, box 143, series 1, subseries 1, GEBA, p. 1.

60. *Handbook of Murfreesboro and Rutherford County, Tennessee* (Murfreesboro: Mutual Realty and Loan Co., [1924]), 92, 94; Wiser, *Rutherford County Schools,* 2:96–100.

61. The burgeoning dairy industry joined corn, hay, and cotton to boost Rutherford to 4th place in gross income in 1925, though farm size was decreasing (from 83 to 60 acres from 1900 to 1925) and tenancy increasing (45 percent to 51 percent between 1910 and 1925). Allred, Watkins, and Hatfield, *Tennessee: Economic and Social,* pt. 2, pp. 54, 58, 82.

62. "Report of O. H. Bernard, State Rural School Agent for Tennessee," May 1925, folder 7, box 270, p. 2; "Report of O. H. Bernard," Oct. 1925, pp. 5–6 (quotations); Dec. 1925; and Jan. 1926, all in TCE.

63. The 1931 Jefferson and 1932 Christiana schools also followed this basic plan. Photographs 1339–43, 1346–47, 1349–50, 1359–60, 1363–64, all in box 38, TBE. School architects and reformers often used an H-shaped plan for larger schools because this shape allowed proper unilateral lighting for all classrooms and easy expansion.

64. James A. Roberts to P. L. Harned, 25 Jan. 1927, and Birdie L. Workman to Harned, 11 Oct. 1927; both in folder 13, box 25, TCE.

65. *Lewis County Herald,* 23 Sept. 1920, 6 and 27 Jan. 1921, 3 Feb. 1927, 7 Apr. 1927, 7 July 1927, and 23 Feb. 1928.

66. Workman to Harned, 11 Oct. 1927, and "State Rural School Building and Repair Fund" [1928], folder 9, box 184, both in TCE; "Rural School Building and Repair Fund," 4.

67. W. W. Brierly to P. L. Harned, 4 June 1926, folder 2, and Frank P. Bachman to Harned, 13 Dec. 1926, folder 3, both in box 11, TCE.

68. *Peabody Bulletin* 3 ([Sept.?] 1914): 9; 3 (June 1914): 76; 4 (Dec. 1915): 10; 6 (Nov. 1917): 15–16; 7 (Sept. 1918): 6; 7 (Mar. 1919): 44.

69. "In Memoriam," 6–8.

70. *UT Record* 19 (Mar. 1916): 30; 20 (Apr. 1917): 94.

71. *UT Record* 23 (Apr. 1920): 75; 25 (June 1922): 103. The education department did not offer the class between 1924 and 1928.

72. *UT Record* 30 (May 1927): 168; 32 (May 1929): 188–89.

73. "Minutes of the State Supervisors of Schoolhouse Construction in the Southern States," 25 Oct. 1928, folder 2, box 314, JRFA; Haskell Pruett, *Rural School Buildings* ([Oklahoma City]: Oklahoma Dept. of Public Instruction, 1928). The National Council on Schoolhouse Construction, formed in 1921, met annually to discuss and adopt building standards. Its work is briefly reviewed in *Guide for Planning School Plants* (National Council on Schoolhouse Construction, [1949?]), v. The National Education Association had already addressed the need for coordinating state standards in its *Report of Committee on School House Planning* (Washington, D.C.: 1925). S. L. Smith served on the committee, which received funding from the GEB.

74. S. L. Smith to Frank P. Bachman, 31 Oct. 1928; S. L. Smith to Alfred K. Stern, 10 Nov. 1928 and 17 Nov. 1928 (quotation); S. L. Smith to W. B. Harrell, 9 Jan. 1929 and 2 Mar. 1929; Bruce R. Payne to S. L. Smith, 31 Oct. 1928; all in folder 2, box 314, JRFA.

75. Fletcher B. Dresslar, "Organization of the Interstate School Building Service," *School Life* 15 (Feb. 1930): 115–16, clipping in Dresslar Papers; Interstate School Building Service, *For Better Schoolhouses* (Nashville, Tenn.: Interstate School Building Service, 1929); Interstate School Building Service, *Proceedings and Approved Suggestions of the 2nd Conference of the Interstate School Building Service* (Nashville, Tenn.: George Peabody College, 1931); Hanchett, "Rosenwald Schools," 423.

76. Tindall, *Emergence of the New South*, 224, 259–64.

77. *Annual Report, TDE, for Scholastic Year Ending June 30, 1924* (Nashville: Ambrose, 1925), 19; *Annual Report, TDE, for Scholastic Year Ending June 30, 1925* (Nashville: Ambrose, 1926), 21; *Annual Report, TDE, 1926*, 24. Dresslar recommended that Tennessee hire a supervisor of school architecture, though he warned against employing a professional architect, who he feared would lack the tact necessary in dealing with recalcitrant rural school boards. See Dresslar, "State Supervision of School Architecture," in Dresslar Papers.

78. P. L. Harned to GEB, 18 Oct. 1928, and W. W. Brierly to Commissioner Harned, 27 Nov. 1928, both in folder 4, box 29; memorandum, P. L. Harned, 23 Nov. 1928, folder 9, box 36; all in TCE.

79. "A One-Teacher School" and "A Home Economics Cottage," in *Annual Report, TDE, for Scholastic Year Ending June 30, 1931–1932* (Jackson, Tenn.: Long-Johnson, 1932).

80. S. L. Smith, "A Decade of Progress in Schoolhouse Construction," folder 2, and "Services Rendered by Division of Schoolhouse Planning," folder 1, both in box 331, JRFA.

3. Building an Ideal

1. Folks, "Schools," 239; Harlan, *Separate and Unequal.* On segregation and its consequences for African American Tennesseans in this period, see Lamon, *Black Tennesseans*; and Cynthia Griggs Fleming, "The Development of Black Education in Tennessee, 1865–1920" (Ph.D. diss., Duke Univ., 1977).

2. S. L. Smith to Julius Rosenwald, 26 Dec. 1921, folder 16, box 127, JRFA.

3. S.L. Smith to Wallace Buttrick, 11 May 1914, folder 1464, box 157, series 1, subseries 1, GEBA.

4. S. L. Smith to James H. Dillard, 8 Apr. 1915, folder 1464, box 157, series 1, subseries 1, GEBA; S. L. Smith, "Report of Some Special Work in Rural Negro Schools for 1919–1920," *Biennial Report, SSPIT, for 1919–20,* 153 (quotation); S. L. Smith, "Brief Report of Some Special Work in Rural Negro Schools for Years 1921–1922," *Biennial Report, SSPIT, for 1921–22,* 272; [Dudley Tanner] to Leo M. Favrot, 10 Aug. 1931, folder 2, box 236, TCE. Tanner reported 24 Jeanes supervisors, but Darlene L. Hutson, "The Jeanes Supervisory Program in Tennessee" (M.A. thesis, Univ. of Tennessee, Knoxville, 1964), 183, counted only 20.

5. S. L. Smith to Buttrick, 16 Mar. 1915, and "Report of S. L. Smith, State Rural School Supervisor for Tennessee, Nov. 1915," both in folder 1468, box 158, series 1, subseries 1, GEBA; photograph 1054, GEBA.

6. Anderson, *Education of Blacks*, chs. 4 and 5, discusses county training schools throughout the region. See also Leo M. Favrot, "The State Agents of Rural Schools for Negroes and Their Relation to Outside Funds Stimulating Negro Public Education," 1928, folder 16, box 202, JRFA; Redcay, *County Training Schools and Public Secondary Education*; Folks, "Schools," 244–46.

7. S. L. Smith, "Report of Some Special Work Among Rural Negro Schools in Tennessee, 1915–16," *Biennial Report, SSPIT, for 1915–16,* 288; S. L. Smith, "Report of Some Special Work in Rural Negro Schools for 1919–1920," 154.

8. S. L. Smith to Abraham Flexner, 16 Feb. 1915, and S. L. Smith to Flexner, 5 Apr. 1915, both in folder 1472, box 158, series 1, subseries 1, GEBA; photograph 1054, Tenn. 126, GEBA; S. L. Smith, "Report of Some Special Work Among Rural Negro Schools in Tennessee, 1915–16," 289.

9. "Equipment for Shelby County Training School," Apr. 1915, folder 1472, box 158; and "Report of S. L. Smith, State Rural Supervisor for Tennessee," Jan. 1916 and Feb. 1916, in folder 1468, box 158; all in series 1, subseries 1, GEBA.

10. "County Training Schools—1916–1917" and "Report of S. L. Smith,

State Rural School Supervisor of Tennessee," Sept. and Nov. 1917, all in folder 1469, box 158, series 1, subseries 1, GEBA.

11. S. L. Smith, "Report of Some Special Work in Rural Negro Schools for 1919–1920," 154–55. Shelby County Training School's agricultural program actually was quite limited, cultivating only one or two acres between 1919 and 1922, and intermittently thereafter. Shop work for boys and home economics instruction for girls, continued with support from the GEB, remained staples of the curriculum. Girls' work, at least, kept alive Principal T. J. Johnson's conception of his school as the county's "big home." See "Summary of Reports, County Training Schools, Tennessee," 1917–18 through 1924–25, folder 1472, box 158, and folders 3064–66, box 294, series 1, subseries 1, GEBA. Agricultural work must have resumed after 1925, for Dudley Tanner was impressed by it and by girls' laundry work when he visited the school in Mar. 1929. See "Report of Dudley Tanner, Rural School Agent for Tennessee," Mar. 1929, folder 2, box 36, TCE.

12. Harry Clark to E. C. Sage, 21 Oct. 1915, folder 1472, box 158, series 1, subseries 1, GEBA.

13. Jackson Davis, "Shelby County Training School," folder 1472, box 158, series 1, subseries 1, GEBA.

14. Leo M. Favrot, *A Study of County Training Schools for Negroes in the South,* John F. Slater Fund Occasional Papers No. 23 (Charlottesville, Va.: [John F. Slater Fund], 1923), 10; S. L. Smith, "Report of Some Special Work Among Rural Negro Schools in Tennessee, 1915–16," 288–89; S. L. Smith, "Report of Some Special Work in Rural Negro Schools for 1919–1920," 154; S. L. Smith to Jackson Davis, 27 Sept. 1915, and "Statement Made at the Conference of Negro Supervisors, Held at Hampton, Nov. 10, 11, 1915," both in folder 1472, box 158, series 1, subseries 1, GEBA. Correspondence on county training school appropriations can be found in folders 1472 and 1473, box 158, and in folders 3064–66, box 294, all in series 1, subseries 1, GEBA.

15. Tennessee was one of the few southern states that located more training schools in urban than in rural areas, according to Redcay, *County Training Schools,* 40, 77, fig. 2; W. E. Turner, "A Survey of Negro High Schools in Tennessee" (M.A. thesis, Univ. of Tennessee, 1933), 35–37. Apart from Memphis and Nashville, Redcay's "urban" locations usually were county seats. Turner's figures include both city and county schools. In 1930, Slater-funded county training schools constituted 78 percent of four-year schools and 92 percent of two-year schools for blacks. Most were one-story brick structures, with 90 percent of four-year schools having ten or fewer classrooms and 83 percent of two-year schools housing eight or fewer classrooms.

16. Charles S. Johnson et al., *Statistical Atlas of Southern Counties* (Chapel Hill: Univ. of North Carolina Press, 1941), 212.
17. All statistical information about schools is derived from *Biennial Report, SSPIT,* for 1913–22; *Annual Report, TDE, for Scholastic Year Ending June 30,* 1923–30.
18. The black population of Lewis County shrank from 11.7 percent to 7.4 percent of the population between 1920 and 1930.
19. "Board of Education Met Here Friday," *Lewis County Herald,* 24 Sept. 1925.
20. When finished, Reaves was the only painted school building in Fayette County. S. L. S[mith], "A Story of the Julius Rosenwald Fund in Tenn. from the Beginning to July 1, 1920," folder 2, box 76, JRFA; *Biennial Report, SSPIT, for 1915–16,* 28; *Biennial Report, SSPIT, for 1917–18,* 15; "Report of S. L. Smith, State Rural School Supervisor for Tennessee, Aug. 1919," folder 1469, box 158, series 1, subseries 1, GEBA.
21. For accounts of the Rosenwald Fund, see Edwin R. Embree, *JRF: Review of Two Decades, 1917–1936* (Chicago: JRF, 1936); Edwin R. Embree and Julia Waxman, *Investment in People: The Story of the JRF* (New York: Harper and Brothers, 1949); S. L. Smith, *Builders of Goodwill: The Story of the State Agents of Negro Education in the South, 1910 to 1950* (Nashville: Tennessee Book Co., 1950); Alfred Gilbert Belles, "The JRF: Efforts in Race Relations, 1928–1948" (Ph.D. diss., Vanderbilt Univ., 1972); and Anderson, *Education of Blacks,* 156–85. On the JRF in Tennessee, see Thomas Beane Stitely, "Bridging the Gap: A History of the Rosenwald Fund in the Development of Rural Negro Schools in Tennessee, 1912–1932" (Ph.D. diss., George Peabody College for Teachers, 1975). For North Carolina, see Hanchett, "Rosenwald Schools," 387–444. For a similar effort at school reform, see Robert J. Taggart, *Private Philanthropy and Public Education: Pierre S. du Pont and the Delaware Schools, 1890–1940* (Newark: Univ. of Delaware Press, 1988).
22. See similar descriptions of the Christiana and Mount Pleasant black schools in Wiser, *Rutherford County Schools,* 2:197, 2:210.
23. "Julius Rosenwald Rural School Fund 1919–1920 Budget, Schedule B," folder 11, box 331, JRFA; listing of Rosenwald schools constructed by July 1, 1930, folder 1, box 343, JRFA; "Rosenwald Schools in Tennessee to June 30, 1925," folder 5, box 270, TCE. African Americans accounted for 30 percent of Rutherford's population in 1920, down from 39 percent in 1900, and for 27 percent of its farmers in 1925, almost three-fourths of whom were tenants. Allred, Watkins, and Hatfield, *Tennessee: Economic and Social,* pt. 2, pp. 25, 52–55, 59, 82, 135; C. S. Johnson, *Statistical Atlas,* 219.
24. Abraham Flexner to Julius Rosenwald, 10 Dec. 1917, and "Brief of

Features of Rural School Audit, Recommendations, and Correspondence on Method of Administering Rural School Construction," n.d., both in folder 1, box 331, JRFA; T. H. Harris to Abraham Flexner, 30 Mar. 1920, folder 2039, box 212, GEBA.

25. F[letcher] B. Dresslar, *Report on the Rosenwald School Buildings*, Bulletin No. 1 (Nashville, Tenn.: JRF, [1920]), 60.

26. Participants in the 1919 planning meeting included the GEB's president Wallace Buttrick, secretary Abraham Flexner, and field agent Jackson Davis; Tuskegee principal R. R. Moton; extension director Clinton J. Calloway; Margaret Murray Washington; state agents for black rural schools S. L. Smith (Tennessee), Leo M. Favrot (Louisiana), J. S. Lambert (Alabama); and Fletcher B. Dresslar. James Leloudis, *Schooling the New South*, 219–20, describes the break with Tuskegee as producing a Rosenwald Fund hierarchy that replicated southern segregation.

27. Dresslar, *Report on the Rosenwald Schools*, 53–54; "Discussion of Rosenwald Schools at Conference of State Agents," 5–6 Jan. 1921, folder 4, box 188, JRFA; "Minutes of the Meeting of the Rosenwald Schoolhouse Building Agents," 15–16 June 1923, folder 12, box 187, JRFA.

28. Jackson Davis to S. L. Smith, 24 Mar. 1927, folder 1, box 331, JRFA; W. T. B. Williams, "The Rosenwald Fund in Negro Education," [1927?], folder 2, box 76, JRFA.

29. "Plan for Distribution of Aid from the JRF for Building Rural Schoolhouses in the South" [1920], and [S. L. Smith,] "Evolution of the Schoolhouse Construction Program by the JRF" [1928], both in folder 1, box 331, JRFA; Ullin Whitney Leavell, *Philanthropy in Negro Education* (Nashville, Tenn.: George Peabody College for Teachers, 1930), 139–43.

30. Wallace Buttrick to Francis W. Shepardson, 17 Apr. 1922, folder 16, box 202, JRFA; Jackson Davis to S. L. Smith, 24 Mar. 1927, folder 1, box 331, JRFA; "Results of the Rosenwald Fund in the South," n.d., folder 2, box 76, JRFA.

31. "Report of S. L. Smith, State Rural School Supervisor for Tennessee, May, 1918," folder 1469, box 158, series 1, subseries 1, GEBA.

32. Dresslar, *Report on the Rosenwald Schools*, 30–31; *Community School Plans* (Nashville, Tenn.: JRF, 1921), folders 2046 and 2047, *Community School Plans*, rev. ed. (Nashville: JRF, 1924), folder 2047, all in box 213, series 1, subseries 1, GEBA; *Community School Plans*, rev. ed. (Nashville: JRF, 1927), folder 4, box 37, TCE; S. L. Smith, *Builders of Goodwill*, 69, 120; Edwin R. Embree, "How Negro Schools Have Advanced Under the Rosenwald Fund," *Nation's Schools* 1 (May 1928): 41. See also Hanchett, "Rosenwald Schools," 401–6. Community School Plan 20-A received praise for its lighting in Fletcher B. Dresslar and Haskell Pruett, *Rural School-houses, School Grounds, and Their Equip-*

ment, U.S. Office of Education Bulletin No. 21 (Washington, D.C.: GPO, 1930), 39–41.

33. "Discussion of Rosenwald Schools at Conference of State Agents," 5–6 Jan. 1921, folder 4, box 188, JRFA; *Community School Plans* (1927), 34.

34. *Community School Plans* (1927), 37; "Discussion of Rosenwald Schools," 1921; "Notes Made at the Conference of State Agents for Negro Rural Schools," 26–28 Nov. 1921, folder 4, box 188, JRFA. The Rosenwald Fund also sponsored an annual "Rosenwald Day," during which parents, children, and teachers cleaned and repaired their school building and grounds and raised money for new projects. "Specifications for Repairs and Improvements for Program for Rosenwald School Day Celebration," folder 12, box 128, JRFA.

35. "Plan for Distribution of Aid from the JRF for Building Rural School-houses in the South," 1922–23, folder 1, box 331, JRFA; Spencer J. Maxcy, "Progressivism and Rural Education in the Deep South, 1900–1950," in *Education and the Rise of the New South,* ed. Ronald K. Goodenow and Arthur O. White (Boston: G. K. Hall, 1981), 65.

36. "Minutes of the Meeting of the Rosenwald Schoolhouse Building Agents," 15–16 Jan. 1923, folder 12, box 187, JRFA; "Conference of State Agents for Negro Rural Schools," 6–9 May 1923, folder 4, box 188, JRFA; S. L. Smith to Alfred K. Stern, 21 Feb. 1927, folder 2, box 336, JRFA.

37. See Leo Favrot's comments in "Notes Made at Hampton, Virginia, Conference [of State Agents for Negro Schools]," 1923, 6, folder 4, box 188, JRFA, and in "The First Rosenwald Buildings in Arkansas and Alabama," n.d., folder 2, box 76, JRFA. "The JRF in the South, 1930–31," folder 2, box 331, JRFA, pp. 1–2, claimed that the National Council on Schoolhouse Construction, the Interstate School Building Service, and "leading school architects" had adopted the principles of its Community School Plans. Although Rosenwald Fund plans appear stark in comparison with urban schools such as those illustrated in William C. Bruce, *Grade School Buildings,* books 1 and 2 (Milwaukee, Wisc.: American School Board Journal, 1914, 1925), those for large rural black schools compare favorably with the simpler Colonial Revival designs in Russell F. Whitehead, *An Architectural Monograph on a Three-Teacher Rural School with Teachers' Cottage* (New York, 1921).

38. O. H. Bernard, "The JRF in Tennessee," [1927], n.p., folder 2, box 76, JRFA.

39. In contrast, Pierre Du Pont's school building project in Delaware spent between $5,000 and $8,000 per room for black schools. Taggart, *Private Philanthropy,* 133–34.

40. *Biennial Report, SSPIT, for 1915–16*, 27–29, 290; *Biennial Report, SSPIT, for 1917–18*, 15.

41. See Leo M. Favrot, "The Service of a Rosenwald Building Agent Is Greatly Needed in Several States," 1928, folder 16, box 202, JRFA.

42. R. E. Clay became Tennessee's first Rosenwald building agent in 1918. Tennessee A&I's President William J. Hale had recommended Clay, who was a friend of Hale's and the president of the Bristol (Tenn.) Negro Business League. While Clay took a leave from Nov. 1922 until Jan. 1925 to work for the Inter-Racial Commission, H. N. Robinson and, briefly, W. L. Porter took over the building agent's responsibilities. H. N. Robinson, "Summary of Work Since Nov. 1, 1922," folder 3, box 269, TCE. Clay's Washingtonian philosophy was too much for some A&I students. See Samuel H. Shannon, "Agricultural and Industrial Education at Tennessee State Univ. During the Normal School Phase, 1912–1922: A Case Study" (Ph.D. diss, George Peabody College for Teachers, 1974), 187–88; S. L. Smith, *Builders of Goodwill*, 45–46; Stitely, "Bridging the Gap," 29.

43. "Report of O. H. Bernard, State Rural School Agent for Tennessee, Oct. 1925," folder 1, box 14, TCE.

44. R. E. Clay to O. H. Bernard, 31 May 1926, folder 1, box 270, TCE; Clay to Bernard, "Special Report," 27 May 1928, folder 3, box 269, TCE.

45. H. N. Robinson used these words to describe the campaign in Henry County in his "Summary of Work, July 1, 1923, to June 30, 1924," 1 July 1924, folder 3, box 269, TCE.

46. Clay to Bernard, 1 Sept. 1925, folder 1, box 270, TCE. In 1925, 67 percent of Haywood farmers were black; overall, farm tenancy had risen from 71 percent in 1910 to 75 percent, according to Allred, Watkins, and Hatfield, *Tennessee: Economic and Social*, pt. 2, pp. 29, 83. Clay joined forces with African American agricultural agent A. M. Dobbins to organize a building campaign for the Prospect and New Hope communities. See Clay to Bernard, 30 Nov. 1925, 1 May 1926, and 30 Nov. 1926, all in folder 1, box 270, TCE. Unlike neighboring Shelby County, Haywood County repressed black political rights, although not black activism. See Richard A. Couto, *Lifting the Veil: A Political History of Struggles for Emancipation* (Knoxville: Univ. of Tennessee Press, 1993). The presence or absence of black political power was important, even in Middle Tennessee's Coffee County, which O. H. Bernard described as being the most racist county in the state. A bond issue expected to be carried by black votes held the prospect of softening white opposition. See "Report of O. H. Bernard, State Rural School Agent for Tennessee, Oct. 1925," folder 1, box 14, TCE.

47. "Monthly Report of Dudley Tanner, State Agent for Negro Schools of Tennessee, Mar. 1930," folder 2, box 36, TCE.

48. H. N. Robinson, "Summary of Work since Nov. 1, 1922," 19 Mar. 1924, folder 3, box 269, TCE; "Report of O. H. Bernard, State Rural School Agent for Tennessee," Oct. 1925 and Nov. 1925, folder 1, box 14, TCE. Bernard stated frankly that new schools for whites paved the way for new schools for blacks, contrary to the Rosenwald Fund's claim. Compare S. L. S[mith], "Story of the Rosenwald Fund in Tenn.," with "Report of O. H. Bernard, State Rural School Agent for Tennessee," May 1926, folder 1, box 14, and Sept. 1926, folder 20, box 13, both in TCE.

49. The counties identified were Maury, Madison, and Sullivan. In the first two counties, R. E. Clay noted that one or two county school board members would have liked to stop the projects as well. In Sullivan County, no school would be built for five years. Clay to Bernard, 10 Dec. 1926, folder 1, box 270, TCE (Maury); "Report of O. H. Bernard, State Rural Agent for Tennessee, Mar. 1924," folder 7, box 270, TCE (Sullivan); A. M. Dobbins, "A Brief Summary of Some of the Accomplishments in Inter-Racial Co-operation within the Past Three Years," folder 2, box 76, JRFA (Madison).

50. "Report of O. H. Bernard, State Rural Agent for Tennessee," Mar. 1924, folder 7, box 270, and Oct. 1925, folder 1, box 14, both TCE; Clay to Bernard, 1 Sept. 1925 and 10 Dec. 1926, both in folder 1, box 270, TCE; "Monthly Report of Dudley Tanner, State Agent for Negro Schools of Tennessee," Mar. 1930, folder 2, box 36, TCE; "Monthly Report for State Rosenwald Agent," Dec. 1930, folder 4, box 269, TCE.

51. H. N. Robinson, "Summary of Work, July 1, 1923, to June 30, 1924," folder 3, box 269, TCE; "Report of O. H. Bernard, State Rural School Agent for Tennessee, Oct. 1925," folder 1, box 14, TCE. Information about Rosenwald-aided schools is derived from the listing of Tennessee schools in folder 1, box 343, JRFA. Hixson replaced an earlier one-room frame school with a bell tower, of a type also seen in a 1916 GEB photograph of an unidentified Hamilton County black school. Hixson school photograph in folder 7, box 559, JRFA, and photograph 1054, Tenn. 126, GEBA.

52. "Report of O. H. Bernard, State Rural School Agent for Tennessee, Oct. 1925," folder 1, box 14, TCE.

53. Clay to Bernard, 1 Oct. 1927, folder 3, box 269, TCE; Lamon, *Black Tennesseans*, 294–96. According to Lamon, Chattanooga was the location of Tennessee's only Garveyite organization. In 1930, blacks accounted for 23 percent of the county population, of which 92 percent lived in Chattanooga. Only 3 percent of black men labored in agriculture, and almost half of black farm operators owned their land. The average value of white schools, almost $16,000, was nearly seven times greater than that of black schools. C. S. Johnson, *Statistical Atlas*, 212.

54. Clay to Bernard, 1 Mar. 1926, folder 1, box 270, TCE; Clay to Bernard, 1 Jan. 1928 and 27 May 1928, both in folder 3, box 269, TCE.

55. Clay to Bernard, 30 Nov. 1925 and 30 Apr. 1927, both in folder 1, box 270, TCE; Clay to Bernard, 30 Sept. 1929, and Clay to Dudley S. Tanner, 31 Oct. 1929, both in folder 3, box 269, TCE.

56. H. N. Robinson, "Report of Rosenwald School Building Agent," Mar. 1924 (quotations) and May 1924, both in folder 3, box 269, TCE; S. L. Smith to P. L. Harned, 29 Mar. 1923, folder 1, box 343, JRFA. In Obion County in 1930, just under 60 percent of black men were farmers, of whom only 15 percent owned their farms. C. S. Johnson, *Statistical Atlas,* 218.

57. H. N. Robinson, "Report of Rosenwald School Building Agent," May 1924 and June 1924, both in folder 3, box 269, TCE; Clay to Bernard, 30 Jan. 1926, folder 1, box 270, TCE.

58. Clay to Bernard, 30 Jan. 1926 and 2 Aug. 1926, both in folder 1, box 270, TCE.

59. Hiland School, photographed in Sept. 1928, also bore asbestos shingling; its design resembles that of the JRF plan 20-A for a two-teacher school with incised corner porch. "Report of O. H. Bernard, State Rural School Agent for Tennessee," Oct. 1926, folder 20, box 13, TCE; photographs 1176 and 1185–86, box 36, TBE.

60. Clay to Bernard, 31 May 1926, 2 Aug. 1926, 1 Sept. 1926, and 31 May 1927, all in folder 1, box 270, TCE.

61. Mrs. M. B. Lane to Clay, 10 Aug. 1927, in folder 3, box 269, TCE; "Report of O. H. Bernard, State Rural School Agent for Tennessee," Nov. 1927, folder 23, box 35, 3, TCE; photographs 1183–94, box 36, TBE.

62. Clay to Bernard, 30 Jan. 1926 and 1 Sept. 1926, both in folder 1, box 270, TCE.

63. Gloria Brown Melton, "Blacks in Memphis, Tennessee, 1920–1955: A Historical Study" (Ph.D. diss., Washington State Univ., 1982), 36–53, 64–76, 88–109; William D. Miller, *Mr. Crump of Memphis* (Baton Rouge: Louisiana State Univ. Press, 1964), 102–4, 133, 204–7, and passim; Miller, *Memphis During the Progressive Era*; Robert A. Lanier, *Memphis in the 1920s: The Second Term of Mayor Rowlett Paine, 1924–1928* (Memphis, Tenn.: Zenda Press, 1979), 18–21, 106–9; Roger Biles, "Robert R. Church, Jr., of Memphis: Black Republican Leader in the Age of Democratic Ascendancy, 1928–1940," *Tennessee Historical Quarterly* 42 (Winter 1983): 362–82; C. S. Johnson, *Statistical Atlas,* 220. Marsha Wedell traces earlier white female reformers in Memphis in *Elite Women and the Reform Impulse in Memphis, 1875–1915* (Knoxville: Univ. of Tennessee Press, 1991).

64. "Report of S. L. Smith, State Rural School Supervisor for Tennessee, Mar. 1917," folder 1469, box 158, series 1, subseries 1, GEBA.

65. "Report of S. L. Smith, State Rural School Supervisor for Tennessee, Oct. 1917," and "Report of S. L. Smith, State Rural School Supervisor for Tennessee, May 1918," both in folder 1469, box 158, series 1, subseries 1, GEBA; S. L. S[mith], "A Story of the JRF in Tenn. From the Beginning to July 1, 1920," folder 2, box 76, JRFA.

66. "Report of O. H. Bernard, State Rural School Supervisor for Tennessee," Oct. 1920, folder 18, box 167, TCE; "A General Statement of the Work of the JRF in the South," [1922], folder 1, box 331, JRFA; listing of Tennessee Rosenwald schools, folder 1, box 343, JRFA. The number of black schools in 1929–30 represents the sum of elementary and high schools reported to the state, but the total may have been lower if they shared facilities.

67. Sue McFall Powers, originally from Montgomery County in Middle Tennessee, moved from the post of principal of Whitehaven High School to become Shelby County superintendent in 1922 and held that position until 1951. Rogers, *Light from Many Candles,* 178–80.

68. H. N. Robinson, "Summary of Work, July 1, 1923, to June 30, 1924," and Clay to Bernard, 31 Jan. 1925, both in folder 3, box 269, TCE.

69. "Jeanes Teachers, 1925–42," and "Extracts from Sept. and Oct. Reports of Jeanes Supervisors in Tennessee" [1929], both in folder 13, box 31, TCE.

70. Clay to Bernard, 1 Oct. 1927, 1 Jan. 1928 (quotations), 1 Mar. 1928, 31 Aug. 1929, all in folder 3, box 269, TCE. Dudley Tanner photographed 3 schools he inspected in Sept. 1930 and another in 1932, indicating that the county continued seeking limited Rosenwald assistance until the JRF building program ended in 1932. See photographs 1405–8, 1411, 1413–14, and 1417, all in box 39, TBE.

71. Clay to Bernard, 30 June 1928, in folder 3, box 269, TCE. Leo Favrot, in "The State Agents of Rural schools for Negroes and Their Relation to Outside Funds Stimulating Negro Public Education," 1928, folder 16, box 202, JRFA, claimed that "the building of Rosenwald schoolhouses has been most active in counties where Jeanes agents are employed to create a demand for better school facilities."

72. Clay to Bernard, 31 Jan. 1925, folder 3, box 269, TCE; Clay to Bernard, 31 July and 31 Dec. 1925, 1 May 1926, all in folder 1, box 270, TCE.

73. H. N. Robinson, "Report of Rosenwald School Building Agent, Month Ending Mar. 31, 1924," 14 Apr. 1924, folder 3, box 269, TCE.

74. Clay to Bernard, 30 Nov. 1926, folder 1, box 270, TCE; Clay to Bernard, 31 Aug. 1929, folder 3, box 269, TCE.

75. H. N. Robinson to Harned, 19 Mar. 1924, folder 3, box 269, TCE.

76. Clay to Bernard, 1 Dec. 1927 and 1 Mar. 1928, folder 3, box 269, TCE.

77. Clay to Bernard, 31 Oct. 1925; "Resolutions," 1 Nov. 1925; Clay to Bernard, 31 May 1926, folder 1, box 270, TCE; Clay to Dudley S. Tan-

ner, 31 Oct. 1929, folder 3, box 269, TCE (quotation). John R. Bond had spoken favorably at Booker T. Washington's visit to Brownsville in 1909; his comments marked him as receptive to race-specific industrial education and deferential race relations. See Couto, *Lifting the Veil*, 95–99.

78. Clay to Bernard, 1 Jan. 1928 and 30 Sept. 1929, both in folder 3, box 269, TCE; Clay to Tanner, 1 Dec. 1932, folder 4, box 269, TCE.

79. Clay to Bernard, 30 Sept. 1929 and 30 Nov. 1929, both in folder 3, box 269, TCE.

80. Clay to Bernard, 31 Oct. 1927, 1 Dec. 1927, and 31 Oct. 1929, all in folder 3, box 269, TCE; Clay to Bernard, 30 Jan. 1926, folder 1, box 270, TCE.

81. Clay to Bernard, 1 Jan. 1928, folder 3, box 269, TCE; Clay to Bernard, 1 Mar. 1926, folder 1, box 270, TCE; S. L. S[mith], "Story of the Rosenwald Fund in Tenn."

82. Clay to I. A. Ligon [chair, Carthage School Board], 18 Oct. 1929; Clay to Dudley S. Tanner, 31 Oct. 1929; Clay to Tanner, 30 Nov. 1929, all in folder 3, box 269, TCE; Clay to Tanner, 1 Dec. 1932, folder 4, box 269, TCE. The local white-owned newspaper covered the African American fair and made favorable remarks about black principal C. E. S. Payne and black schoolchildren, but did not mention the Rosenwald campaign. "Big Colored Fair to Be Held in Carthage Soon," 10 Oct. 1929; "Colored Fair in Carthage Oct. 21st to 26th," 17 Oct. 1929; and "Carthage Colored Fair Being Held This Week," 24 Oct. 1929, all *Carthage (Tenn.) Courier*.

83. Clay to Bernard, 31 Dec. 1925 and 30 June 1926, both in folder 1, box 270, TCE.

84. S. L. S[mith], "Story of the Rosenwald Fund in Tenn."

85. Clay to Bernard, 31 Aug. 1929, folder 3, box 269, TCE; Clay to Tanner, 31 May 1930, 1 Oct. 1930, and 29 Dec. 1930, all in folder 4, box 269, TCE. Three-quarters of Fayette's farmers were black; just over 90 percent of them were tenants. Allred, Watkins, and Hatfield, *Tennessee: Economic and Social*, pt. 2, pp. 29; C. S. Johnson, *Statistical Atlas*, 211.

86. William A. Link, "Making the Inarticulate Speak," 69–71.

87. Clay to Bernard, 1 May 1926 and 4 Apr. 1927, both in folder 1, box 270, TCE. See also Clay to Bernard, 30 Nov. 1926, folder 1, box 270, TCE; 1 Jan. 1928 and 31 Oct. 1929, both in folder 3, box 269, TCE. H. N. Robinson found the same difficulties in Denmark, Madison County, and in Sweetwater, Monroe County. See his "Summary of Work Since Nov. 1, 1922," and his "Summary of Work July 1, 1923, to June 30, 1924."

88. Clay to Bernard, 30 Sept. 1925, folder 1, box 269, TCE; Clay, "Monthly Report, State Rosenwald Agent," Apr. 1933, folder 5, box 269, TCE.

89. Clay to Bernard, "Special Report," 27 May 1928, folder 3, box 269, TCE. This instance concerned a Baptist preacher who used a personal relationship with the Tipton County superintendent to keep a teaching position for his daughter.

90. Clay to Bernard, 31 July 1925, 30 Sept. 1925, and 30 Oct. 1926, all in folder 1, box 270, TCE.

91. Clay to Bernard, 30 Nov. 1929, in folder 3, box 269, TCE. Clay's philosophy and class shaped his condescending attitudes toward some African Americans, although he may have exaggerated his own sentiments in order to appeal to his white supervisors. He described black migrants to Knoxville as "a shiftless element" and believed that African Americans in Hardeman County had been "neglected," making them "very backward and dull." He concluded that "it is going to take some time to organize and teach them what to do and how to do it." Yet they were already raising money for a school. Clay to Bernard, 1 Oct. 1927, folder 3, box 269, TCE, and 30 Apr. 1927, folder 1, box 270, TCE. In a variation on his usual sermon, Clay told Huntingdon, Carroll County, African Americans that if they couldn't resolve their differences, they "would never get the white people to do anything for them." Clay to Bernard, 31 May 1926, in folder 1, box 270, TCE.

92. Clay to Bernard, 31 May 1926. In seeking out surviving Rosenwald schools in Tennessee, I have found a number of them located adjacent, or close, to a church.

93. W. T. B. Williams, "The Rosenwald Fund in Negro Education," [1927], folder 2, box 78, JRFA; Anderson, *Education of Blacks,* 156, 172.

94. In 1925, 51.7 percent of all southern counties had a Rosenwald school, but there were only 17 in the 65 Tennessee counties having black populations of less than 12.5 percent, according to S. L. Smith to [Francis W.] Shepardson, 20 Aug. 1925, folder 1, box 331, JRFA. S. L. Smith, *Builders of Goodwill,* 26; [S. L. Smith] to P. L. Harned, 3 May 1928 and 15 June 1928, and [S. L. Smith] to O. H. Bernard, 11 July 1928, all in folder 1, box 343, JRFA; S. L. Smith to Alfred K. Stern, 31 Aug. 1928; Stern to S. L. Smith, 6 Sept. 1928; and S. L. Smith to Walter B. Hill, 7 Nov. 1928; all in folder 4, box 331, JRFA.

95. The revival of the Ku Klux Klan in Lewis County in 1926 may have lengthened delays for rural black schools. Hohenwald Rosenwald School would have been eligible for state rural school building fund aid and consolidation assistance as well. *Lewis County Herald,* 18 Feb. and 14 Oct. 1926; S. L. Smith to P. L. Harned, 8 June 1928, folder 1, box 36, TCE; "Report Showing by States the First Rosenwald School Built in Counties of 5 Per Cent Negro Population Stimulated by Extra Aid of 50 Per Cent, Nov. 1928 to July 1930," folder 2, box 331, JRFA; listing

of Tennessee Rosenwald schools, folder 1, box 343, JRFA; photographs 907–8, TBE.

96. *Annual Report, TDE, for Scholastic Year Ending June 30, 1927,* 17–18; *Annual Report, TDE, for Scholastic Year Ending June 30, 1928,* 20; *Annual Report, TDE, for Scholastic Year Ending June 30, 1930* (Nashville: Ambrose, 1931), 18.

97. "Conference of State Agents of Rural Schools for Negroes," 8–9 June 1928, folder 4, box 188, JRFA.

98. Bernard to S. L. Smith, 31 Mar. 1928, and P. L. Harned to S. L. Smith, 2 Apr. 1928, both in folder 1, box 343, JRFA.

99. Southern states postponed fully funding a black school official until the fund abruptly stopped aid in 1932. See unidentified correspondent to S. L. Smith, 5 May 1927; S. L. Smith to Alfred K. Stern, 13 Apr. 1928; S. L. Smith to Stern, 6 Jan. 1932; all in folder 5, box 331, JRFA.

100. "A Decade of Increase in Schoolhouse Property for Negroes, 1920 to 1930," and "Summary of Completed Buildings from Beginning to July 1, 1932," both in folder 2, box 331, JRFA.

4. Building a Bridge between School and Home Life

1. For reformers' attitudes, see Ellwood P. Cubberly, *Rural Life and Education: A Study of the Rural-School Problem as a Phase of the Rural-Life Problem* (Boston: Houghton Mifflin, 1914), 172; "The Objectives of Country Life," *Proceedings of the First National Country Life Conference* (Ithaca, N.Y.: National Country Life Association, 1919), 17–18; and O. G. Brim, "Handicaps of the Rural Child," *Proceedings of the Fifth National Country Life Conference* (New York: Association Press, 1923). Progressive prescriptions for rural women have been described and critiqued for their gendered assumptions by, among others, Joan M. Jensen, *With These Hands: Women Working on the Land* (Old Westbury, N.Y.: Feminist Press, 1981), 148–52, 165–70; Fink, *Agrarian Women*; Katherine Jellison, *Entitled to Power: Farm Women and Technology, 1913–1963* (Chapel Hill: Univ. of North Carolina Press, 1993); Jane Adams, *The Transformation of Rural Life: Southern Illinois, 1890–1990* (Chapel Hill: Univ. of North Carolina Press, 1994); Neth, *Preserving the Family Farm*; and Marilyn Irvin Holt, *Linoleum, Better Babies and the Modern Farm Woman, 1890–1930* (Albuquerque: Univ. of New Mexico Press, 1995).

2. Mary Meek Atkeson, *The Woman on the Farm* (New York: Century, 1924), 174–86.

3. Henrietta W. Calvin, "Report of Committee on the Rural Home," *Proceedings of the Third National Country Life Conference* (Chicago: Univ.

of Chicago Press, 1921), 163. Henrietta W. Calvin and Carrie A. Lyford coauthored *Home Economics, 1916* (Washington, D.C.: GPO, 1916).

4. *Biennial Report, SSPIT, for 1913–14,* 36–37, 243–51 (quotation on 249). In 1914, 67 Tennessee cities and towns reported to the U.S. Bureau of Education that their schools offered some type of home economics classes. Benjamin R. Andrews, "Education for the Home," pt. 4, U.S. Bureau of Education Bulletin, 1914, No. 39 (Washington, D.C.: GPO, 1915), 58.

5. *Outline on Rural School Supervision,* n.p. Despite Keffer's promise, the Tennessee Extension Service's work among blacks, especially black women, was extremely limited. To compensate for state neglect, the GEB set up the program of black Home Makers Clubs discussed in ch. 5 of this volume. "Report of S. L. Smith, Rural School Supervisor for Tennessee for Aug. 1914," and "Report of S. L. Smith, Rural School Supervisor, State of Tennessee, Sept. 1914," both in folder 1468, box 158, series 1, subseries 1, GEBA.

6. "Report of S. L. Smith, Rural School Supervisor for Tennessee for Aug., 1914," and "Report of S. L. Smith, Rural School Supervisor, State of Tennessee, Sept. 1914," both in folder 1468, box 158, series 1, subseries 1, GEBA.

7. S. L. Smith, "Report of Some Special Work in Rural Negro Schools for 1915–16," *Biennial Report, SSPIT, for 1915–16,* 290–91, and S. L. Smith, "Report of Some Special Work in Rural Negro Schools for 1919–1920," *Biennial Report, SSPIT, for 1919–20,* 155–56. See also the correspondence between P. L. Harned and GEB officials in folder 2, box 11, TCE; folder 2, box 236, TCE; and folder 1, box 239, TCE.

8. S. L. Smith to James H. Dillard, 8 Apr. 1915, folder 1464, box 157, series 1, subseries 1, GEBA; S. L. Smith, "Report of Some Special Work in Rural Negro Schools for 1919–1920," 153; S. L. Smith, "Brief Report of Some Special Work in Rural Negro Schools for Years 1921–1922," *Biennial Report, SSPIT, for 1921–22,* 272; [Dudley Tanner] to Leo M. Favrot, 10 Aug. 1931, folder 2, box 236, TCE.

9. "Report of S. L. Smith, Rural School Supervisor, State of Tennessee, Nov. 1918," folder 1469, box 158, series 1, subseries 1, GEBA.

10. Folks, "Schools," 183; "Some Phases of Vocational Home Economics," *Tennessee Educational Bulletin* 1 (Apr. 1922): 3; "Work of State Division of Home Economics," *Tennessee Educational Bulletin,* 4 (Oct.–Dec. 1925): 6; "Annual Report of the State Supervisors of Vocational Education to the State Board for Vocational Education," 1925, folder 3, box 420, TCE, p. 53.

11. Calvin, "Report of Committee on the Rural Home"; Geraldine Jonçich Clifford, "'Marry, Stitch, Die, or Do Worse': Educating Women for Work," in *Work, Youth, and Schooling: Historical Perspectives on*

Vocationalism in American Education, ed. James D. Anderson, Harvey Kantor and David B. Tyack (Stanford, Calif.: Stanford Univ. Press, 1982), 258; Matthews, *"Just a Housewife,"* 158–59; Laura Shapiro, *Perfection Salad: Women and Cooking at the Turn of the Century* (New York: Farrar, Strauss and Giroux, 1986), 218–19. Also see Nancy F. Cott, *The Grounding of Modern Feminism* (New Haven, Conn.: Yale Univ. Press, 1987), 162–65, 170–71.

12. "Smith-Hughes Requirements for Home Economics in All-Day Schools," *Tennessee Educational Bulletin* 1 (Mar. 1922): 3–4; *Biennial Report, SSPIT, for 1921–22,* 305; "Tentative Two-Year Course of Study for Vocational Home Economics," [1922–23], folder 3, box 196, TCE, pp. 1, 8, 12–13; *Biennial Report, SSPIT, for 1921–22,* 308; *Annual Report, TDE, for Scholastic Year Ending June 30, 1923* (Nashville, 1924), 179; "Annual Report of the State Supervisors of Vocational Education," 1925, p. 57.

13. "Annual Report of the State Supervisor of Home Economics [for the Year Ending 30 June 1924]," sect. 3, pp. 1, 5–6, 7–9; "Vocational Home Economics in Tennessee Evening School Classes," [1924], 3, both in folder 9, box 160, TCE.

14. Requests for, and reports summarizing, GEB contributions to county training schools can be found in: folders 1472 and 1473, box 158, series 1, subseries 1, GEBA, folders 3064, 3065, and 3066, box 294, series 1, subseries 1, GEBA; folders 1 and 4, box 236, TCE. For an itemized list of equipment for each school, see "Proposed Apportionment of Equipment Fund for County Training Schools in Tennessee, 1927–28," folder 2, box 236, TCE. On the Slater Fund, see Bernard to James Hardy Dillard, 4 Aug. 1925, folder 11, box 273, TCE.

15. "Report of S. L. Smith, Rural School Supervisor of Tennessee, Month of Oct. 1914," folder 1468, box 158, series 1, subseries 1, GEBA, p. 2.

16. Marie White to P. L. Harned, 9 Mar. 1927, and Edith Thomas to Marie White, 16 Mar. 1927 (quotations), both in folder 7, box 12, TCE; Marie White to W. J. Hale, 14 Oct. 1929, folder 10, box 22, TCE; "Annual Descriptive Report of the State Board of Vocational Education," 1927–28, sect. 3: "Home Economics," folder 11, box 39, TCE, p. 1. See also "A Study of Home-Economics Education in Teacher-Training Institutions for Negroes," Federal Board for Vocational Education Bulletin No. 79, Home Economics Series No. 7 (Washington, D.C.: GPO, 1923).

17. Marie White, "Home Economics News," *Tennessee Educational Bulletin* 4 (Feb. 1925): 4; "Home Economics Education," *Annual Report, TDE, 1927,* 211; "Your Home Economics Rooms," *Home Economics News Letter* (Nashville, Tenn.: Division of Vocational Education, Sept. 1928), folder 9, box 39, TCE, p. 3; Edith M. Thomas to Marie White, 12 Oct. 1926, folder 7, box 12, TCE. On the George-Reed Act, see Alfred

Charles True, *A History of Agricultural Education in the United States, 1785–1925* (Washington, D.C.: GPO, 1925; reprint, New York: Arno Press, 1969), 322–82; Lloyd E. Blauch, *Federal Cooperation in Agricultural Extension Work, Vocational Education, and Vocational Rehabilitation* (Washington, D.C.: GPO, 1935; reprint, New York: Arno Press, 1969), 50–121, 228–29; Adelaide S. Baylor, "Vocational Education in Home Economics Under the George-Reed Act," *Journal of Home Economics* 21 (Sept. 1929): 645–49.

18. Folks, "Schools," 152–53; "Smith-Hughes Requirements," 4; "Annual Report of the Division of Extension," 1918, *ESART*, roll 3, p. 341; "Doings of County Agricultural and Home Demonstration Agents," a series of articles in *TAER*: 3 (1 Jan. 1920): 4; 3 (June 1920): 4; 4 (Aug. 1920): 3; 4 (Jan. 1921): 3; 4 (1 May 1921): 3; 5 (Sept. 1921): 2; "Women Build and Equip Club House," *TAER* 10 (Feb. 1927): 4. Black agents and their constituents undertook similar projects. An example is described in "Colored Community Builds Splendid School," *TAER* 5 (Nov. 1921): 2.

19. *UT Record* 17 (Apr. 1914): 102 (quotation); 20 (Apr. 1917): 92, 94; 23 (Apr. 1920): 75; 25 (June 1922): 103, 104; 26 (June 1923): 115; 30 (May 1927): 141–42, 144.

20. *UT Record* 19 (Mar. 1916): 27; 23 (Apr. 1920): 102–03; 28 (May 1925): 158; 30 (May 1927): 121.

21. *5th Annual Report to Congress of the Federal Board for Vocational Education, 1921,* in *House Documents,* 67th Cong., 2d Sess., No. 240 (also Serial 8085, Washington, D.C., 1921), 71–72; *8th Annual Report to Congress of the Federal Board for Vocational Education, 1924,* in *House Documents,* 68th Cong., 2d Sess., No. 456 (also Serial 8503, Washington, D.C., 1924), 62; *10th Annual Report to Congress of the Federal Board for Vocational Education, 1926,* in *House Documents,* 69th Cong., 2d Sess., No. 534 (also Serial 8805, Washington, D.C., 1926), 34–40. See also Myrl Jeannette Obert, "Growth of Home Economics in State Teachers Colleges" (M.A. thesis, George Peabody College for Teachers, 1929), 27.

22. *UT Record* 20 (Apr. 1917): 58–59, 74, 122–24; 21 (Apr. 1918): 44; 22 (Apr. 1919): 60, 103–5.

23. *UT Record* 23 (Apr. 1920): 49–51, 104–5.

24. *UT Record* 27 (May 1924): 93–95; 27 (Nov. 1924): 22–23 (quotation on 23); 29 (Nov. 1926): 7, 23–24; 31 (July 1928): 29–30; 31 (Nov. 1928): 35.

25. *UT Record* 31 (May 1928): 124–27; 176–79; 31 (Nov. 1928): 35 (quotations); "UT Announces Course for Home Demonstration Agents," *TAER* 10 (Apr. 1927): 1; "Clothing and Household Management," 1928, *ESART,* roll 21, pp. 1–2.

26. *Peabody Bulletin* 1 (Sept. 1912): 7. For further discussion of Peabody's home economics program, see Mary S. Hoffschwelle, "The Science of Domesticity: Home Economics at George Peabody College for Teachers, 1914–1939," *Journal of Southern History* 57 (Nov. 1991): 659–80.

27. *Peabody Bulletin* 1 (Apr. 1913): 7, 98–99; 3 (Jan. 1915): 11; [Bruce R. Payne], "Report of the President of George Peabody College for Teachers," 19 Jan. 1915, box 9, PA; Cullum, "George Peabody College for Teachers," 43–46. Peabody hosted the 2nd Annual National Conference for Training Rural Teachers in 1915. See "Declaration of Principles," *School and Society* 3 (22 Jan. 1916): 137–40.

28. "The Seaman A. Knapp School of Country Life," *Tennessee Agriculture* 3 (1 Sept. 1914): 331; *Peabody Bulletin* 1 (Jan. 1913): 4. See also Otis W. Caldwell, "Home Economics and Rural Extension," *Journal of Home Economics* 6 (Apr. 1914): 100–101, 105.

29. [Payne], "Report of the President," 1912, box 9, PA; W. K. Tate, "Report of the Treasurer," 1914, box 45, PA; Ruth Gillespie, "Home Economics at George Peabody College for Teachers," box 49, PA; "By-Laws of the Faculty of George Peabody College for Teachers," 3 Dec. 1915, in box "Faculty Minutes, 1914–1936," PA; Ada M. Field, "Home Economics Building at George Peabody College for Teachers," *Journal of Home Economics* 7 (Oct. 1915): 418–20; *Peabody Bulletin* 3 (June 1915): 81–82; 4 (Dec. 1915): 8–10, 14; 6 (Mar. 1918): 12–13.

30. "The Knapp School of Country Life—Its Aim," *Peabody Summer School News* 1 (12 July 1916): 1, 3; *Peabody Bulletin* 4 (Sept. 1915): 17–21.

31. "Special Winter Courses at the George Peabody College for Teachers," *School and Society* 2 (25 Dec. 1915): 918; *Peabody Bulletin* 5 (Dec. 1916): 7–16.

32. *Peabody Bulletin* 6 (Nov. 1917): 17; "Four-Year Course Leading to the Degree of Bachelor of Science and Diploma in Home Demonstration Work," pasted in "Faculty Minutes," 8 May 1918, in box "Faculty Minutes 1914–1936," PA; *Peabody Bulletin* 7 (Nov. 1918): 3.

33. "Four Year Course . . . in Home Demonstration Work"; [Bruce R. Payne], "President's Report," 1918, Box 9, PA; Payne to W. W. Brierly, 4 Feb. 1918, folder 1358, box 147, series 1, subseries 1, GEBA.

34. *Biennial Report, SSPIT, for 1919–20*, 19–20, 166–67; *Peabody Bulletin* 9 (Sept. 1920): 24; 10 (Nov. 1921): 6; 11 (Mar. 1922): 9; 11 (Jan. 1923): 56; 12 (Mar. 1924): 83. See also Joseph F. Kett, "The Adolescence of Vocational Education," in Kantor and Tyack, *Work, Youth, and Schooling*, 82. As late as 1927, the Univ. of Tennessee was the only federally approved and funded teacher training institution in the state, according to Gladys Alee Branegan, *Home Economics Teacher Training Under the Smith-Hughes Act, 1917 to 1927* (New York: Teachers College, Columbia Univ., 1929), 91; but the Tennessee Board of Education

did accept a master's degree in vocational education as being equivalent to the Univ. of Tennessee program for teachers in its school programs funded by Smith-Hughes. See Rhey Boyd Parsons, *Teacher Education in Tennessee* (Chicago: Univ. of Chicago Libraries, 1935), 124.

35. Ruth Schwartz Cowan, "Two Washes in the Morning and a Bridge Party at Night: The American Housewife Between the Wars," in *Decades of Discontent: The Women's Movement, 1920–1940*, ed. Lois Scharf and Joan M. Jensen (Westport, Conn.: Greenwood Press, 1983), 179–83; Shapiro, *Perfection Salad,* 218–20.

36. *Peabody Bulletin* 15 (May 1926): 11 and 16 (Mar. 1927): 12; "Faculty Minutes," 12 Jan. 1927, in box "Faculty Minutes, 1914–1936," PA; *Suggested Curricula* (Nashville: George Peabody College for Teachers, 1927); *Annual Report of the GEB, 1928–1929* (New York: GEB, 1929), 11, 13, 76–77.

37. [Bruce R. Payne,] "President's Report," 8 June 1921, PA, 3–4.

38. *Peabody Bulletin* 10 (Nov. 1921): 6 and 10 (Mar. 1922): 78–79.

39. William W. Force, *Payne of Peabody: An Apostle of Education* (Nashville, Tenn.: Printed by the Author, 1985), 42; *Peabody Bulletin* 11 (Mar. 1923): 85–86 and 14 (May 1925): 92. Beginning with the 1929–30 academic year, the *Peabody Bulletin* contains no reference to a home demonstration degree program, although "Organization of Home Demonstration" and "Food Preservation" courses were offered until the summer of 1932. Knapp Farm operated as a certified seed-corn station for the state of Tennessee and as a site for college social activities until its sale in 1965.

40. S. L. Smith to Abraham Flexner, 20 Sept. 1915; "Summary of Monthly Reports of Agents for Home Makers' Clubs for Negroes—Season 1915, Tennessee"; S. L. Smith to E. C. Sage, 1 Sept. 1916; S. L. Smith, "Report of Homemakers' Club Work of Tennessee, 1916"; S. L. Smith to Flexner, 16 Aug. 1917; "Summarized Statement of Home Makers' Club Work for the Summer of 1917 in the State of Tennessee"; S. L. Smith to Sage, 15 Aug. 1918; "Summarized Statement of Home Makers Club Work for the Summer of 1918 in the State of Tennessee"—all in folder 1474, box 158, series 1, subseries 1, GEBA; S. L. Smith, "Report of Some Special Work Among Rural Negro Schools in Tennessee, 1915–16," *Biennial Report, SSPIT, for 1915–16,* 288, 293; and S. L. Smith, "Report of Some Special Work in Rural Negro Schools for 1919–1920," *Biennial Report, SSPIT, for 1919–20,* 153, 157.

41. S. L. Smith, "Brief Report of Some Special Work in Rural Negro Schools for Years 1921–1922," *Biennial Report, SSPIT, for 1921–22,* 272; O. H. Bernard to Albert Williams, 25 Jan. 1921, folder 18, box 167, TCE; "Jeanes Teachers, 1925–42," folder 6, box 246, TCE; "Extracts from Sept. and Oct. Reports of Jeanes Supervisors in Tennessee" [1928–29], folder 13, box 31,

TCE; "Annual Report of Home Demonstration Agent of Hamilton County," 1921, roll 5, and "Home Demonstration Agent, District Three," 1922, roll 7, p. 272, both in *ESART.* Fagala graduated from Atlanta Univ. and studied at Tennessee A&I Normal School. She worked in Hamilton County until 1938. See Hutson, "Jeanes Supervisory Program," 207.

42. True, *History of Agricultural Education,* 374–77; "Annual Report of the Division of Extension," 1918, *ESART,* roll 3, p. 10.

43. Tennessee Home Economics Association, *Home Economics Heritage in Tennessee,* 30; Harry Clark to Brown Ayres, 1 Nov. 1914, folder 1424, box 143, series 1, subseries 1, GEBA; "Summary of Reports of Mr. J. B. Brown, State Agent for Rural Schools in Tennessee, July 1, 1915, to Jan. 1, 1916," folder 1463, box 157, series 1, subseries 1, GEBA; Almon J. Sims, *History of Extension Work,* 14; "Annual Report of Home Demonstration Work for Women and Girls, Calendar Year 1919," Hamilton County, *ESART,* roll 3.

44. "Supervision," *Biennial Report, SSPIT, for 1921–22,* 271; "Annual Report of Home Demonstration Agent of Hamilton County, 1921," roll 5, and "Home Demonstration Agent, District Three," 1922, roll 7, both in *ESART*; "Mrs. Reagan Nominated for Hall of Fame," *TAER* 13 (Aug. 1929): 2.

45. Lula H. Crim to Wallace Buttrick, 27 Apr. 1919, and Charl O. Williams to Buttrick, 6 June 1919, both in folder 1477, box 159, series 1, subseries 1, GEBA; S. L. Smith to Buttrick, 6 May 1919, folder 1464, box 157, series 1, subseries 1, GEBA. Lula Crim previously had been a missionary, worked in Africa, and taught at Payne College; she received a fellowship at the Bethlehem House settlement in Nashville while studying at George Peabody College for Teachers. See Neverdon-Morton, *Afro-American Women of the South,* 168.

46. Crim to E. C. Sage, 21 June 1920, and "Report of Work in Negro Schools, July 1, 1919–Jan. 1, 1921," both in folder 1477, box 159, series 1, subseries 1, GEBA; J. B. Brown to Albert Williams, 26 Jan. 1921, folder 15, box 183, TCE.

47. Albert Williams to Wallace Buttrick, 6 Feb. 1922, folder 1477, box 159, series 1, subseries 1, GEBA.

48. "Annual Report of the Division of Extension for the Fiscal Year Ending June 30, 1918," roll 3, p. 356; "Annual Report of Home Demonstration Work for Women and Girls, Calendar Year 1919," roll 3; narrative report appended to "Annual Report of Home Demonstration Agent, Shelby County," 1921, roll 6, p. 3, all in *ESART.*

49. Tennessee Home Economics Association, *Home Economics Heritage,* 191; Cara L. Harris, "Teaching Foods in Rural Schools," *Journal of Home Economics* 13 (Sept. 1921): 426–27. The same themes recur in Cara L. Harris, "Organization of Homemaking Courses in Country High

Schools and Rural Elementary Schools," *Journal of Home Economics* 15 (Mar. 1923): 118–19.

50. "Summary of Shelby County Lunch Room Survey, 1925–1926," *ESART*, roll 18.

51. "Annual Report of the Division of Extension for the Fiscal Year Ending June 30, 1918," *ESART*, roll 3, p. 341; Tennessee Home Economics Association, *Home Economics Heritage*, 190.

52. "Annual Report of Home Demonstration Work for Women and Girls," 1919, Obion County, *ESART*, roll 3, p. 4 and map.

53. "Obion County Organized Temporary Council," *TAER* 3 (11 Oct. 1919): 8; "Annual Report of Home Demonstration Work for Women and Girls," 1920, Obion County, *ESART*, roll 4.

5. Better Homes on Better Farms

1. "President's Address" in "Proceedings of the Middle Tennessee Home-Makers' Association," *Tennessee Agriculture* 3 (1 Nov. 1914): 464.

2. T[homas] F. Peck, "Community Cooperation," *Tennessee Agriculture* 3 (1 June 1914): 225.

3. The gendered division of labor in extension service programs and rural women's responses are analyzed in Deborah Fink, *Open Country, Iowa: Rural Women, Tradition and Change* (Albany: State Univ. of New York Press, 1986); Sarah Elbert, "Women and Farming: Changing Structures, Changing Roles," in *Women and Farming: Changing Roles, Changing Structures,* ed. Wava G. Haney and Jane B. Knowles, 245–64 (Boulder, Colo.: Westview Press, 1988); Kathleen R. Babbitt, "The Productive Farm Woman and the Extension Home Economist in New York State, 1920–1940," *Agricultural History* 67 (Spring 1993): 83–101; Jellison, *Entitled to Power*; Adams, *Transformation of Rural Life*; and Neth, *Preserving the Family Farm*. For a Tennessee context for these issues, see Melissa Walker, "'All We Knew Was To Farm': Gender, Class, Race and Change Among East Tennessee Farm Women, 1920–1941" (Ph.D. diss., Clark Univ., 1996).

4. Other studies suggest the persistence of traditional house forms. Sally McMurry found that farm houses remained the same, while their interiors incorporated mass-produced consumer goods in McMurry, *Transforming Rural Life: Dairying Families and Agricultural Change, 1820–1885* (Baltimore, Md.: Johns Hopkins Univ. Press, 1995), 205–6; and Jane Adams, *Transformation of Rural Life*, 201–14, finds that farm houses in southern Illinois did not change significantly from the late nineteenth century to the 1950s. Conversely, farm families adopting the suburban bungalow style still used traditional floor plans, according to Susan Mulcahey Chase, "Rural Adaptations of Suburban Bungalows,

Sussex County, Delaware," in *Gender, Class, and Shelter,* Perspectives in Vernacular Architecture No. 5, ed. Elizabeth Collins Cromley and Carter L. Hudgins (Knoxville: Univ. of Tennessee Press, 1995), 179–89. I would add that the emphasis on domestic furnishings reflects the selection of women as the agents of domestic reform (compared to state and county governments as the agents of school reform); given the gender division of authority, farm women could not demand a new house, but they could rearrange and refurbish interiors.

5. On the Smith-Lever Act and its provisions, see Blauch, *Federal Cooperation in Agricultural Extension Work,* 52–94; Roy V. Scott, *Reluctant Farmer.* On the early years of the Tennessee Division of Extension, see Moore, "Review of a Few Steps," 16–17, 28–32; and M[aurice] C. Burritt, *The County Agent and the Farm Bureau* (New York: Harcourt, Brace, and Co., 1922), 168.

6. Joan M. Jensen, "Crossing Ethnic Barriers in the Southwest: Women's Agricultural Extension Education, 1914–1940," *Agricultural History* 60 (Spring 1986): 169–81; Cynthia Sturgis, "'How're You Gonna Keep 'Em Down on the Farm? Rural Women and the Urban Model in Utah," *Agricultural History* 60 (Spring 1986): 182–99; Dorothy Schwieder, "Education and Change in the Lives of Iowa Farm Women, 1900–1940," *Agricultural History* 60 (Spring 1986): 200–15; Powers, "The 'Girl Question' in Education," 21–57; Rury, *Education and Women's Work,* 131–74.

7. See, e.g., Jellison, *Entitled to Power,* and Neth, *Preserving the Family Farm.* For examples of the prescriptive literature critiqued by these historians, see Warren H. Wilson, "The Producer and Consumer in the Home," in *6th Annual National Country Life Conference* (Chicago: Univ. of Chicago Press, 1923), 113–21; Clarence Beaman Smith and Meredith Chester Wilson, *The Agricultural Extension System of the United States* (New York: Wiley and Sons, 1930).

8. Bradford Knapp and Mary E. Cresswell, "The Effect of Home Demonstration Work on the Community and the County in the South," *Yearbook of the U.S. Dept. of Agriculture, 1916* (Washington, D.C.: GPO, 1917), 251; see also Marilyn I. Holt, *Linoleum, Better Babies,* 76–77.

9. J. A. Evans was chief of the federal Office of Extension, South, at the time of its merger in 1921 with the Office of Extension, North and West. Evans, *Recollections of Extension History,* 24–29; Clarence Beaman Smith and Meredith Chester Wilson, *Agricultural Extension System,* 28–40, 209; Kathleen C. Hilton, "'Both in the Field, Each with a Plow': Race and Gender in USDA Policy, 1907–1929," in *Hidden Histories of Women in the New South,* ed. Virginia Bernhard, Betty Brandon, Elizabeth Fox-Genovese, Theda Perdue, and Elizabeth Hayes Turner, 114–33 (Columbia: Univ. of Missouri Press, 1994); Lynne A. Rieff, "'Go

Ahead and Do All You Can': Southern Progressives and Alabama Home Demonstration Clubs, 1914–1940," in *Southern Women: Hidden Histories of Women in the New South*, ed. Virginia Bernhard, Betty Brandon, Elizabeth Fox-Genovese, Theda Perdue, and Elizabeth H. Turner, 134–49 (Columbia: Univ. of Missouri Press, 1994).

10. Moore, "Review of a Few Steps," 17; Almon J. Sims, *History of Extension Work*, 17, 31–32; "Report of the Division of Extension of the College of Agriculture of the Univ. of Tennessee for the Year Ending June 30, 1915," *ESART*, roll 1, p. 12; Virginia P. Moore, "Report of Canning Club Work in Tennessee for Year 1914," *ESART*, roll 1, p. 5. According to Clarence Beaman Smith and Meredith Chester Wilson, *Agricultural Extension System*, 35–36, female demonstration work advanced more rapidly in the South than in other regions before 1917.

11. James L. Sibley, "Homemakers' Clubs for Negro Girls," *Southern Workman* 44 (Feb. 1915): 81–86. The Smith-Lever Act did not mandate whether or how federal money should be divided between white and black land-grant colleges; provisions for black extension programs depended on the largess of individual states. Mabel Myers was one of the first graduates of the two-year teacher training course at Tennessee State A&I Normal School in 1914, according to Starlene Johnson Taylor, "The History of the Teacher Education Program at Tennessee State University" (Ed.D. diss., Tennessee State Univ., 1988), 43.

12. S. L. Smith to County Superintendents, 18 Feb. 1915, folder 1464, box 157; "Summary of Monthly Reports of Agents for Home Makers' Clubs for Negroes—Season 1915"; and "Report of Homemakers' Club Work of Tennessee, 1916," folder 1474, box 158, all in series 1, subseries 1, GEBA.

13. Virginia P. Moore, "Review of a Few Steps," 17; "Statement of S. L. Smith, State Rural School Supervisor for Tennessee, June 1915," folder 1468, box 158, series 1, subseries 1, GEBA; S. L. Smith, "Report of Some Special Work Among Rural Negro Schools in Tennessee, 1915–16," in *Biennial Report, SSPIT, for 1915–16*, 287 (quotations).

14. H[arcourt] A. and H. K. Bryson, *Rural Organization: Community, County, Division, State*, Division of Extension Publication No. 10 (Knoxville: Univ. of Tennessee College of Agriculture, Nov. 1915). Their proposals, and the place of the home in the community club, follow Thomas N. Carver, "The Organization of a Rural Community," *Yearbook of the U.S. Dept. of Agriculture, 1914* (Washington, D.C.: GPO, 1915), 135–37. On the central place of the home in rural life, see Leonarda Goss, "The Countryside—Its Home," in *Balancing Country Life*, by Young Men's Christian Association, 3–12 (New York: Association Press, 1917).

15. Moore, "Report of Canning Club Work in Tennessee for Year 1914," *ESART*, roll 1, p. 5; Louise G. Turner, *Home Work for Winter Months*

for *Canning Club Girls of Tennessee: Kitchen Rules, Setting the Table, Beverages,* Division of Extension Publication No. 2 (Knoxville: Univ. of Tennessee College of Agriculture, Nov. 1914); Louise G. Turner, *What to Do When Cleaning House,* Division of Extension Publication No. 5 (Knoxville: Univ. of Tennessee College of Agriculture, Feb. 1915).

16. Mary Geneva Conway to C. A. Keffer, 19 June 1916, *ESART,* roll 1. Club membership figures are summarized in Hoffschwelle, "Rebuilding the Rural Southern Community," tables 3, 4, and 7, pp. 498–99, 502.

17. Typical of rural East Tennessee, the vast majority of Hamilton's farm owners and tenants were white and, on average, farmed roughly equal holdings (75 acres). Tenancy increased slightly from 35 percent to 37 percent in the 1910s. Allred, Watkins, and Hatfield, *Tennessee: Economic and Social,* pt. 2, pp. 29, 53–54, 58, 82, 84; C. S. Johnson, *Statistical Atlas,* 212.

18. "Report of County Collaborator, Hamilton County," and "Report of Girls' Canning Clubs of Tennessee up to Dec. 19, 1912," both in *ESART,* roll 1; 1912 Hamilton County club report, folder 16, box 1, Moore Papers; photograph "After the Day's Work—Canning Party, Hamilton Co.," folder 17, box 4, Moore Papers; Knapp and Cresswell, "Effect of Home Demonstration Work," 256.

19. Knapp and Cresswell, "Effect of Home Demonstration Work," 256.

20. Elizabeth M. Lauderbach to O. B. Martin, 25 Mar. 1915; "Ten Leading Club Girls Graded According to Uniform Score Card" [1914–15]; "Two Leading Girls in Canning Club Work—Tennessee" [1915]; "Home Economics Work in Tennessee" [1915]; all in *ESART,* roll 1.

21. Knapp and Cresswell, "Effect of Home Demonstration Work," 257, 258.

22. Ibid., 256–57, 258.

23. Morgan and Bryson, *Rural Organization,* 6. On labor-saving household conveniences, see T[homas] F. Peck, "Farm Conveniences," *Tennessee Agriculture* 3 (1 Feb. 1914): 77–79; Carver, "Organization of a Rural Community," 133–35; Crow, *American Country Girl,* 126–34; Cromwell, *Agriculture and Life,* 283–86; Mary E. Cresswell, "The Home Demonstration Work," *Annals of the American Academy of Political and Social Sciences* 67 (Sept. 1916): 247–48.

24. Mrs. J. H. May, "Economy in the Home Life" in "Proceedings of the Middle Tennessee Home-Makers' Association," *Tennessee Agriculture* 3 (1 Nov. 1914): 464–67, 471; Mrs. Deaderick, "The Practical Equipment of Our Country Homes," *East Tennessee Farmers' Convention Program and Proceedings,* 1914 and 1915.

25. "Annual Report, Home Demonstration Work in Tennessee, Year Ending 1916," *ESART,* roll 1. For statistical information on home convenience, home management, and home furnishings projects, see Hoffschwelle, "Rebuilding the Rural Southern Community," tables 5–6 and 8–25, pp. 500–501, 503–18.

26. "Annual Report of the Division of Extension," 1918, *ESART,* roll 3, pp. 10, 341; Moore, "Review of a Few Steps," 22.

27. "Annual Report of the Division of Extension," 1917, *ESART,* roll 2, p. 7; "Report in Home Demonstration Work for Year Ending June 30, 1917," *ESART,* roll 2, pp. 1–2; "Report of Home Demonstration Work in Tennessee, 1917," *ESART,* roll 2, p. 7; "Annual Report of the Division of Extension," 1918, *ESART,* roll 3, p. 344; "Women Do Patriotic Work," *TAER* 2 (14 Sept. 1918): 1. Despite the war-related emphasis on foodstuffs, women's work received but passing mention in the Tennessee Dept. of Agriculture's *Biennial Reports* for 1917–18 and 1918–20. *Biennial Reports* for 1913–14 and 1915–16 also had reported on home extension topics and farm women's meetings, but after the war, these subjects disappeared, apart from a brief mention in the department's official report in 1923–24.

28. [S. L. Smith,] "Summarized Statement of Home Makers' Club Work for the Summer of 191[8] in the State of Tennessee," folder 1474, box 158, series 1, subseries 1, GEBA, 1–3.

29. "Work of Farm Women in War: Home Makers Now See the Dignity and Power in Their Great Labor," *Knoxville Sentinel,* 14 May 1918, and "How Farm Women in Our Section Are Responding to the Call of War Work," *Knoxville Sentinel,* 15 May 1918, newspaper clippings in *East Tennessee Farmers' Convention Program and Proceedings,* 1918.

30. "Annual Report of the Division of Extension," 1918, *ESART,* roll 3, p. 387.

31. Ibid., 390.

32. "Annual Report of the Division of Extension," 1918, *ESART,* roll 3, pp. 392–93; "Hits Keynote of Convention: President Shaw Urges Farmers to Organize," *Knoxville Journal and Tribune,* 15 May 1918, newspaper clipping in *East Tennessee Farmers' Convention Program and Proceedings,* 1918; "County Councils of Agriculture," *TAER* 3 (27 Sept., 11 and 25 Oct. 1919): 8; Thomas Freeman Dixon, *The County Council of Agriculture,* Division of Extension Publication No. 91 (Knoxville: Univ. of Tennessee College of Agriculture, Nov. 1920).

33. Wartime expansion of extension programs resulted in their increased acceptance in Iowa, according to Dorothy Schweider, *Seventy-Five Years of Service: Cooperative Extension in Iowa* (Ames: Iowa State Univ. Press, 1993), 34–36; Marilyn Holt, *Linoleum, Better Babies,* 73–76, argues that wartime agents and clubs persisted in the South; and Keith, *Country People in the New South,* 143–69, suggests that the war gave Tennessee Progressives temporary power and lasting organizational experience.

34. Dixon, *County Council,* 2, 4; Evans, *Recollections of Extension History,* 32–35; "Temporary State Farm Bureau Federation Formed," *TAER* 5 (Aug. 1921): 2; Burritt, *County Agent and Farm Bureau,* 228–29, 241–44; S. G. Abernathy, comp., *Brief History of Farm Bureau in Tennes-*

see, 1921–1949 [Columbia: Tennessee Farm Bureau Federation, 1949?], 9–14; "Narrative Report of Elizabeth M. Lauderbach, County Home Demonstration Agent, Hamilton County, Tennessee, 1923," *ESART,* roll 10, pp. 4–5, 17; "Narrative Report of Elizabeth M. Lauderbach, County Home Demonstration Agent, Hamilton County, Tennessee, 1924," *ESART,* roll 12, pp. 1–2. Of southern states, only the Tennessee and Alabama extension services encouraged farm bureau organization, according to Gladys Baker, *The County Agent* (Chicago: Univ. of Chicago Press, 1939), 20. Tennessee agents even organized themselves into the first state professional association for extension workers. See "They Have Their Feet Under the Council Table of the Division," *TAER* 3 (1 Apr. 1920): 9.

35. "Annual Report of the Division of Extension for the Fiscal Year Ending June 30, 1918," 344–45, 347–49, 414; "Annual Report for Girls' Club and Home Demonstration Work," Lewis County, 1918; both in *ESART,* roll 3.

36. Home economics classes had entered the Lewis High School curriculum in 1920, with no discernible impact on girls' or women's clubs. Boilerplate articles on progressive farming techniques and home improvements, as well as notices of state extension service initiatives, appeared regularly in the county newspaper. But without an active club network, Lewis offered no response to further state, regional, or national home improvement campaigns. Not until the county hired a male agricultural agent in 1929 would country girls have the opportunity to join a club. Allred, Watkins, and Hatfield, *Tennessee: Economic and Social,* pt. 2, p. 101; Tennessee Home Economics Association, *Home Economics Heritage,* 117; *Lewis County Herald,* 19 Aug. 1920, 11 Aug. 1921, 22 June 1922, 24 Aug. 1922, 21 May 1925, 14 Mar. 1928.

37. "Annual Report of the Division of Extension for the Fiscal Year Ending June 30, 1918," *ESART,* roll 3, pp. 344–45, 347–49, 414; "Annual Report for Girls' Club and Home Demonstration Work, Rutherford County, 1918," *ESART,* roll 3; Hattie Ross Neblett, "Annual Narrative Report," 1926, *ESART,* roll 17, p. 2.

38. Evans, *Recollections of Extension History,* 31–32; Almon J. Sims, *History of Extension Work,* 32–34; Burritt, *County Agent and Farm Bureau,* 168, 180. On the general postwar agricultural situation, see James H. Shideler, *Farm Crisis, 1919–1923* (Berkeley: Univ. of California Press, 1957).

39. Moore, "Review of a Few Steps," 23; Flora Melissa Byrd, "Annual Report of Home Demonstration Work for Women and Girls Calendar Year 1919," Bradley County, *ESART,* roll 3, p. 4; "Annual Report of the Director, Agricultural Extension Service," 1922, *ESART,* roll 7, p. 282.

40. "Home Demonstration Bears Fruit in the South," *Yearbook of the U.S.*

Dept. of Agriculture, 1920 (Washington, D.C.: GPO, 1921), 111–23 (quotation, 123).

41. Moore, "Review of a Few Steps," 22–23. Moore, whose health suffered from the effects of influenza, resigned in Aug. 1919 to care for her invalid mother and the family farm. She joined the Florida Extension Service as home improvement specialist after her mother's death in 1923. For agents' comments on home improvement work, see 1919 reports from Bradley, Greene, Hamilton, Johnson, Lake, Sevier, and Unicoi counties in *ESART,* roll 3; "With County Agents," *TAER* 2 (31 May 1919): 4, and 3 (12 July 1919): 2.

42. "More Home Conveniences," *TAER* 4 (Oct. 1920): 8.

43. Mary Geneva Conway, *Make the Farm Kitchen Convenient,* Division of Extension Publication No. 71 (Knoxville: Univ. of Tennessee College of Agriculture, Aug. 1918). For another discussion of farm kitchens, see Thomas E. French and Frederick W. Ives, *Agricultural Drawing and the Design of Farm Structures* (New York: McGraw-Hill, 1915), 82–84, 117.

44. "More Home Conveniences," 8. Even in the more affluent northern and western states, 61 percent of farm women had to carry their own water an average of 39 feet to the house; 96 percent did their own washing, and 57 percent possessed washing machines. See Florence E. Ward, "The Farm Woman's Problems," *Journal of Home Economics* 12 (Oct. 1920): 441, 443; Florence E. Ward, *The Farm Woman's Problems,* USDA Circular 148 (Washington, D.C.: GPO, Nov. 1920). Unfortunately, Ward did not survey southern farm households.

45. Maude Guthrie, *Home Economics Projects for Women's Home Demonstration Clubs in Tennessee,* Division of Extension Publication No. 89 (Knoxville: Univ. of Tennessee College of Agriculture, Sept. 1920), 2, 4. On power appliances, see also A. M. Daniels, "Electric Light and Power in the Farm Home," *Yearbook of the U.S. Dept. of Agriculture, 1919* (Washington, D.C.: GPO, 1920), 223–38.

46. "Annual Report of the Division of Extension," 1918, *ESART,* roll 3, p. 424; "Annual Report of Home Demonstration Work for Women and Girls, Calendar Year 1920" for Lake and McMinn counties, *ESART,* roll 4.

47. "Annual Report of Home Demonstration Agent, Weakley County," 1921, *ESART,* roll 6, reverse of p. 10. Weakley County's predominantly (94 percent) white farmers grew corn, hay, and cotton. They had prospered in the years 1910–19, when aggregate farm property value rose from $12 million to almost $29 million, only to fall back to $16 million by 1925; gross farm income fell by over $2 million between 1920 and 1925. Meanwhile, tenancy declined from 38 percent to 32 percent, then rose again to 38 percent. Allred, Watkins, and Hatfield, *Tennessee: Economic and Social,* pt. 2, pp. 29, 54, 82, 135, 137. This difficult decade and its place in the transformation of the farm woman into the farm

homemaker, as well as the disparity between the experiences of white and black club women, are also explored in Melissa Walker, "'A Smile on Her Face and a Song on Her Lips': Home Extension Work Among East Tennessee Farm Women During the Agricultural Depression of the 1920s," *Southern Historian* 15 (Spring 1994): 51–67.

48. S. L. Smith to Wallace Buttrick, 19 May 1918, folder 1464, box 157, series 1, subseries 1, GEBA; Mabel Myers, Stella Richards, and Lillian White, *Home-made Brooms, Rugs and Mattresses,* Division of Extension Publication No. 77 (Knoxville: Univ. of Tennessee College of Agriculture, May 1919); "Negro Work Firmly Established," *TAER* 3 (1 May 1920): 9; Melissa Walker, "Home Extension Work Among African Americans in East Tennessee, 1920–1939," *Agricultural History* 70 (Summer 1996): 487–502.

49. F. M. McRee, quoted in unidentified newspaper clipping, "Farmers in 47th Convention Report Alarmingly Bad Crop Conditions in This Section," in *East Tennessee Farmers' Convention Program and Proceedings,* 1920; Charles E. Gibbons, "Rural Life," in *Child Welfare in Tennessee: An Inquiry by the National Child Labor Committee for the Tennessee Child Welfare Commission* (Nashville: Tennessee Child Welfare Commission, [1920]), 360–61.

50. "Efficient Farm Homes," *TAER* 4 (June 1921): 8.

51. "Annual Report of the Director, Agricultural Extension Service," 1922, *ESART,* roll 7, pp. 5–7. The state extension division consistently favored white agricultural agents over white female and especially African American agents. Director Keffer justified the division's preference for placing male agents in new counties as a necessary first step that would increase farm income and so create demand for better farm homes and women agents. "Annual Report 1924," *ESART,* roll 11, pp. 7, 26, 90; "Annual Report of the Director of the Agricultural Extension Service," 1928, *ESART,* roll 21, p. 9; "County Agent Work," *ESART,* roll 21, p. 12.

52. "Home Demonstration Work," 1928, *ESART,* roll 21, p. 1. Two years' intensive lobbying by the American Home Economics Association and General Federal of Women's Clubs won a provision for the hiring of male and female agents "in fair and just proportions." Even so, Capper-Ketcham funds did not redress the numerical imbalance between the two groups. On the Capper-Ketcham Act, see Blauch, *Federal Cooperation in Agricultural Extension Work,* 136, and "Increases in Extension Work," *Southern Ruralist* 35 (15 Oct. 1928): 20. The *Southern Ruralist* called for equal salaries as well as equal numbers.

53. "Home Demonstration Work," 1929, *ESART,* roll 24, p. 2; M. Lloyd Downen, "An Overview," in *Proud Past, Promising Future: A Narrative History of the Tennessee Agricultural Extension Service, 1914–1989* ([Knoxville:] Tennessee Agricultural Extension Service, [1989]), 10.

54. "Annual Narrative Report," Marshall, Giles, Bedford, and Davidson counties, 1924, *ESART,* roll 13, p. 5.
55. "Annual Report," 1924, *ESART,* roll 11, p. 94. For examples of club plans including such work, see those accompanying the 1924 reports from Cheatham, Davidson, Franklin, Montgomery, and Shelby county white agents, and Hattie L. Ross's report for black women's clubs in Marshall, Giles, Bedford, and Davidson counties, *ESART,* rolls 12–13. Weakley County bucked the trend because farm families had foregone household expenditures in anticipation of a bad harvest. See ARCEW, 1924, Weakley County, *ESART,* roll 14, p. 23.
56. In their reports, agents catalogued the number of clubs and members enrolled in these projects, method demonstrations given by the agent herself, and "result demonstrations" or actual project work done by club members. Under home management, women and girls could elect to follow a systematized plan of housework, keep a budget, or improve laundry methods. Records of labor-saving devices added or kitchens planned and rearranged offered tangible measurements of home management improvements. Home furnishings records detailed the numbers of women and girls who improved the selection and arrangement of furnishings or repaired and renovated them, and who redid room surfaces, as well as the number of rooms receiving these improvements. Home agents, like their male counterparts, recorded assistance with home construction and remodeling under "Rural Engineering," although their form included only poultry houses in addition to work on dwellings. Nevertheless, their figures were not always reliable. Agents complained that club members neglected to submit reports; they themselves fudged numbers for the sake of appearances. On home management, see Florence E. Ward, "The Educational Needs of the American Farm Woman," in *Country Community Education: Proceedings of the Fifth National Country Life Conference* (New York: Association Press, 1922), 205–6. On the questionable accuracy of the ARCEW reporting system, see Baker, *County Agent,* 116–18.
57. "Annual Report of Home Demonstration Agent of Wilson County," 1921, *ESART,* roll 7, p. 6 of appended narrative.
58. "Annual Report," 1923, *ESART,* roll 9, p. 128; "Annual Narrative Report of [Negro] Extension Work" for Anderson, Blount, Greene, Hamblen, Jefferson, Knox, Loudon, Sullivan counties, 1924, *ESART,* roll 13, p. 7.
59. "Special Report of Work Done by Negro Home Demonstration Agent, Tennessee, 1921," filed by Mattie L. Barr Keith, Lillian White, Rebecca Davis, and Sallie Duvall, *ESART,* roll 5.
60. "Report of the Work of the County Agent, Calendar Year 1921," Montgomery and Robertson counties, *ESART,* roll 6; "Report of Work of the

County Agent," Montgomery and Robertson counties, 1922, *ESART,* roll 8; "Report of Work of the County Agent," Davidson, Sumner, and Williamson counties, 1922, *ESART,* roll 8, p. 8; "Report of the Work of the County Agent," Madison and Haywood counties, 1922, *ESART,* roll 8, p. 38. Their reports echo Thomas Monroe Campbell, *The Movable School Goes to the Negro Farmer* (Tuskegee Institute, Ala.: Tuskegee Institute Press, 1936; reprint, New York: Arno Press, 1969); Howard W. Odum, "Health and Housing," in *Cooperation in Southern Communities,* ed. T. J. Woofter, Jr., and Isaac Fisher (Atlanta, Ga.: Commission on Interracial Cooperation, [1922]), 41–44; E. H. Swinn, *Agricultural Instruction: A Means of Establishing Better Racial Relations in Southern Communities,* Extension Service Circular No. 68 (Washington, D.C.: U.S. Dept. of Agriculture, Feb. 1928); and Benjamin F. Hubert, "The Country Life Movement for Negroes," *Rural America* 7 (May 1929): 4.

61. "Annual Report 1922," *ESART,* roll 7, pp. 250–51, 261, 262, 286.

62. Untitled narrative preceding "Annual Report of Home Demonstration Work," Wilson County, 1922, *ESART,* roll 9, pp. 7–8; "Anderson County Home Demonstration Agent Annual Report," 1924, *ESART,* roll 11, p. 7.

63. Anderson County's farmers, almost all of whom were white, harvested corn and hay on farms of between 80 and 90 acres; tenancy had declined since 1910, but annual gross farm income also fell from $1.6 million to $1.4 million between 1920 and 1925; cash income per family in 1925 was $899, almost $50 less than the state average. Allred, Watkins, and Hatfield, *Tennessee: Economic and Social,* pt. 2, pp. 29, 37, 82, 135, 137, 140; C. S. Johnson, *Statistical Atlas,* 207.

64. See "Annual Report 1923," *ESART,* roll 9; 1923 narrative reports for Jefferson, Sullivan, and Van Buren counties, *ESART,* roll 11; 1924 narrative reports for Bedford, Madison, McMinn, Shelby, Sullivan, Sumner, and Wilson counties, *ESART,* rolls 12–14; 1923 narrative reports of black demonstration work for Madison, Fayette, Hardeman, and Haywood counties, *ESART,* roll 10; 1924 narrative reports for Roane, Rhea, and White counties (quotation) and Madison, Hardeman, and Fayette counties, *ESART,* roll 13; "Clothing and Household Management," 1924, *ESART,* roll 11. In 1927, District 2 agent Mary Geneva White reported that the budget project had failed but that club women had "over 100% success" in adding one convenience to each of their homes. "Agent, District 2," *ESART,* roll 19, p. 24.

65. Jean Gordon and Jan McArthur, "American Women and Domestic Consumption, 1800–1920: Four Interpretive Themes," in *Making the American Home: Middle-Class Women and Domestic Material Culture, 1840–1940,* ed. Marilyn Ferris Motz and Pat Browne, 27–47 (Bowling Green, Ohio: Bowling Green State Univ. Popular Press, 1988); Mary

Corbin Sies, "The Domestic Mission of the Privileged American Subur-
ban Homemaker, 1877–1917: A Reassessment," in Motz and Browne,
Making the American Home, 193–210; Spencer-Wood, "Diversity and
Nineteenth-Century Domestic Reform," 175–208. On women's roles in
redesigning rural homes in the nineteenth century, see Sally McMurry,
*Families and Farmhouses in Nineteenth-Century America: Vernacular
Design and Social Change* (New York: Oxford Univ. Press, 1988).

66. Narrative report for Marshall County, 1923, *ESART,* roll 10, p. 7.

67. "Annual Report 1923," *ESART,* roll 9, p. 151; see also 1923 narrative
reports for Wilson County and for black club work in Roane, Rhea, and
White counties, *ESART,* roll 11; ARCEW, 1924, Wilson County, *ESART,*
roll 14, p. 24; "Van Buren County 1926," *ESART,* roll 19, p. 3; "Many
Colored Homes Improved," *TAER* 10 (Sept. 1926): 3.

68. For useful summaries of design principles applied to rural homes, see
Helen Atwater, "Selection of Household Equipment," in *Yearbook of
Agriculture, 1914,* 339–62; Atkeson, *Woman on the Farm,* 47–57.

69. "Annual Report 1923," *ESART,* roll 9, p. 151; ARCEW, Negro work
in Anderson, Blount, Campbell, Hamblen, Jefferson, Knox, Loudon, and
Sullivan counties, 1925, *ESART,* roll 15, p. 24. See the 1923 narrative
reports for Jefferson and Van Buren counties, *ESART,* rolls 10–11; 1924
reports for Montgomery, Sullivan, Williamson, and Wilson counties,
ESART, rolls 13 and 14; ARCEW, 1924, Van Buren County, *ESART,* roll
14, p. 24; 1925 narrative reports from white agents for Dyer, Fayette,
Franklin, Knox, Lawrence, Sullivan, Sumner, and Van Buren counties
and ARCEW forms from Roane and Van Buren counties, all in *ESART,*
rolls 14–16; "Annual Report," Davidson County, 1929, *ESART,* roll 24,
p. 9. In 1927, club girl Lois Wallace refinished family pieces for her prize-
winning bedroom project; see "Annual Report of Home Demonstration
Work in Anderson County," *ESART,* roll 19, pp. 7–8 and photographs;
"Dressing Up Old Furniture," *Southern Ruralist* 36 (1 May 1929): 22;
Univ. of Tennessee, Knoxville, Agricultural Extension Service, Home
Demonstration Dept., *Improved Country Homes in Tennessee* (Nashville: Tennessee Dept. of Agriculture, 1928), 8.

70. "Annual Report of Home Demonstration Agent, Rhea County," 1921,
ESART, roll 6; "Home Demonstration Agent, District 4," 1922, *ESART,*
roll 7, p. 286; "Home Demonstration Agent Annual Report 1922,"
Sullivan County, *ESART,* roll 8. The 1919 program for girls' clubs included housework and home improvement. A revamped program in
1921 dropped these topics, although sewing projects included bedroom
sets. Agents elaborated these into projects in bedroom decoration. See
Virginia P. Moore, *Girls' Home Demonstration Clubs in Tennessee,*
Division of Extension Publication No. 76 (Knoxville: Univ. of Tennessee, College of Agriculture, Apr. 1919); Margaret A. Ambrose, comp.,

Four-Year Program of Work for Girls' Home Demonstration Clubs in Tennessee, Division of Extension Publication No. 94 (Knoxville: Univ. of Tennessee College of Agriculture, June 1921); and photograph entitled "Bedroom of Isabel Matthews, Madison County, Home Demonstration Club Girl," in *Improved Country Homes,* 29.

71. Ellen Latting, "My Home Demonstration Work," quoted in "Home Demonstration Work," 1928, *ESART,* roll 21, pp. 10–11.

72. "Clothing and Household Management," 1929, *ESART,* roll 24, p. 4; "Clothing and Household Management," in *Annual Report, 1930* (Knoxville: Univ. of Tennessee College of Agriculture, Division of Extension, 1930), 348.

73. "Home Demonstration" [Greene County], *TAER* 7 (Jan. 1924): 3; "Home Demonstration" [Marshall County], *TAER* 7 (May 1924): 1; "Make Baskets" [Knox County], *TAER* 8 (May 1925): 6; photograph of Knox County 4-H market, *TAER* 10 (Dec. 1926): 4; "Home Demonstration Notes" [McMinn County], *TAER* 11 (Sept. 1927): 4; "Baskets from Bulrushes" [White County], *TAER* 12 (July 1928): 2; "Annual Report," Lawrence County, 1925, *ESART,* roll 15, p. 8; 1925 narratives from Fayette and Sumner counties, *ESART,* rolls 15 and 16; *Four-Year Program of Work for Members of Girls' Home Demonstration Clubs,* 69–74; "Summary of Year's Work—1925," Franklin County, *ESART,* roll 15, p. 1; "Narrative of Home Demonstration Work," Hamilton County, 1925, ibid., 1. See also "Narrative Summary of Annual Report," Sullivan County, 1928, *ESART,* roll 24, p. 3; Lula Ledbetter Brigham, "An Old Handicraft Brought Up to Date," *Southern Ruralist* 35 (1 May 1928): 24; Ola Powell Malcolm, "Home Industries for Farm Women and Girls Numerous," in *Yearbook of the U.S. Dept. of Agriculture, 1926* (Washington, D.C.: GPO, 1927), 429–30; Ola Powell Malcolm, "Women Market 4-H Brand Products in Increasing Volume," in *Yearbook of the U.S. Dept. of Agriculture, 1928* (Washington, D.C.: GPO, 1929), 617.

74. Bradford and Cresswell, "Home Demonstration Work in the South," 260–61; "Home Demonstration Agent, District 3," 1922, p. 272; ARCEW, 1923, Hamilton County, *ESART,* roll 10.

75. "Narrative of Home Demonstration Work," 1925, Hamilton County, *ESART,* roll 15; Malcolm, "Home Industries," 428–29.

76. "Making Hooked Rugs," *TAER* 10 (Aug. 1926): 1; "Narrative Report of Claiborne—Union—Hancock Counties," 1929, *ESART,* roll 24, p. 9.

77. "Narrative Report of Elizabeth M. Lauderbach," 1927, *ESART,* roll 20, p. 4.

78. Babbitt, "Productive Farm Woman," 88–101; "Annual Report of Colored Home Demonstration Work in District 3," *ESART,* roll 22, p. 4.

79. 1929 ARCEW form and narrative report from Sumner County, *ESART*, roll 26; photograph of Mrs. J. E. Phillips, winner of Lincoln County clothing contest, surrounded by her handmade trays, baskets, and vases, *TAER* 11 (Dec. 1928): 3.

80. "Annual Narrative Report," Marshall County, 1927, *ESART*, roll 20, p. 7; "Narrative Report, Williamson County," 1927, *ESART*, roll 21, p. 16; 1928 narrative reports from Dyer, Lincoln, Sullivan, and Williamson counties, *ESART*, rolls 22–24; 1929 ARCEW forms and narrative reports from Sumner and Williamson counties, *ESART*, rolls 26 and 27; "Handicraft," *TAER* 14 (Aug. 1930): 2.

81. "Wide Interest in Home Improvement," *TAER* 9 (Mar. 1926): 1; "Supplementary Report for Shelby County," 1925, *ESART*, roll 16, p. 57; "Annual Narrative Report," 1926, Negro work in Giles, Bedford, Davidson, and Rutherford counties, *ESART*, roll 17, p. 3; "Annual Narrative Report," Montgomery County, 1927, *ESART*, roll 21, p. 27; "Narrative Annual Report," Dyer County, 1927, *ESART*, roll 20, p. 5; "Narrative Report," Negro work in Anderson, Blount, Campbell, Hamblen, Jefferson, Knox, Loudon, McMinn, and Sullivan counties, *ESART*, roll 20, p. 5; 1928 narrative reports from Dyer and Sullivan counties and for Negro work in Hamilton, Rhea, Roane, Warren, and White counties, *ESART*, rolls 22 and 24; 1929 narrative reports from Montgomery and Sumner counties, *ESART*, roll 26. See also Lois P. Dowdle, "Does a Picture Tell a Story to You?" *Southern Ruralist* 35 (15 Oct. 1928): 20. Grace E. Frysinger, "Needed Changes in Home Demonstration Work," *Rural America* 6 (Jan. 1928): 7, voiced the extension service's taste in art when she expressed the hope that discussions of color and line in clothing projects would lead to art study and thence to an appreciation of the similarities between rural America and landscapes by Millet and Corot. For a discussion of women's picture study across the nation, see Karen J. Blair, *The Torchbearers: Women and the Amateur Arts Associations in America, 1890–1930* (Bloomington: Indiana Univ. Press, 1994).

82. *Southern Ruralist* 35 (1 Apr. 1928): 31.

83. "Personal Mention," *TAER* 13 (Aug. 1929): 1; "Report of Home Demonstration Work in Decatur County," 1929, *ESART*, roll 24, p. 1.

6. Domestic Consumption and Competition

1. "With the County Agents" and "With the Departments of the Division," *TAER* 4 (Nov.–Dec. 1920): 4–5; "Home Improvement Day in Loudon County," *TAER* 5 (Aug. 1921): 2; "Annual Report 1921," *ESART*, roll 5, p. 281.

2. The 1926 events in Sumner and Dyer counties each claimed 500 women

in attendance. "Greene Co. 1924 Report," *ESART,* roll 12; "Annual Report 1924," *ESART,* roll 11, pp. 95, 255. On such events in other counties, see the 1924 narrative reports for McNairy, Roane, White, and Williamson counties, *ESART,* rolls 13–14; "What the Agents Say in Their Reports," *TAER* 7 (May 1924): 1, *TAER* 8 (July 1924): 3, and *TAER* 8 (Nov. 1924): 4; "Home Demonstration Items of Interest," *TAER* 8 (Mar. 1925): 5; "Home Improvement Day in Dyer," *TAER* 9 (May 1926): 3 and photos; "Home Improvement Day in Sumner," *TAER* 10 (Aug. 1926): 1.

3. "Annual Report of Home Demonstration Work for Women and Girls," 1919 and 1920, Greene County, *ESART,* roll 3.

4. "Division of Extension Annual Report, 1921," ESART, roll 5, p. 281; "Annual Report of Home Demonstration Agent," 1921, Greene County, ESART, roll 5; unidentified newspaper clipping, "Greene County Women's Day Was Great Success," in "Greene County, Home Demonstration Annual Report, 1923," ESART, roll 10.

5. "Greene Co. 1924 Report," *ESART,* roll 12. In 1925, Sumner County's Chamber of Commerce orchestrated a full page of advertisements in the local newspaper inviting women to Home Improvement Day. "Papers Boost Home Improvement Day," *TAER* 7 (June 1925): 9.

6. Unidentified newspaper clipping, "Home Improvement Day in County Great Success," in "Greene Co. 1924 Report," *ESART,* roll 12. Only some Greene County farm women had money to spend; although total farm property value dropped only slightly from 1920 to 1925, in the same years the county fell from second in the state for its gross farm income to twelfth, and tenancy increased from just over one-fourth to one-third of farm operators. Allred, Watkins, and Hatfield, *Tennessee: Economic and Social,* pt. 2, pp. 54, 82, 135, 137.

7. ARCEW, 1924, Greene County, *ESART,* roll 12.

8. Mary Neth, in *Preserving the Family Farm,* 187–213, calls this paradox "Making Do in a Consumer Culture"; see also Rieff, "Go Ahead and Do All You Can," 147, and Walker, "A Smile on Her Face," 57–66.

9. "Home Demonstration Work," in "Annual Report, 1924," *ESART,* roll 12, p. 95.

10. "Franklin County Home Demonstration Annual Report 1923," *ESART,* roll 10; "Home Convenience Day in Franklin Marked Success," *TAER* 7 (Oct. 1923): 2; "Annual Report 1923," *ESART,* roll 9, pp. 293–94, followed by unidentified clipping and photographs of model dining room and bedroom at the Anderson County Home Improvement Day.

11. Mary Neth, *Preserving the Family Farm,* 133–35, explains how, from its inception, the Country Life movement promoted commercial agricultural interests and how the USDA and Farm Bureau continuously reinforced urban, middle-class, pro-business attitudes among prosperous

farmers. Pete Daniel, *Breaking the Land: The Transformation of Cotton, Tobacco, and Rice Cultures since 1880* (Urbana: Univ. of Illinois Press, 1985): 16–18, chronicles USDA extension director Bradford Knapp's turmoil over an early corporate alliance, which set a precedent for agricultural agents' cooperation with commercial interests. Jean Gordon and Jan McArthur, "American Women and Domestic Consumption," 37–39, describes the trend toward rationalized domestic consumption that peaked in the 1920s.

12. Holt, *Linoleum, Better Babies,* 85–89; "Greene County Home Demonstration Annual Report 1923," *ESART,* roll 10.

13. "Kitchen Improvement," 1923, Greene County, *ESART,* roll 10. The Doty family had passed down their Greene County farm since 1783. They engaged in subsistence farming until William D. B. Doty added sheep and tobacco at the turn of the century. See Carroll Van West, *Tennessee Agriculture: A Century Farms Perspective* (Nashville: Tennessee Dept. of Agriculture, 1986), 43.

14. ARCEW and "Narrative Report Giles County 1924," *ESART,* roll 12, pp. 7–8; "Kitchen Contest," *TAER* 8 (Nov. 1924): 1; "Giles County Has First Kitchen Contest," *TAER* 8 (Jan. 1925): 3–4.

15. Ruth Van Deman, *The Well-Planned Kitchen,* USDA Circular 189 (Washington, D.C.: GPO, Sept. 1921; rev. Aug. 1923); Meredith Chester Wilson, *Kitchen Arrangement and Equipment,* USDA Extension Service Circular 30 ([Washington, D.C.: United States Dept. of Agriculture,] Dec. 1926). For other references to kitchen contests, see Mrs. John H. Dyer, "The Farm Woman's Viewpoint," in *The Rural Home: Proceedings of the 6th National Country Life Conference* (Chicago: Univ. of Chicago Press, 1924), 164; Atkeson, *Woman on the Farm,* 42–46; "Home Improvement Work," *Journal of Rural Education* 4 (Feb.–Mar. 1925): 318–19. For some general prescriptions for rural kitchens, see Crow, *American Country Girl,* 126–34; Jane S. McKimmon, "Woman's Part in Rural Development," in *East Tennessee Farmers' Convention Program and Proceedings,* 1923, [2]; Lois P. Dowdle, "How to Break Your Back" and "Necessary Equipment for the Kitchen," *Southern Ruralist* 36 (1 Aug. 1929): 15, 16; Leonore Dunnigan, "Kitchens in Color: The Housewife's Modern Workshop Combines Beauty and Utility," *Farmer's Wife* 32 (June 1929): 10, 28; Bess M. Rowe, "Your Kitchen and You," *Farmer's Wife* 32 (Dec. 1929): 11, 33.

16. "Giles County Has First Kitchen Contest," *TAER* 8 (Jan. 1925): 4; "Annual Report 1925," *ESART,* roll 14, p. 4; "Home Demonstration Work, District 3," *ESART,* roll 14, p. 8.

17. See 1925 narrative reports from Anderson, Bradley, Cheatham, Franklin, Knox, Lawrence, Madison, Roane, and Van Buren counties, *ESART,* rolls 14–16.

18. 1925 narrative reports for Bradley, Cheatham, and Montgomery counties, *ESART,* rolls 14–15; "Model Kitchen Shown at Jackson Fair," *TAER* 9 (Oct. 1925): 2. District 3 agent Lizzie Reagan and Mrs. C. O. Browder portrayed campaign participants in a skit performed at several meetings and fairs, including the East Tennessee Farmers' Convention, according to an unidentified clipping, "Convention Dialogue Portrays Big Task Facing Farm Women," in *East Tennessee Farmers' Convention Program and Proceedings,* 1925.

19. For agents' remarks, see 1925 narrative reports of white agents from Anderson, Bradley, Cheatham, Davidson, Montgomery, Roane, and Van Buren counties, and reports of black agents for Fayette, Hardeman, Madison, Rhea, Roane, and White counties; for remarks of participating demonstrators, see the 1925 narrative reports by white agents from Anderson, Gibson, Greene, Maury, and McMinn counties, as well as Lillian Keller's report, all in *ESART,* rolls 14–16.

20. See 1925 narrative reports of white club work in Davidson, Franklin, Greene, Madison, McMinn, Montgomery, Van Buren, and Weakley counties, and black club work in Rhea, Roane, and White counties, in *ESART,* rolls 14–16.

21. Completed questionnaires are included with 1925 reports from Bradley, Cheatham, Montgomery, and Shelby counties, *ESART,* rolls 14–16.

22. "Annual Report, Home Demonstration Agent Davidson County Tennessee, 1925," 20; ARCEW, 1925, McMinn County, 23; "Narrative of Home Demonstration Work," Hamilton County, 5, 7, 9; all in *ESART,* rolls 14 and 15.

23. "A Model Kitchen," *TAER* 8 (May 1925): 6; untitled photograph and caption, *TAER* 9 (Dec. 1925): 3.

24. Letter from "An Enthusiastic Contestant," McMinn County, in Lillian L. Keller, "Annual Report," 1925, *ESART,* roll 14, p. 4; "Narrative Summary of Annual Report," Sullivan County, 1925, *ESART,* roll 16, p. 10.

25. "What the Kitchen Campaign Has Meant to Me," in "Clothing and Household Management," 1925, *ESART,* roll 15, pp. 6 and 7.

26. Ibid. African American women displayed the house dresses they made as part of their kitchen improvement projects in a fashion parade at the 1927 West Tennessee Farmer's Institute. "Colored Work," *TAER* 11 (Sept. 1927): 4.

27. On 1920s urban housewives and their roles in the culture of consumption and the family's emotional adjustment, see Matthews, *Just a Housewife,* 177–83, 187–92; Cowan, "Two Washes in the Morning," 178–82, 186–91.

28. "What the Kitchen Campaign Has Meant to Me," 6; clipping, "Tennessee Farm Women Have Much Better Kitchens"; "What I Have Done to

Improve My Kitchen"; narrative report and photographs of farm kitchens in "Greene Home Demonstration Agent Annual Report, 1925"; all
in *ESART,* roll 15, pp. 3, 6–9.

29. Lillian L. Keller, *The Living Room That Is Livable,* Division of Exten-
sion Publication No. 134 (Knoxville: Univ. of Tennessee College of Ag-
riculture, Dec. 1925); "Clothing and Household Management," 1926,
ESART, roll 16, pp. 2 and 3; "Better Living in the Farm Home Aim of
Agents," *TAER* 9 (Jan. 1926): 2; "Wide Interest in Home Improvement,"
TAER 9 (Mar. 1926): 1, 4, and *TAER* 9 (May 1926): 1.

30. Keller, *Living Room,* 3 and 4.

31. Ibid., 4–11, quotation on 8.

32. "Home Improved," *TAER* 9 (May 1926): 3. For white agents' accounts
of the campaign, see esp. 1926 narrative reports and ARCEW forms for
Davidson, Dyer, Franklin, Greene, Hamilton, Lawrence, Knox, McMinn,
Maury, Montgomery, Roane, Shelby, Sumner, and Williamson counties;
for black agents' work, see 1926 reports of Hattie Ross Neblett, Kate
B. Gresham, and Rebecca Davis; all in *ESART,* rolls 17–19.

33. "Home Demonstration Agent," Greene County, 1926, *ESART,* roll 17,
p. 3; "Narrative Annual Report," Dyer County, 1926, *ESART,* roll 17,
p. 7; "Annual Report of Knox County Home Dem Agt 1926," *ESART,*
roll 17, p. 4; "Annual Narrative Report," Negro work in Giles, Bedford,
Davidson, and Rutherford counties, 1926, *ESART,* roll 17, p. 5.

34. 1926 narrative reports and ARCEW forms for Anderson, Bradley,
Hardeman, Lincoln, Sullivan, and Van Buren counties, all in *ESART,* roll
17.

35. "Annual Narrative Report," Giles County, 1926, and "Narrative Annual Report," Dyer County, 1925 (quotation on p. 7), both in *ESART,*
roll 17; 1928 narrative reports, Hamblen and Hamilton counties,
ESART, roll 22; "Club Improving Kitchens," *TAER* 13 (Sept. 1929): 4.

36. Annual narrative reports, 1926, from Knox, McMinn, and Shelby counties, and for Negro work in Bedford, Davidson, Giles, and Rutherford
counties, *ESART,* rolls 17–19; annual narrative reports, 1927, from
Fayette, Greene, Knox, Lawrence, and Madison counties, *ESART,* rolls
19–20; annual narrative reports, 1928, for Cocke, Lawrence, Montgomery, Sullivan, and White counties, *ESART,* rolls 22–24; annual narrative
reports, 1929, from Maury, Sullivan, and Williamson counties, *ESART,*
rolls 26–27; "With the Colored Agents," *TAER* 9 (Mar. 1926): 4; "Improve Kitchens at Small Cost," *TAER* 11 (May 1928): 4; "To Improve
Homes," *TAER* 12 (Mar. 1929): 3; "Kitchen Improved," *TAER* 13 (Sept.
1929): 1; "Club Improving Kitchens," *TAER* 13 (Sept. 1929): 4; Oma
Worley, "Better Kitchens Now," *Southern Ruralist* 35 (1 Jan. 1929): 22.
For USDA commentaries, see George M. Warren, "Plumbing on Farms
Inadequate," in *Yearbook of Agriculture, 1926,* 584–87; Hildegarde

Kneeland, "Abolishing the Domestic Lockstep—The Scientific Kitchen," in *Housing Problems in America: Proceedings of the 10th National Conference on Housing* (New York: National Housing Association, 1929), 19–24.

37. District 1 agent narrative, 1927, and narrative reports, 1927, for Davidson, Dyer, Fayette, Franklin, Lawrence, Marshall, Montgomery, Rhea, Shelby, Weakley, and Williamson counties, and for Negro work in Madison, Hardeman, Haywood, and Fayette counties, all in *ESART,* rolls 19–21. District 1 agent narrative, 1928, and narrative reports, 1928, for Dyer, Hamblen, Hamilton, Knox, Lincoln, Marshall, and Warren counties, and for Negro work in Hamilton, Rhea, Roane, Warren, and White counties, all in *ESART,* rolls 22–24. "Clothing and Household Management," 1928, *ESART,* roll 24, p. 3; "Home Demonstration Work," 1929, *ESART,* roll 24, p. 17. Annual narrative reports, 1929, from Marshall, Montgomery, Sullivan, Sumner, and White counties, *ESART,* rolls 26–27; "Inter-State Has Splendid H.D. Exhibition" and "Club Girl Has Prize Bed Room Exhibit," *TAER* 11 (Nov. 1927): 3; "Club Makes Excellent Home Improvement Record," *TAER* 12 (Sept. 1928): 4; Lucille Blanche Lee, "The Work of the Home Demonstration Agent in Tennessee" (M.S. thesis, Univ. of Tennessee, 1930), 70–72. See also Grace E. Frysinger, "Home Life on the Farm," in *Yearbook of Agriculture, 1926,* 431–32.

38. Janet Ann Hutchison, "American Housing, Gender, and the Better Homes Movement, 1922–1935" (Ph.D. diss., Univ. of Delaware, 1989), chs. 1 and 7; Jellison, *Entitled to Power,* 38–39. For contemporary discussions of better farm homes, see reports from the National Farm Homes Conference in *Agricultural Engineering* 7 (Apr. 1926); "The Farm Home" and "The Rural Home," in *A Decade of Rural Progress: Proceedings of the 10th and 11th National Country Life Conferences* (Chicago: Univ. of Chicago Press, 1928), 36–42; John M. Gries and James Ford, eds., *Farm and Village Housing* (Washington, D.C.: President's Conference on Home Building and Home Ownership, 1932) [conference held in 1928].

39. "Madison County Home Demonstration Report, 1923," *ESART,* roll 10, p. 4; "Madison County 1924 Narrative Report of Home Demonstration Work," *ESART,* roll 13, p. 11; "What the Agents Say in Their Reports," *TAER* 7 (July 1923): 3.

40. Annual narrative reports, 1925, from Bradley, Cheatham, Dyer, Shelby, White, and Williamson counties, *ESART,* rolls 14–16. Agents also combined county Home Improvement Days with Better Homes observances.

41. "Wide Interest in Home Improvement," *TAER* 9 (Mar. 1926): 1, and *TAER* 11 [9] (May 1926): 1; "Montgomery County Better Homes Campaign Summarized," *TAER* 9 (June 1926): 3; untitled photographs and

caption describing Williamson demonstration house, *TAER* 10 (Jan. 1927): 3; "Tennessee Home Wins Prize," *TAER* 11 (Sept. 1927): 1; annual narrative reports, 1926, from Montgomery and Williamson counties, *ESART,* rolls 18–19; "Home Demonstration Work, District 4," 1927, *ESART,* roll 19, p. 50; "Clothing and Household Management," 1928, *ESART,* roll 21; "Clothing and Household Management," 1929, *ESART,* roll 24; Mrs. P. W. Walters, "The House, Its Settings and Furnishings," in *East Tennessee Farmers' Convention Program and Proceedings,* 1928, pp. 1–2.

42. "Narrative of Hamblen County Home Demonstration Agent's Annual Report, 1928," *ESART,* roll 22, p. 8. See also Lawrence County ARCEW, 1928, *ESART,* roll 23, p. 24.

43. See, e.g., the Delphi's and Finley community club plans for 1925, attached to narrative report for Dyer County, *ESART,* roll 15; annual narrative report, 1927, Knox County, *ESART,* roll 20; annual narrative report, 1929, Sullivan County, *ESART,* roll 26.

44. "Supplementary Report for Shelby County," 1925, *ESART,* roll 16, pp. 55–57, 124–26; "Clothing and Household Management" and annual narrative reports, 1926, from Hamilton, Madison, Montgomery, and Williamson counties and on Negro work in Madison County, *ESART,* rolls 16–19; annual narrative reports, 1927, for Knox, Shelby, and Sullivan counties, *ESART,* rolls 20–21; "Clothing and Household Management," "Home Demonstration Work, District 4," and annual narrative reports, 1928, for Greene, Hamblen, Hamilton, Knox, Lawrence, Robertson, and Shelby counties, and on Negro work in Blount County, *ESART,* rolls 21–23; "Clothing and Household Management," 1929, *ESART,* roll 24.

45. Bungalows served as demonstration houses in 1925 in Dyersburg, Dyer County, and Raleigh and Millington, Shelby County; and in 1927 in Sullivan County. Montgomery County won second prize in 1926 with an English and a colonial cottage; the 1927 fourth prize winner in Fountain City, Knox County, was an unadorned colonial cottage. Knox County Better Homes workers turned a wing-and-gable cottage into a colonial one in 1929.

46. Annual narrative reports from Maury County: 1927, *ESART,* roll 20; 1928, *ESART,* roll 23; and 1929, *ESART,* roll 26; "Narrative Report of Home Demonstration Work in Robertson County," 1928, *ESART,* roll 23.

47. Annual narrative reports, 1927, from Shelby and Williamson counties, *ESART,* roll 21; "Better Homes Tour in Williamson," *TAER* 10 (June 1927): 2.

48. Annual narrative report, 1926, for Negro work in Madison County, *ESART,* roll 17, p. 2; "Williamson County Narrative Report," 1926,

ESART, roll 19, pp. 10–11; "Home Demonstration Work, District 4," 1928, *ESART,* roll 21, p. 62 (quotation); "Report of Home Demonstration Work in Shelby County," 1928, *ESART,* roll 23, pp. 3–4. Hutchison, "American Housing," 220–27, and Hutchison, "Better Homes and Gullah," *Agricultural History* 67 (Spring 1993): 102–18, discuss African American Better Homes projects on St. Helena Island, S.C.

49. Mrs. Robert Burt, "The Better Homes Movement in Clarksville," reprint of address delivered at Tennessee A&I College, 29 June 1930, in folder 3, box 383, TCE.

50. *Southern Ruralist's Home Improvement Project* (Atlanta, Ga.: Southern Ruralist, 1929), 4; [Lois P. Dowdle], "Is Your Home One To Be Proud Of?" *Southern Ruralist* 34 (1 Feb. 1928): 26; [Lois P. Dowdle], "Is Your Name Written There?" *Southern Ruralist* 35 (1 Apr. 1928): 26; [Lois P. Dowdle], "A Second Home Improvement Contest," *Southern Ruralist* 35 (1 Oct. 1928): 20; [Lois P. Dowdle], "Home Improvement Results," *Southern Ruralist* 35 (15 Jan. 1929): 24; [Lois P. Dowdle], "As Is the Home, So Is the Child," *Southern Ruralist* 36 (1 Aug. 1929): 14. The journal's annual home improvement issue featured USDA photographs of model projects. See "Your Home Can Be Modern, Too," and "Beauty and Comfort for Farm Home," *Southern Ruralist* 35 (1 Aug. 1928): 2, 23; "Better Equipment, Brighter Homes," *Southern Ruralist* 36 (1 Aug. 1929): 2.

51. Lois P. Dowdle, "All About Home Improvement Score Card," *Southern Ruralist* 35 (15 Feb. 1929): 35; Lois P. Dowdle, "Home Improvement Contest Winners," *Southern Ruralist* 36 (15 May 1929): 21; Mabel Worley, "The Joy of Winning," *Southern Ruralist* (1 July 1929): 17; *Southern Ruralist's Home Improvement Project,* 5, 8, 12; "Hamilton Home Wins First Prize in Southern Contest," *TAER* 12 (May 1929): 1; Walker, "Home Extension Work," 60. On Tennessee contestants, see "Clothing and Household Management," 1928, and annual narrative reports, 1928, from Knox, Madison, and Shelby counties, *ESART,* rolls 21–23; "Clothing and Household Management," 1929, and annual narrative report, 1929, Warren County, *ESART,* roll 27; "To Improve Homes," *TAER* 12 (Mar. 1929): 3.

52. [Lois P. Dowdle], "Southern Home and Our Pledge," *Southern Ruralist* 34 (15 Jan. 1928): 22; Lois P. Dowdle, "Home Improvement Contest Winners," 21.

53. *Southern Ruralist's Home Improvement Project,* 3. Editors lured advertisers with $86,000 of documented expenditures by contestants and unrecorded thousands of dollars spent by others who did not submit final reports.

54. "A Key to the Door of Recognition," and Bess M. Rowe, "Master Farm Homemakers," *Farmer's Wife* 31 (Apr. 1928): 1, 7; Bess M. Rowe, "Ever

Widening: Master Farm Homemaker Movement Reaches Far in Its In-fluence," *Farmer's Wife* 32 (June 1929): 13, 22, 27; "Clothing and Household Management," "Home Demonstration Work, District 4," and "Annual Report of Knox County Home Dem. Agent," 1928, all in *ESART*, rolls 21–22; "Farm Women Spend Week at UT," *TAER* 11 (Feb. 1928): 1. See also Holt, *Linoleum, Better Babies*, 89–90; Neth, *Preserving the Family Farm*, 228–36. On Master Farmers, who earned 150 of 1,000 points for home life, see Clifford B. Gregory, "The Master Farmer Movement," *Rural America* 5 (Oct. 1927): 15–16.

55. "Clothing and Household Management," 1928, *ESART*, roll 21, p. 4; Rowe, "Master Farm Homemakers," 7–8; "Who Are the Master Home-makers?" *Farmer's Wife* 31 (Apr. 1928): 59 (quotation); "Time Savers in the Homes of Master Homemakers," *Farmer's Wife* 32 (Mar. 1929): 43.

56. Rowe, "Master Farm Homemakers," 7–8; "Who Are the Master Home-makers?" 59; Rowe, "Ever Widening," 27; Rowe, "Two Years: They Make the Master Farm Homemaker Movement Truly National," *Farmer's Wife* 32 (Nov. 1929): 12.

57. *Improved Country Homes*; "'Better Homes on Better Farms' Slogan Adopted by Tennessee Agricultural Extension Workers," *TAER* 11 (Dec. 1927–Jan. 1928): 1; Margaret A. Ambrose, "'Name the Farm Home' Slogan," *Southern Ruralist* 35 (1 Jan. 1929): 21.

58. *Improved County Homes*, 5; "Clothing and Household Management," *ESART*, roll 24, p. 2.

Selected Bibliography

Archives and Manuscript Sources

Claxton, Philander P. Papers. MS-278. Univ. of Tennessee Archives. Hoskins Library, Knoxville.

Commonwealth Fund Archives. Rockefeller Archive Center, Sleepy Hollow, New York.

Dresslar, Fletcher B. Papers. Vanderbilt Univ. Special Collections and Archives. Jean and Alexander Heard Library, Nashville, Tennessee.

General Education Board. Rockefeller Foundation Archives. Rockefeller Archive Center, Sleepy Hollow, New York.

Julius Rosenwald Fund Archives. Fisk Univ. Special Collections. Fisk Univ. Library, Nashville, Tennessee.

Moore, Virginia P. Papers. MS-1546. Univ. of Tennessee Special Collections. Hoskins Library, Knoxville.

Mustard, Harry S. Photographic Album, 1925–30. Tennessee Historical Society Collection. Tennessee State Library and Archives, Nashville.

Payne, Bruce R. Papers. Vanderbilt Univ. Special Collections and Archives. Jean and Alexander Heard Library, Nashville, Tennessee.

Peabody Archives. Vanderbilt Univ. Special Collections. Jean and Alexander Heard Library, Nashville, Tennessee.

Rockefeller Sanitary Commission. Rockefeller Foundation Archives. Rockefeller Archive Center, Sleepy Hollow, New York.

Tennessee Board of Education. Records. Record Group 91. Tennessee State Library and Archives, Nashville.

Tennessee Commissioner of Education. Records. Record Group 92. Tennessee State Library and Archives, Nashville.

U.S. Federal Extension Service. Records. *Extension Service Annual Reports: Tennessee,* 1910–29. Record Group 33, Microfilm T-889, Rolls 1–27. National Archives.

University of Tennessee. Summer School of the South. Records. AR-249.
    Univ. of Tennessee Archives. Hoskins Library, Knoxville.

Newspapers, Periodicals, Annual Reports

American Country Life Association. *Proceedings of the National Country
    Life Conference.* 1918–28.
East Tennessee Farmers' Convention Program and Proceedings. 1912, 1914–
    29.
Farmer's Wife. Volumes 31–32 (1928–30).
George Peabody College for Teachers. *Bulletin.* Volumes 1–17 (1912–29).
Lewis County (Tenn.) Herald. 1914–30.
Southern Ruralist. Volumes 34–36 (1928–30).
Tennessee Agricultural Extension Review. Volumes 1–4 (1918–21).
Tennessee Agriculture. Volumes 2–3 (1913–14).
Tennessee Dept. of Education. *Annual Report of the Department of Educa-
    tion for the Scholastic Year Ending June 30.* 1923–30.
Tennessee Dept. of Public Instruction. *Biennial Report of the State Superin-
    tendent of Public Instruction of Tennessee for the Scholastic Years
    Ending June 30.* 1911–12 through 1921–22.
Tennessee Educational Bulletin. Volumes 1–7 (1922–28).
Tennessee Extension Review. Volumes 5–13 (1921–29).
United States Dept. of Agriculture. *Yearbook of the United States Depart-
    ment of Agriculture.* Washington, D.C.: Government Printing
    Office, 1914–30.
University of Tennessee Record. Knoxville, Tennessee. Volumes 6–33 (1903–
    30).

Published Primary Sources: Books, Articles, Reports

Adams and Alsup. *Plans and Specifications for Public School Buildings.*
    Nashville: Tennessee Dept. of Public Instruction, 1907.
Ambrose, Margaret A., comp. *Four-Year Program of Work for Girls' Home
    Demonstration Clubs in Tennessee.* Division of Extension Pub-
    lication No. 94. Knoxville: Univ. of Tennessee, College of Agri-
    culture, June 1921; 2d ed., Nov. 1924.
Atkeson, Mary Meek. *The Woman on the Farm.* New York: Century, 1924.
Ayres, May; Jesse F. Williams; and Thomas D. Wood. *Healthful Schools: How
    to Build, Equip, and Maintain Them.* Boston: Houghton Mifflin,
    1918.
Building Plans for Rural School Houses: State of Tennessee. Nashville: State
    Dept. of Education, 1928.

Burritt, M[aurice] C. *The County Agent and the Farm Bureau.* New York: Harcourt, Brace and Co., 1922.

Caldwell, Otis W. "Home Economics and Rural Extension." *Journal of Home Economics* 6 (Apr. 1914): 99–109.

Child Welfare in Tennessee: An Inquiry by the National Child Labor Committee for the Tennessee Child Welfare Commission. Nashville: Child Welfare Commission, [1920].

Community School Plans. Nashville, Tenn.: Julius Rosenwald Fund, 1921; revised editions, 1924, 1927, 1931.

Conway, Mary Geneva. *Make the Farm Kitchen Convenient.* Division of Extension Publication No. 71. Knoxville: Univ. of Tennessee, College of Agriculture, Aug. 1918.

Cresswell, Mary E. "The Home Demonstration Work." *Annals of the American Academy of Political and Social Sciences* 67 (Sept. 1916): 247–48.

Cromwell, Arthur D. *Agriculture and Life: A Text-book for Normal Schools and Teachers' Reading Circles.* Philadelphia: J. B. Lippincott, 1915.

Crow, Martha Foote. *The American Country Girl.* New York: Frederick A. Stokes Company, 1915.

Cubberly, Ellwood P. *Rural Life and Education: A Study of the Rural-School Problem as a Phase of the Rural-Life Problem.* Boston: Houghton Mifflin Company, 1914.

Dixon, Thomas Freeman. *The County Council of Agriculture.* Division of Extension Publication No. 91. Knoxville: Univ. of Tennessee, College of Agriculture, Nov. 1920.

Dresslar, Fletcher B. *American Schoolhouses.* U.S. Bureau of Education Bulletin No. 5, 1910. Washington, D.C.: Government Printing Office, 1911.

———. "The Hygiene of Rural Schools." In *Journal of Proceedings of the 50th Annual Meeting of the National Education Association,* 1103–11. Chicago: Univ. of Chicago Press, 1912.

———. *Report on the Rosenwald School Buildings.* Bulletin No. 1. Nashville, Tenn.: Julius Rosenwald Fund, [1920].

———. *Rural Schoolhouses and Grounds.* U.S. Bureau of Education Bulletin No. 12. Washington, D.C.: Government Printing Office, 1914.

———. *School Hygiene.* New York: Macmillan, 1925.

Dresslar, Fletcher B., and Haskell Pruett. *Rural School-houses, School Grounds, and Their Equipment.* U.S. Office of Education Bulletin No. 21. Washington, D.C.: Government Printing Office, 1930.

Embree, Edwin R. "How Negro Schools Have Advanced Under the Rosenwald Fund." *Nation's Schools* 1 (May 1928): 41.

Farm Housing in Tennessee, with Regional Comparisons. Rural Research Series Monograph 26. Knoxville: Univ. of Tennessee, Agricultural Economics Dept., [1930s].

Favrot, Leo M. *A Study of County Training Schools for Negroes in the South.* John F. Slater Fund Occasional Papers No. 23. Charlottesville, Va.: [John F. Slater Fund], 1923.

Ferrell, J[ohn] A. *The Rural School and Hookworm Disease.* U.S. Bureau of Education Bulletin No. 20. Washington, D.C.: Government Printing Office, 1914.

Field, Ada M. "Home Economics Building at George Peabody College for Teachers." *Journal of Home Economics* 7 (Oct. 1915): 418–20.

French, Mrs. L[izzie] Crozier. *Home-Making Efficiency.* Nashville, Tenn., 1912.

Frysinger, Grace E. "Needed Changes in Home Demonstration Work." *Rural America* 6 (Jan. 1928): 7.

Furbringer, M. H. *Domestic Architecture.* Memphis, Tenn.: W. C. Jones, M. H. Furbringer, 1916.

The General Education Board: An Account of Its Activities, 1902–1914. New York: General Education Board, 1915.

Gillette, John M. "Conditions and Needs of Country Life." *Annals of the American Academy of Political and Social Science* 40 (Mar. 1912): 7.

Guthrie, Maude. *Home Economics Projects for Women's Home Demonstration Clubs in Tennessee.* Division of Extension Publication No. 89. Knoxville: Univ. of Tennessee, College of Agriculture, Sept. 1920.

Handbook of Murfreesboro and Rutherford County, Tennessee. Murfreesboro: Mutual Realty and Loan Co., [1924].

Harris, Cara L. "Organization of Homemaking Courses in Country High Schools and Rural Elementary Schools." *Journal of Home Economics* 15 (Mar. 1923): 118–19.

———. "Teaching Foods in Rural Schools." *Journal of Home Economics* 13 (Sept. 1921): 426.

Hubert, Benjamin F. "The Country Life Movement for Negroes." *Rural America* 7 (May 1929): 4.

Interstate School Building Service. *For Better Schoolhouses.* Nashville, Tenn.: Interstate School Building Service, 1929.

———. *Proceedings and Approved Suggestions of the Second Conference of the Interstate School Building Service.* Nashville, Tenn.: George Peabody College, 1931.

Johnson, D. B. "The Conference on Education of Women in the Country." In *Education in the South,* 40–43. U.S. Bureau of Education

Bulletin No. 30. Washington, D.C.: Government Printing Office, 1913.

Keller, Lillian L. *The Living Room That Is Livable*. Division of Extension Publication No. 134. Knoxville: Univ. of Tennessee, College of Agriculture, Dec. 1925.

"The Knapp School of Country Life—Its Aim." *Peabody Summer School News* 1 (12 July 1916): 1, 3.

McKeever, William A. *Farm Boys and Girls*. New York: Macmillan, 1913.

Moore, Virginia P. *Girls' Home Demonstration Clubs in Tennessee*. Division of Extension Publication No. 76. Knoxville: Univ. of Tennessee, College of Agriculture, Apr. 1919.

———, comp. "Canning Club Work in Tennessee." *Tennessee Tomato Club Bulletin* 1 (1913): 9–10.

Morgan, H[arcourt] A., and H. K. Bryson. *Rural Organization: Community, County, Division, State*. Division of Extension Publication No. 10. Knoxville: Univ. of Tennessee, College of Agriculture, Nov. 1915.

Mulligan, Catharine A. *A Brief Course in Domestic Science for State Institutes of Tennessee*. Nashville: Superintendent of Public Instruction, 1913.

Mustard, Harry S. *Cross-Sections of Rural Health Progress*. New York: Commonwealth Fund, 1930.

Myers, Mabel; Stella Richards; and Lillian White. *Home-made Brooms, Rugs and Mattresses*. Division of Extension Publication No. 77. Knoxville: Univ. of Tennessee, College of Agriculture, May 1919.

Odum, Howard W. "Health and Housing." In *Cooperation in Southern Communities*, edited by T. J. Woofter, Jr., and Isaac Fisher, 41–44. Atlanta, Ga.: Commission on Inter-racial Cooperation, [1922].

Outline of Organization and Plan of Operation of Agriculture and Home Economics Demonstration and Teaching on the Farms and in the County High Schools of Tennessee. Division of Extension Publication No. 1. Knoxville: Univ. of Tennessee, College of Agriculture, July 1914.

Outline on Rural School Supervision. Bulletin No. 1. Nashville: State Dept. of Public Instruction, 1916.

Perkins, Dwight H. "The Relation of Schoolhouse Architecture to the Social Center Movement." In *Journal of Proceedings of the 50th Annual Meeting of the National Education Association*, 234–39. Chicago: Univ. of Chicago Press, 1912.

Pruett, Haskell. *Rural School Buildings*. [Oklahoma City]: Oklahoma Dept. of Public Instruction, 1928.

Quick, Herbert. "The Social Center and the Rural Community." In *Journal of Proceedings and Addresses of the 50th Annual Meeting of the National Education Association,* 436–49. Chicago: Univ. of Chicago Press, 1912.

Report of the Commission on Country Life. New York: Sturgis and Walton, 1911; reprint, Chapel Hill: Univ. of North Carolina Press, 1944.

Shaw, Edward R. *School Hygiene.* New York: Macmillan, 1911.

Sibley, James L. "Homemakers' Clubs for Negro Girls." *Southern Workman* 44 (Feb. 1915): 81–86.

Smith, C. B. "The Agricultural Extension Program." *Rural America* 5 (Nov. 1927): 11–12.

"Special Winter Courses at the George Peabody College for Teachers." *School and Society* 2 (25 Dec. 1915): 918.

"Standardization of the Rural School Plant." *School and Society* 1 (13 Feb. 1915): 222–25.

"Standardized School House Design: Part I." *American Architect* 114 (6 Nov. 1918): 559–64.

"Standardized School House Design: Part II." *American Architect* 114 (13 Nov. 1918): 598–91.

Steward, Mrs. Clarence S. *Mountain Settlement Work in the East Tennessee Mountains.* [Tennessee Federation of Women's Clubs, 1925?].

Strayer, George D., and N. L. Englehardt. *Report of the Survey of Certain Aspects of the School System of Chattanooga and Hamilton County.* New York: Teachers College, Columbia Univ. Bureau of Publications, 1929.

Swinn, E. H. *Agricultural Instruction: A Means of Establishing Better Racial Relations in Southern Communities.* Extension Service Circular 68. [Washington, D.C.: United States Dept. of Agriculture,] Feb. 1928.

Tennessee. Dept. of Public Instruction. *Rural School Situation in Tennessee.* Nashville: McQuiddy Printing Company, 1911.

Terman, Lewis M. *The Hygiene of the School Child.* Boston: Houghton Mifflin, 1914.

Turner, Louise G. *Home Work for Winter Months for Canning Club Girls of Tennessee: Kitchen Rules, Setting the Table, Beverages.* Division of Extension Publication No. 2. Knoxville: Univ. of Tennessee, College of Agriculture, Nov. 1914.

———. *What to Do When Cleaning House.* Division of Extension Publication No. 5. Knoxville: Univ. of Tennessee, College of Agriculture, Feb. 1915.

Univ. of Tennessee, Knoxville, Agricultural Extension Service, Home Demonstration Dept. *Improved Country Homes in Tennessee.* Nashville: Tennessee Dept. of Agriculture, 1928.

Van Deman, Ruth. *The Well-Planned Kitchen*. United States Dept. of Agriculture Circular 189. Washington, D.C.: Government Printing Office, Sept. 1921; revised Aug. 1923.

Ward, Edward J. "The Schoolhouse as the Civic and Social Center of the Community." In *Journal of Proceedings and Addresses of the 50th Annual Meeting of the National Education Association*, 250–57. Chicago: Univ. of Chicago Press, 1912.

Ward, Florence E. "The Farm Woman's Problems." *Journal of Home Economics* 12 (Oct. 1920): 437–57.

———. *The Farm Woman's Problems*. United States Dept. of Agriculture Circular 148. Washington, D.C.: Government Printing Office, 1920.

Whitfield, J. L. "An Indictment of the Rural School." In *Education in the South*, 43–44. U.S. Bureau of Education Bulletin No. 30. Washington, D.C.: Government Printing Office, 1913.

Wilson, Meredith Chester. *The Effectiveness of Home-Economics Extension Work in Reaching Farm Women*. United States Dept. of Agriculture Circular 101. [Washington, D.C.: United States Dept. of Agriculture,] Apr. 1929.

———. *Kitchen Arrangement and Equipment*. United States Dept. of Agriculture Circular 30. [Washington, D.C.: United States Dept. of Agriculture,] Dec. 1926.

Wright, Luther L. "The Rural School Plant." Abstracted by Frederick K. Noyes. In *Current Educational Topics No. 2*, 23–24. U.S. Bureau of Education Bulletin No. 15. Washington, D.C.: Government Printing Office, 1912.

Secondary Sources

Abernathy, S. G., comp. *Brief History of the Farm Bureau in Tennessee, 1921–1949*. [Columbia: Tennessee Farm Bureau Federation, 1949?].

Adams, Jane. *The Transformation of Rural Life: Southern Illinois, 1890–1990*. Chapel Hill: Univ. of North Carolina Press, 1994.

Allred, C. E.; S. W. Watkins; and G. H. Hatfield. *Tennessee, Economic and Social*, part 2: *The Counties*. Knoxville: Univ. of Tennessee, 1929.

Anderson, James D. *The Education of Blacks in the South, 1865–1935*. Chapel Hill: Univ. of North Carolina Press, 1988.

———. "Northern Philanthropy and the Shaping of Southern Black Rural Education, 1902–1935." *History of Education Quarterly* 18 (Winter 1978): 371–96.

Ash, Stephen V. *Middle Tennessee Society Transformed, 1860–1870: War and Peace in the Upper South*. Baton Rouge: Louisiana State Univ. Press, 1988.

Babbitt, Kathleen R. "The Productive Farm Woman and the Home Economist in New York State, 1920–1940." *Agricultural History* 67 (Spring 1993): 83–101.

Bailey, Joseph Cannon. *Seaman A. Knapp: Schoolmaster of American Agriculture*. New York: Columbia Univ. Press, 1945.

Biles, Roger. "Robert R. Church, Jr., of Memphis: Black Republican Leader in the Age of Democratic Ascendancy, 1928–1940." *Tennessee Historical Quarterly* 42 (Winter 1983): 362–82.

Blauch, Lloyd E. *Federal Cooperation in Agricultural Extension Work, Vocational Education, and Vocational Rehabilitation*. Washington, D.C.: Government Printing Office, 1935.

Bowers, William L. *The Country Life Movement in America, 1900–1920*. Port Washington, N.Y.: Kennikat Press, 1974.

———. "Country Life Reform, 1900–1920: A Neglected Aspect of Progressive Era History." *Agricultural History* 45 (July 1971): 211–21.

Branegan, Gladys Alee. *Home Economics Teacher Training Under the Smith-Hughes Act, 1917 to 1927*. New York: Teachers College, Columbia Univ., 1929.

Campbell, Thomas Monroe. *The Movable School Goes to the Negro Farmer*. Tuskegee, Ala.: Tuskegee Institute Press, 1936; reprint, New York: Arno Press, 1969.

Chambers, Clarke A. *Seedtime of Reform: American Social Service and Social Actions, 1918–1933*. Minneapolis: Univ. of Minnesota Press, 1963.

Chatfield, E. Charles. "The Southern Sociological Congress: Organization of Uplift." *Tennessee Historical Quarterly* 19 (Dec. 1960): 328–38.

———. "The Southern Sociological Congress: Rationale of Uplift." *Tennessee Historical Quarterly* 20 (Mar. 1961): 51–64.

Clark, Clifford Edward, Jr. *The American Family Home, 1800–1960*. Chapel Hill: Univ. of North Carolina Press, 1986.

Cohen, Lizabeth A. "Embellishing a Life of Labor: An Interpretation of the Material Culture of American Working-Class Homes, 1885–1915." In *Common Places: Readings in American Vernacular Architecture*, edited by Dell Upton and John Michael Vlach, 261–78. Athens: Univ. of Georgia Press, 1986.

Cohn, Jan. *The Palace or the Poorhouse: The American House as a Cultural Symbol*. East Lansing: Michigan State Univ. Press, 1979.

Conway, Jill. "Women Reformers and American Culture, 1870–1930." *Journal of Social History* 5 (Winter 1971–72): 162–77.

Cott, Nancy. *The Grounding of Modern Feminism*. New Haven, Conn.: Yale Univ. Press, 1987.

Cowan, Ruth Schwartz. *More Work for Mother: The Ironies of Household*

Technology, from the Open Hearth to the Microwave. New York: Basic Books, 1983.

Cremin, Lawrence A. *The Transformation of the School: Progressivism in American Education, 1876–1957.* New York: Alfred A. Knopf, 1964.

Cutler, William W., III. "Cathedral of Culture: The Schoolhouse in American Thought and Practice Since 1820." *History of Education Quarterly* 29 (Spring 1989): 1–40.

Dabney, Charles William. *Universal Education in the South,* vol. 2: *The Southern Education Movement.* Chapel Hill: Univ. of North Carolina Press, 1936.

Danbom, David B. *Born in the Country: A History of Rural America.* Baltimore, Md.: Johns Hopkins Univ. Press, 1995.

———. *The Resisted Revolution: Urban American and the Industrialization of Agriculture, 1900–1930.* Ames: Iowa State Univ. Press, 1979.

Davis, Allen F. *Spearheads of Reform: The Social Settlements and the Progressive Movement, 1890–1914.* New York: Oxford Univ. Press, 1967.

Dittmer, John. *Black Georgia in the Progressive Era, 1900–1920.* Urbana: Univ. of Illinois Press, 1977.

Doyle, Don H. *New Men, New Cities, New South: Atlanta, Nashville, Charleston, Mobile, 1860–1910.* Chapel Hill: Univ. of North Carolina Press, 1990.

Eigelsbach, William B. "The Rise and Fall of a Summer School." *Library Development Review, 1987–88* (Knoxville: Univ. of Tennessee, 1987): 16–19.

Embree, Edwin R. *Julius Rosenwald Fund: Review of Two Decades, 1917–1936.* Chicago: Julius Rosenwald Fund, 1936.

Embree, Edwin R., and Julia Waxman. *Investment in People: The Story of the Julius Rosenwald Fund.* New York: Harper and Brothers, 1949.

Ettling, John. *The Germ of Laziness: Rockefeller Philanthropy and Public Health in the New South.* Cambridge, Mass.: Harvard Univ. Press, 1981.

Evans, J. A. *Recollections of Extension History.* Extension Circular No. 224. Raleigh: North Carolina State College of Agriculture and Engineering, 1938.

Fass, Paula. *Outside In: Minorities and the Transformation of American Education.* New York: Oxford Univ. Press, 1989.

Filene, Peter G. "An Obituary for 'The Progressive Movement.'" *American Quarterly* 22 (Spring 1970): 20–34.

Fink, Deborah. *Open Country, Iowa: Rural Women, Tradition and Change.* Albany: State Univ. of New York Press, 1986.

————. *Agrarian Women: Wives and Mothers in Rural Nebraska, 1880–1940.* Chapel Hill: Univ. of North Carolina Press, 1992.

Fitzpatrick, Ellen. *Endless Crusade: Women Social Scientists and Progressive Reform.* New York: Oxford Univ. Press, 1990.

Force, William W. *Payne of Peabody: An Apostle of Education.* Nashville, Tenn.: Published by the Author, 1985.

Forderhase, Nancy. "'Limited Only by Earth and Sky': The Louisville Women's Club and Progressive Reform, 1900–1920." *Filson Club History Quarterly* 59 (July 1985): 327–43.

Fosdick, Raymond B. *Adventure in Giving: The Story of the General Education Board.* New York: Harper and Row, 1962.

Fredrickson, George M. *The Black Image in the White Mind: The Debate on Afro-American Character and Destiny, 1817–1914.* New York: Harper and Row, 1971.

Freedman, Estelle B. "The New Woman: Changing Views of Women in the 1920s." *Journal of American History* 61 (Sept. 1974): 372–93.

Fuller, Wayne E. "Changing Concepts of the Country School as a Community Center in the Midwest." *Agricultural History* 58 (July 1984): 423–41.

————. *One-Room Schools of the Middle West: An Illustrated History.* Lawrence: Univ. Press of Kansas, 1994.

Glassberg, David. *American Historical Pageantry: The Uses of Tradition in the Early Twentieth Century.* Chapel Hill: Univ. of North Carolina Press, 1990.

Gowans, Alan. *The Comfortable House: North American Suburban Architecture, 1890–1930.* Cambridge, Mass.: MIT Press, 1986.

Grantham, Dewey W. "The Contours of Southern Progressivism." *American Historical Review* 86 (Dec. 1981): 1035–59.

————. *Hoke Smith and the Politics of the New South.* Baton Rouge: Louisiana State Univ. Press, 1957.

————. *The Regional Imagination: The South and Recent American History.* Nashville, Tenn.: Vanderbilt Univ. Press, 1979.

————. *Southern Progressivism: The Reconciliation of Progress and Tradition.* Knoxville: Univ. of Tennessee Press, 1983.

Gulliford, Andrew. *America's Country Schools.* Washington, D.C.: Preservation Press, 1990.

Hanchett, Thomas W. "The Rosenwald Schools and Black Education in North Carolina." *North Carolina Historical Review* 65 (Oct. 1988): 387–444.

Haney, Wava G., and Jane B. Knowles, eds. *Women and Farming: Changing Roles, Changing Structures.* Boulder, Colo.: Westview Press, 1988.

Harlan, Louis R. *Separate and Unequal: Public School Campaigns and Rac-*

ism in the Southern Seaboard States, 1901–1915. Chapel Hill: Univ. of North Carolina Press, 1958.

Hawley, Ellis W. *The Great War and the Search for a Modern Order: A History of the American People and Their Institutions, 1917–1933.* New York: St. Martin's Press, 1979.

Hayden, Dolores. *The Grand Domestic Revolution: A History of Feminist Design for American Homes, Neighborhoods, and Cities.* Cambridge, Mass.: MIT Press, 1981.

Hays, Samuel P. *The Response to Industrialism, 1885–1914.* Chicago: Univ. of Chicago Press, 1957.

Heath, Kingston. "A Dying Heritage: One-Room Schools of Gallatin County, Montana." In *Perspectives in Vernacular Architecture,* edited by Camille Wells, 201–16. Columbia: Univ. of Missouri Press, 1987.

Hilton, Kathleen C. "'Both in the Field, Each with a Plow': Race and Gender in USDA Policy, 1907–1929." In *Hidden Histories of Women in the New South,* edited by Virginia Bernhard, Betty Brandon, Elizabeth Fox-Genovese, Theda Perdue, and Elizabeth Hayes Turner, 114–33. Columbia: Univ. of Missouri Press, 1994.

Hine, Darlene Clark. "'We Specialize in the Wholly Impossible': The Philanthropic Work of Black Women." In *Lady Bountiful Revisited: Women, Philanthropy, and Power,* edited by Kathleen D. McCarthy, 70–93. New Brunswick, N.J.: Rutgers Univ. Press, 1990.

Holt, Andrew David. *The Struggle for a State System of Public Education in Tennessee, 1903–1936.* New York: Teachers College, Columbia Univ. Bureau of Publications, 1938.

Holt, Marilyn Irvin. *Linoleum, Better Babies, and the Modern Farm Woman, 1890–1930.* Albuquerque: Univ. of New Mexico Press, 1995.

Jenkins, William D. "Housewifery and Motherhood: The Question of Role Change in the Progressive Era." In *Woman's Being, Woman's Place: Female Identity and Vocation in American History,* edited by Mary Kelley, 142–53. Boston: G. K. Hall, 1979.

Jensen, Joan M. "Crossing Ethnic Barriers in the Southwest: Women's Agricultural Extension Education, 1914–1940." *Agricultural History* 60 (Spring 1986): 169–81.

———. *With These Hands: Women Working on the Land.* Old Westbury, N.Y.: Feminist Press, 1981.

Johnson, Charles S. *Statistical Atlas of Southern Counties.* Chapel Hill: Univ. of North Carolina Press, 1941.

Jones, Lance G. E. *The Jeanes Teacher in the United States, 1908–1933.* Chapel Hill: Univ. of North Carolina Press, 1937.

Kantor, Harvey, and David B. Tyack. *Learning to Earn: School, Work, and Vocational Reform in California, 1880–1930.* Madison: Univ. of Wisconsin Press, 1988.

———. *Work, Youth, and Schooling: Historical Perspectives on Vocationalism in American Education.* Stanford, Calif.: Stanford Univ. Press, 1982.

Keith, Jeanette. *Country People in the New South: Tennessee's Upper Cumberland.* Chapel Hill: Univ. of North Carolina Press, 1995.

Kett, Joseph F. "Women and the Progressive Impulse in Southern Education." In *The Web of Southern Social Relations: Women, Family, and Education,* edited by Walter J. Fraser, Jr.; R. Frank Saunders, Jr.; and Jon Wakelyn, 166–80. Athens: Univ. of Georgia Press, 1985.

Kirby, Jack Temple. *Darkness at the Dawning: Race and Reform in the Progressive South.* Philadelphia: J. B. Lippincott, 1972.

Kirschner, Don S. *The Paradox of Professionalism: Reform and Public Service in Urban America, 1900–1940.* New York: Greenwood Press, 1986.

Kousser, J. Morgan. *The Shaping of Southern Politics: Suffrage Restriction and the Establishment of the One-Party South, 1880–1910.* New Haven, Conn.: Yale Univ. Press, 1974.

Lamon, Lester. *Black Tennesseans, 1900–1930.* Knoxville: Univ. of Tennessee Press, 1977.

———. "The Tennessee Agricultural and Industrial Normal School: Public Higher Education for Black Tennesseans." *Tennessee Historical Quarterly* 32 (Spring 1973): 42–58.

Lanier, Robert A. *Memphis in the 1920s: The Second Term of Mayor Rowlett Paine, 1924–1928.* Memphis, Tenn.: Zenda Press, 1979.

Leavell, Ullin Whitney. *Philanthropy in Negro Education.* Nashville, Tenn.: George Peabody College for Teachers, 1930.

Leloudis, James L., II. *Schooling the New South: Pedagogy, Self and Society in North Carolina, 1880–1920.* Chapel Hill: Univ. of North Carolina Press, 1996.

———. "The Woman's Association for the Betterment of Public School Houses in North Carolina, 1902–1919." *Journal of American History* 69 (Mar. 1983): 886–909.

Lewis, Charles Lea. *Philander Priestley Claxton: Crusader for Public Education.* Knoxville: Univ. of Tennessee Press, 1948.

Link, Arthur S. "The Progressive Movement in the South, 1870–1914." *North Carolina Historical Review* 23 (Apr. 1946): 172–95.

———. "What Happened to the Progressive Movement in the 1920s?" *American Historical Review* 64 (July 1959): 833–51.

Link, Arthur S., and Richard L. McCormick. *Progressivism.* Arlington Heights, Ill.: Harlan-Davidson, 1983.

Link, William A. *A Hard Country and a Lonely Place: Schooling, Society, and Reform in Rural Virginia, 1870–1920.* Chapel Hill: Univ. of North Carolina Press, 1986.

———. "'The Harvest Is Ripe, but the Laborers Are Few': The Hookworm Crusade in North Carolina, 1909–1915." *North Carolina Historical Review* 67 (Jan. 1990): 1–27.

———. "Making the Inarticulate Speak: A Reassessment of Public Education in the Rural South, 1870–1920." In *History of Education in the South,* edited by Clinton B. Allison and Chipman B. Stuart, 63–75. Norman: Univ. of Oklahoma Press, 1983.

———. *The Paradox of Southern Progressivism, 1880–1930.* Chapel Hill: Univ. of North Carolina Press, 1992.

———. "Privies, Progressivism, and Public Schools: Health Reform and Education in the Rural South, 1909–1920." *Journal of Southern History* 54 (Nov. 1988): 623–42.

———. "The Social Context of Southern Progressivism, 1880–1930." In *The Wilson Era: Essays in Honor of Arthur S. Link,* edited by John Milton Cooper, Jr., and Charles E. Neu, 55–82. Arlington Heights, Ill.: Harlan-Davidson, 1991.

Livingood, James W. *Hamilton County.* Memphis, Tenn.: Memphis State Univ. Press, 1981.

Maxcy, Spencer J. "Progressivism and Rural Education in the Deep South, 1900–1950." In *Education and the Rise of the New South,* edited by Ronald K. Goodenow and Arthur O. White, 47–71. Boston: G. K. Hall, 1981.

May, Bridget A. "Progressivism and the Colonial Revival: The Modern Colonial House, 1900–1920." *Winterthur Portfolio* 26 (Summer-Autumn 1991): 107–22.

McCormick, Richard L. "The Discovery That Business Corrupts Politics: A Reappraisal of the Origins of Progressivism." *American Historical Review* 86 (Apr. 1981): 247–74.

McKenzie, Robert Tracy. *One South or Many? Plantation Belt and Upcountry in Civil War–Era Tennessee.* Cambridge, England: Cambridge Univ. Press, 1994.

McMurry, Sally. *Families and Farmhouses in Nineteenth-Century America.* New York: Oxford Univ. Press, 1988.

———. *Transforming Rural Life: Dairying Families and Agricultural Change, 1820–1885.* Baltimore, Md.: Johns Hopkins Univ. Press, 1995.

Miller, William D. *Memphis During the Progressive Era.* Memphis, Tenn.: Memphis State Univ. Press, 1957.

———. *Mr. Crump of Memphis.* Baton Rouge: Louisiana State Univ. Press, 1964.

Mitchell, Theodore R. "From Black to White: The Transformation of Educational Reform in the New South, 1890–1910." *Educational Theory* 39 (Fall 1989): 337–50.

Mitchell, Theodore R., and Robert Lowe. "To Sow Contentment: Philanthropy, Scientific Agriculture and the Making of the New South: 1906–1920." *Journal of Social History* 24 (Winter 1990): 317–40.

Motz, Marilyn Ferris, and Pat Browne, eds. *Making the American Home: Middle-Class Women and Domestic Material Culture, 1840–1940*. Bowling Green, Ohio: Bowling Green State Univ. Popular Press, 1988.

Muncy, Robyn. *Creating a Female Dominion in American Reform, 1890–1935*. New York: Oxford Univ. Press, 1991.

Neth, Mary. *Preserving the Family Farm: Women, Community, and the Foundations of Agribusiness in the Midwest, 1900–1940*. Baltimore, Md.: Johns Hopkins Univ. Press, 1995.

Neverdon-Morton, Cynthia. *Afro-American Women of the South and the Advancement of the Race, 1895–1925*. Knoxville: Univ. of Tennessee Press, 1989.

Obion County History. Vol. 1. Union City, Tenn.: Obion County Historical Society, 1981.

Parsons, Rhey Boyd. *Teacher Education in Tennessee*. Chicago: Univ. of Chicago Libraries, 1935.

Palmer, Phyllis. *Domesticity and Dirt: Housewives and Domestic Servants in the United States, 1920–1945*. Philadelphia: Temple Univ. Press, 1989.

Peterson, Fred W. "Vernacular Building and Victorian Architecture: Midwestern Farm Homes." *Journal of Interdisciplinary History* 12 (Winter 1982): 409–27.

Plank, David N., and Rick Ginsberg, eds. *Southern Cities, Southern Schools: Public Education in the Urban South*. New York: Greenwood Press, 1990.

Proud Past, Promising Future: A Narrative History of the Tennessee Agricultural Extension Service, 1914–1989. [Knoxville]: Tennessee Agricultural Extension Service, [1989].

Prown, Jules David. "Mind in Matter: An Introduction to Material Culture Theory and Method." *Winterthur Portfolio* 17 (Spring 1982): 1–19.

———. "Style as Evidence." *Winterthur Portfolio* 15 (Autumn 1980): 197–210.

Quandt, Jean B. *From the Small Town to the Great Community: The Social Thought of Progressive Intellectuals*. New Brunswick, N.J.: Rutgers Univ. Press, 1970.

Quimby, Ian M. G., ed. *Material Culture and the Study of American Life*. New York: Norton, 1978.

Redcay, Edward E. *County Training Schools and Public Secondary Educa-*

tion for Negroes in the South. Washington, D.C.: John F. Slater Fund, 1935.

Reese, William J. *Power and the Promise of School Reform: Grass-Roots Movements During the Progressive Era*. Boston: Routledge and Kegan Paul, 1986.

Rieff, Lynne A. "'Go Ahead and Do All You Can': Southern Progressives and Alabama Home Demonstration Clubs, 1914–1940." In *Hidden Histories of Women in the New South*, edited by Virginia Bernhard, Betty Brandon, Elizabeth Fox-Genovese, Theda Perdue, and Elizabeth Hayes Turner, 134–49. Columbia: Univ. of Missouri Press, 1994.

Roberts, Mrs. Everett Bryan, comp. *Tennessee Congress of Parents and Teachers History: Thirty-One Years in Retrospect, 1911–1942*. Memphis: Murdock-Johnston Printing Company, [1942].

Robertson, Cheryl. "House and Home in the Arts and Crafts Era: Reforms for Simpler Living." In *"The Art That Is Life": The Arts and Crafts Movement in America, 1875–1920*, edited by Wendy Kaplan et al., 336–57. Boston: Little, Brown, and Company, 1987.

———. "Male and Female Agendas for Domestic Reform: The Middle-Class Bungalow in Gendered Perspective." *Winterthur Portfolio* 26 (Summer-Autumn 1991): 123–42.

Rodgers, Daniel T. "In Search of Progressivism." *Reviews in American History* 10 (Dec. 1982): 113–32.

Rogers, Lucille. *Light from Many Candles: A History of Pioneer Women in Education in Tennessee*. Nashville: Xi State, Delta Kappa Gamma, 1960.

Rury, John L. *Education and Women's Work: Female Schooling and the Division of Labor in Urban America, 1870–1930*. Albany: State Univ. of New York Press, 1991.

Salem, Dorothy C. *To Better Our World: Black Women in Organized Reform, 1890–1920*. Brooklyn, N.Y.: Carlson Publishers, 1990.

Schlereth, Thomas J. "Material Culture Studies and Social History Research." *Journal of Social History* 16 (Summer 1983): 111–43.

———. *Material Culture Studies in America*. Nashville, Tenn.: American Association for State and Local History, 1982.

Schwieder, Dorothy. "Education and Change in the Lives of Iowa Farm Women, 1900–1940." *Agricultural History* 60 (Spring 1986): 200–215.

Scott, Anne Firor. "Most Invisible of All: Black Women's Voluntary Associations." *Journal of Southern History* 56 (Feb. 1990): 3–22.

———. *Natural Allies: Women's Associations in American History*. Urbana: Univ. of Illinois Press, 1991.

————. *The Southern Lady: From Pedestal to Politics, 1830–1930.* Chicago: Univ. of Chicago Press, 1970.

————. "Women's Voluntary Associations: From Charity to Reform." In *Lady Bountiful Revisited: Women, Philanthropy, and Power,* edited by Kathleen D. McCarthy, 41–46. New Brunswick, N.J.: Rutgers Univ. Press, 1990.

Scott, Roy V. *The Reluctant Farmer: The Rise of Agricultural Extension to 1914.* Urbana: Univ. of Illinois Press, 1970.

Shapiro, Laura. *Perfection Salad: Women and Cooking at the Turn of the Century.* New York: Farrar, Strauss and Giroux, 1986.

Sims, Almon J. *A History of Extension Work in Tennessee: Twenty-Five Years of Service to Rural Life, 1914–1939.* Publication 223. [Knoxville]: Univ. of Tennessee, 1939.

Sims, Anastatia. *The Power of Femininity in the New South: Women's Organizations and Politics in North Carolina, 1880–1930.* Columbia: Univ. of South Carolina Press, 1997.

Smith, Samuel L. *Builders of Goodwill: The Story of the State Agents of Negro Education in the South, 1910 to 1950.* Nashville: Tennessee Book Company, 1950.

Strasser, Susan. *Never Done: A History of American Housework.* New York: Pantheon, 1982.

Sturgis, Cynthia. "'How're You Gonna Keep 'Em Down on the Farm?' Rural Women and the Urban Model in Utah." *Agricultural History* 60 (Spring 1986): 182–99.

Taggart, Robert J. *Private Philanthropy and Public Education: Pierre S. du Pont and the Delaware Schools, 1890–1940.* Newark: Univ. of Delaware Press, 1988.

Tennessee Home Economics Association. *Home Economics Heritage in Tennessee, 1909–1959.* [Nashville]: n.p., 1959.

Tindall, George Brown. *The Emergence of the New South, 1913–1945.* Baton Rouge: Louisiana State Univ. Press, 1967.

True, Alfred Charles. *A History of Agricultural Education in the United States, 1785–1925.* Washington, D.C.: Government Printing Office, 1925; reprint, New York: Arno Press, 1969.

Tyack, David, and Elisabeth Hansot. *Learning Together: A History of Co-education in American Schools.* New Haven, Conn.: Yale Univ. Press, 1990.

Walker, Melissa. "'A Smile on Her Face and a Song on Her Lips': Home Extension Work Among East Tennessee Farm Women During the Agricultural Depression of the 1920s." *Southern Historian* 15 (Spring 1994): 51–67.

————. "Home Extension Work Among African Americans in East Tennessee, 1920–1939." *Agricultural History* 70 (Summer 1996): 487–502.

Wedell, Marsha. *Elite Women and the Reform Impulse in Memphis, 1875–1915*. Knoxville: Univ. of Tennessee Press, 1991.

Werner, Morris R. *Julius Rosenwald: The Life of a Practical Humanitarian*. New York: Harper and Row, 1939.

West, Carroll Van. *Tennessee Agriculture: A Century Farms Perspective*. Nashville: Tennessee Dept. of Agriculture, 1986.

Whisnant, David E. *All That Is Native and Fine: The Politics of Culture in an American Region*. Chapel Hill: Univ. of North Carolina Press, 1983.

White, Robert Hiram. *Development of the Tennessee State Educational Organization, 1796–1929*. Kingsport, Tenn.: Southern Publishers, Inc., 1929.

Wiebe, Robert H. *The Search for Order, 1877–1920*. New York: Hill and Wang, 1967.

Williams, Mildred M.; Kara Vaughn Jackson; Madie A. Kiney; Susie W. Wheeler; Rebecca Davis; Rebecca A. Crawford; Maggie Forte; and Ethel Bell. *The Jeanes Story: A Chapter in the History of American Education, 1908–1969*. Jackson, Miss.: Southern Education Foundation, 1979.

Winters, Donald L. *Tennessee Farming, Tennessee Farmers: Antebellum Agriculture in the Upper South*. Knoxville: Univ. of Tennessee Press, 1994.

Wiser, Louise Houck, comp. *A History of Rutherford County Schools to 1972*. Vols. 1 and 2. Murfreesboro, Tenn.: Rutherford County Historical Society, 1986.

Woodward, C. Vann. *Origins of the New South, 1877–1913*. Baton Rouge: Louisiana State Univ. Press, 1951.

Wright, Gwendolyn. *Building the Dream: A Social History of Housing in America*. Cambridge, Mass.: MIT Press, 1981.

———. *Moralism and the Model Home: Domestic Architecture and Cultural Conflict in Chicago, 1873–1913*. Chicago: Univ. of Chicago Press, 1980.

Theses and Dissertations

Belles, Alfred G. "The Julius Rosenwald Fund: Efforts in Race Relations, 1928–48." Ph.D. diss., Vanderbilt Univ., 1972.

Cullum, Edward Neely. "George Peabody College for Teachers, 1914–1937." Ed.D. diss., George Peabody College for Teachers, 1963.

Fleming, Cynthia Griggs. "The Development of Black Education in Tennessee, 1865–1920." Ph.D. diss., Duke Univ., 1977.

Frances, Ellen E. "Progressivism and the American House: Architecture as an Agent of Social Reform." Master's thesis, Univ. of Oregon, 1982.

Hanson, Susan Atherton. "Home Sweet Home: Industrialization's Impact on Rural Households, 1865–1925." Ph.D. diss., Univ. of Maryland, 1986.

Hardin, Martin Leander. "A Study of Rural School Buildings and Grounds, with Special Reference to Union County, Tennessee." Master's thesis, Univ. of Tennessee, 1923.

Hutchison, Janet Ann. "American Housing, Gender, and the Better Homes Movement, 1922–1935." Ph.D. diss., Univ. of Delaware, 1989.

Hutson, Darlene L. "The Jeanes Supervisory Program in Tennessee." Ed.D. diss., Univ. of Tennessee, 1964.

Lee, Lucille Blanche. "The Work of the Home Demonstration Agent in Tennessee." Master's thesis, Univ. of Tennessee, 1930.

May, Martha Elizabeth. "Home Life: Progressive Social Reformers' Prescriptions for Social Stability, 1890–1920." Ph.D. diss., State Univ. of New York at Binghamton, 1984.

Melton, Gloria Brown. "Blacks in Memphis, Tennessee, 1920–1955: A Historical Study." Ph.D. diss., Washington State Univ., 1982.

Powers, Jane Bernard. "The Girl Question in Education: Vocational Training for Young Women in the Progressive Era." Ph.D. diss., Stanford Univ., 1987.

Shahan, Joe Michael. "Reform and Politics in Tennessee, 1906– 1914." Ph.D. diss., Vanderbilt Univ., 1981.

Shannon, Samuel H. "Agricultural and Industrial Education at Tennessee State Univ. During the Normal School Phase, 1912–1922: A Case Study." Ph.D. diss., George Peabody College for Teachers, 1974.

Simpson, Evelyn Shipe. "The Development of Home Economics at the Univ. of Tennessee." Ed.D. diss., Univ. of Tennessee, 1961.

Slater, Margaret. "The Evolution of Schoolhouse Architecture in Tennessee." Master's thesis, Middle Tennessee State Univ., 1987.

Stitely, Thomas Beane. "Bridging the Gap: A History of the Rosenwald Fund in the Development of Rural Schools in Tennessee, 1912–1932." Ph.D. diss., George Peabody College for Teachers, 1975.

Taylor, Starlene Johnson. "The History of the Teacher Education Program at Tennessee State University." Ed.D. diss., Tennessee State Univ., 1988.

Turner, W. E. "A Survey of Negro High Schools in Tennessee." Master's thesis, Univ. of Tennessee, 1933.

Walker, Melissa. "'All We Knew Was To Farm': Gender, Class, Race and Change Among East Tennessee Farm Women, 1920–1941." Ph.D. diss., Clark Univ., 1996.

Index

Adams and Alsup, 24, 25
African-Americans, 2, 3–4, 6, 10, 13, 14, 15, 27, 61–62, 76–87, 89, 92, 109, 145, 146, 148; women, 85–86, 99–100, 114, 116; *see also* agricultural agents, Better Homes movement, education, extension agents, farmers, home demonstration, home demonstration agents, home economics, secondary schools, vocational education
Agricultural agents, 105, 107, 116, 130, 145; African American, 82, 118, 144, 164n.70; white, 102, 118
Agriculture and Home Economics Cooperative Extension Act, 117
Ambrose, Margaret A., 114–15, 118, 129, 130, 132
American Country Life Association, 14
American Farm Bureau Federation, 99, 113, 130, 132, 143, 195n.34
American Public Health Association, 55
Anderson County, 38, 119, 199n.63
Anna T. Jeanes Foundation, 28, 61, 63, 92; *see also* Jeanes industrial supervising teachers

Bedford County, 77, 85
Benton County, 32
Bernard, Ollie H., 48, 50, 51–52, 55, 59, 75, 76, 79, 80, 88, 100, 177n.46, 178n.48
Better Homes movement, 9–10, 122, 127, 137–40, 143, 144, 208n.45; African Americans in, 138, 140, 149
Blount County, 138, 140
Bond, John R., 85, 181n.77
Bradley County, 114

Brister, John W., 22, 47
Brown, John B., 36–37, 52, 63, 92
Bungalow style, 24, 75, 138, 148, 208n.45
Business progressivism, 35, 59, 62, 89, 91, 105
Buttrick, Wallace, 16, 21, 28, 175n.26

Capper-Ketcham Act, 117, 197n.52
Chattanooga, 8, 24, 77–78, 110, 123, 124, 178n.53
Church, Robert R., Jr., 81
Clark, Harry, 23, 43–44, 65, 95
Classical Revival style, 24, 40, 41, 43
Claxton, Philander P., 2, 19, 20, 28–29
Clay, Robert E., 62, 67, 76–80, 82–87, 89, 177n.42, 178n.49, 182n.91
Coffee County, 77, 177n.46
Collaborators. *See* home demonstration agents
Colonial Revival style, 52, 54, 56, 59, 71, 75, 121, 123, 124, 138, 141, 142, 148, 149, 169n.53, 175n.37, 208n.45
Colored Methodist Episcopal (CME) Church, 80, 83, 84, 87
Commission for Interracial Cooperation, 4; *see also* Tennessee Inter-Racial League
Commission on Country Life, 14, 18, 29
Community School Plans, 45, 46, 71, 72–74, 77, 176n.37
Conference for Education in the South, 15–17, 18, 19, 31, 61
Conway (Mary) Geneva, 109, 115
Cooperative Education Association, 23
Council of Agriculture, 102, 113
Country Life movement, 8, 14, 24, 107, 118, 203–4n.11
Country Life programs, 96–97, 99, 146; *see*

Country Life programs, *cont.*
    also Seaman A. Knapp School of
    Country Life
Country Life reformers, 14, 15, 19, 32, 33,
    95, 104, 120, 135, 144, 169n.54
County training schools, 28, 64–66, 81, 93,
    94, 101, 173n.11, 173n.15
Craftsman style, 52, 53, 71
Credle, William F., 57
Cresswell, Mary, 107, 110
Crim, Lula H., 101, 189n.45
Crockett County, 87
Crump, Edward Hull, 9, 81
Curry, Jabez Lamar Monroe, 15–16

Dabney, Charles W., 2, 16, 19, 20, 21–22,
    29
Davidson County, 28, 121, 133
Davis, Jackson, 65, 175n.26
Decatur County, 84, 126
Demonstration method, 30–31; *see also*
    extension agents, home demonstration
Dillard, James Hardy, 28
Dresslar, Fletcher B., 2, 24, 26, 45, 57–58,
    59, 63, 64, 68–69, 71, 171n.77, 175n.26
Dyer County, 77, 136, 208n.45
DuBois, W. E. B., 15

Education, 7, 14–17, 19–20; African
    American attitudes about, 71, 87, 89,
    147; prescribed for African Americans,
    61, 65, 67; *see also* vocational education
Embree, Edwin, 88, 89, 147
Evans, J. A., 107, 191n.9
Extension agents, 5, 105, 146; African
    American, 84, 92; white, 92; *see also*
    agricultural agents, home demonstration
    agents

Fagala, Albura Henderson, 84, 100
Farm Bureau. *See* American Farm Bureau
    Federation
Farmers, 13–14, 31; African American, 3, 6;
    economic conditions of, 3, 5–6, 55, 109,
    115–17, 165–66n.15, 166n.18, 168n.38;
    and gender division of labor, 65, 105,
    107, 190n.3; and tenancy, 1, 3, 6, 10,
    15, 132; *see also* individual counties
Fayette County, 6, 67, 86, 181n.85
Federal Board for Vocational Education, 95
First World War, 98, 102, 111, 113, 117

Fisk University, 2
Flexner, Abraham, 36, 175n.26
Folks, Gertrude, 61, 95
Franklin County, 130
French, Lizzie Crozier, 29
Fuller, Wayne, 17

General Education Act of 1909, 6, 19, 20
General Education Board (GEB), 2, 16, 20,
    21, 28, 65, 68, 82, 97, 145; and African
    American education, 61, 89, 92; and
    demonstration work, 31–32, 107, 108,
    112, 116; and industrial education, 17,
    63, 64, 94, 101; and school agents, 23,
    33, 36, 57, 58, 62, 75; and school
    buildings, 58, 59–60, 147
George Peabody College for Teachers, 2, 21,
    26, 27, 33, 45, 57, 58, 59, 63, 92, 95,
    97–99, 111–12, 145, 147, 188n.39
George-Reed Act, 95
Gibson County, 84–85
Giles County, 6, 87, 119, 120, 132, 136
Great Depression, 88, 147
Greene County, 8, 39–42, 44, 66, 128–29,
    131–32, 134–35, 148, 149, 166n.18,
    166n.20, 203n.6

Hale, William J., 21, 94, 177n.42
Hamblen County, 138
Hamilton County, 8, 24, 63, 77–78, 84, 99–
    100, 109, 113, 123, 124, 138, 141, 149,
    178n.51, 178n.53
Hampton Institute, 16, 92
Handicrafts, 106, 123–24, 149
Hardin County, 85
Harlan, Louis R., 17, 61
Harned, Perry L., 44, 50, 51, 88
Hatch Act, 95
Haywood County, 77, 84, 85, 118, 177n.46
High schools. *See* secondary schools
Highways. *See* roads
Hohenwald, 9, 56, 87, 182n.95
Home conveniences, 106, 109, 110–11,
    114–18, 125, 128, 129, 164n.71
Home decoration and furnishings, 29–30, 98,
    117–23, 125, 130; Progressive standards
    and designs for, 105–6, 119–21, 131–32,
    133, 134–36, 138–40, 169n.53; *see also*
    Better Homes movement, Bungalow style,
    Classical Revival style, Colonial Revival
    style, Craftsman style

Home demonstration, 9, 10, 33, 99, 105–26, 147, 149; African-American programs, 108, 114, 116, 117, 132, 164n.71, 184n.5, 205n.26; wartime programs, 111–14

Home demonstration agents, 8, 9, 10, 31, 33, 91, 95, 96, 97–98, 100, 105–26, 127–44, 145, 164n.70, 198n.56; African American, 85, 108–9, 117, 118, 119, 121, 124; white, 101, 112, 119, 133

Home demonstration clubs, for girls, 7, 31, 32, 91, 102, 105, 107, 108, 109–10, 112, 113, 121–23, 128–29, 200n.70; for women, 9, 95, 101, 102, 105, 107, 109, 110, 112, 113, 129

Home economics, 7, 8, 10, 11, 15, 17–18, 29, 63, 82, 90–103, 107, 119, 143, 146–47; for African Americans, 92, 93, 94, 99–100, 102; in higher education, 95–99; in public schools, 91–95, 184n.4, 195n.36

Home improvement, 10, 11, 106, 108, 116, 117–19, 127, 129, 137, 143–44; contests, 127–28, 131–42, 149; state campaigns, 131–37, 138, 143; see also Better Homes movement, home decoration and furnishings, Home Improvement days

Home Improvement days, 128–31, 138, 139, 149

Home Makers Clubs, 99, 108–9, 112, 184n.5

Home-Makers Associations, 29, 30, 32, 104, 111, 112, 143

Homes, 5, 93, 108, 116, 190–91n.4; role in rural reform, 31, 32, 104–5, 115, 146

Hoover, Herbert, 111, 137

Industrial education. See vocational education

Interstate School Building Service (ISBS), 2, 35, 58–59, 60, 147, 176n.37

Jeanes industrial supervising teachers, 27–28, 63, 64, 82, 83, 84, 85, 92, 101, 102, 108, 145, 149, 180n.71; see also Anna T. Jeanes Foundation

John F. Slater Fund, 15–16, 17, 28, 61, 63, 64, 65–66, 92, 94, 173n.15

Jones, Robert L., 21, 23

Jones and Furbringer, 43

Julius Rosenwald Fund (JRF), 51, 58–59, 64, 66, 67, 75, 76, 82, 87, 88, 89, 94, 145, 176n.34; rural school program of, 2, 58, 62, 66, 67–89, 147, 148, 180n.70; see also Rosenwald agent, Rosenwald schools

Keffer, Charles A., 92, 100, 184n.5, 197n.51

Keith, Jeanette, 35

Keller, Lillian L., 117, 122–23, 124, 129, 130, 132, 135, 141, 142, 144

Kett, Joseph, 35

Knapp, Bradford, 107, 110

Knapp, Seaman A., 30–31, 107

Knox County, 122, 123, 138, 140, 208n.45

Knoxville College, 20

Ku Klux Klan, 3, 182n.95

Lake County, 115

Lauderbach, Elizabeth Michael Bourges (Mrs. J. B.), 100, 109–11, 113

Lauderdale County, 77

Lewis County, 8–9, 37, 39, 44, 56–57, 66, 87, 113, 148, 165–66n.15, 174n.18, 182n.95, 195n.36

Link, William A., 17, 35, 86

Loudon County, 28

Madison County, 84, 85, 118, 138, 140, 143, 178n.49, 181n.87

Mahan, George, Jr., 51, 52, 53–54, 59, 169n.54

Marshall County, 6, 120, 124

Martin, O. B., 114

Mason, Clara Boone, 104, 144

Master Farm Homemakers, 142–43, 149

Maury County, 77, 85, 133, 134, 178n.49

McKenzie, Robert Tracy, 3

McMinn County, 28, 115, 133

Memphis, 3, 9, 43, 65, 81, 122

Montgomery County, 24, 62–63, 125, 138

Moore, Virginia Pearl, 23–24, 30, 31, 32–33, 107, 111, 112, 114, 144, 159n.41, 163n.70, 196n.41

Morrill Acts, 14, 20

Murphy, Edgar Gardner, 16–17

Myers, Mabel, 108, 116, 192n.11

Mynders, Seymour, 19, 26

Nashville, 21, 28, 70, 75

National Council on School Construction, 58, 171n.73, 176n.37

National Country Life Conference, 91
National Home Economics Association, 18

Obion County, 9, 46–51, 52, 78–80, 102,
148, 168n.38, 179n.56
Ogden, Robert Curtis, 16

Page, Walter Hines, 33
Parent-Teacher Asscociations, 24, 85, 86,
95, 143, 144, 160n.42
Payne, Bruce R., 2, 21, 97
Peabody Education Fund, 2, 15, 19, 21, 36
Peabody Normal College, 19, 20, 21
Peay, Austin, 5
Peck, Thomas F., 104, 144
Picture study, 123, 124–25, 202n.81
Polk County, 33
Porter, W. L., 67, 177n.42
Powell, Ola, 114
Powers, Sue M., 81, 82, 180n.67
Progressive reforms and reformers, 1, 5, 8,
10–11, 13–14, 26–27, 60, 145; concerns
about race, 15–17, 61–62, 70; concerns
about the South, 1, 7, 14–17; strategies
of, 7, 17, 28, 34–35, 90–91, 105–6,
145–49; see also business progressivism,
Country Life movement, Country Life
programs, Country Life reformers
Public health, 26–27
Putnam County, 32

Railroads, 5, 8–9
Reagan, Lizzie B. (Mrs. James A.), 30, 120–
21, 123, 163n.70, 205n.18
Richards, Stella (Estelle), 108, 116
Roads, 5, 8, 9, 55, 116, 123
Robinson, H. N., 67, 81, 84, 177n.42,
181n.87
Rockefeller, John D., 2, 16
Rockefeller, John D., Jr., 16
Rockefeller Foundation, 88
Rockefeller Sanitary Commission (RSC), 2,
20, 27
Roosevelt, Franklin D., 1
Roosevelt, Theodore, 14
Rose, Wickliffe, 2, 20, 21
Rosenwald, Julius, 28, 33, 67, 68, 69–70,
76
Rosenwald agent, 67, 76–78, 83, 84, 145
Rosenwald schools, community campaigns
for, 68, 70, 78–81, 84–87, 181n.82;

designs for, 68–69, 75, 79; reformers'
claims for, 70–71, 75; white reactions to,
70, 75, 76–81, 85, 89; see also Community School Plans
Rutherford County, 8, 9, 46, 52, 55, 67–68,
71, 113–14, 170n.61, 174n.23

School agents, 145, 146, 149; for black
rural schools, 36, 47, 55, 59, 62, 63, 76,
77, 92, 100, 108; for secondary schools,
23, 36, 47, 55, 65, 95; for white rural
schools, 36, 63, 92; see also Rosenwald
agent
School architecture, 40; Progressive
standards and designs for, 7, 10–11, 22–
27, 34–35, 36–37, 43, 45–46, 47–50,
52, 53–54, 55, 56, 57–60, 63–64, 71–
75, 79, 87; vernacular standards and
designs, 37, 39, 50, 79, 87; see also
Community School Plans, Fletcher B.
Dresslar, Interstate School Building
Service, Rosenwald schools, Samuel L.
Smith, Tennessee Division of Schoolhouse Planning
School consolidation, 22, 23, 34–35, 36–40,
42, 43–44, 47, 48, 50, 51, 55, 63, 81,
87, 156n.18; opposition to, 39, 86
School improvement, 23–24, 28, 63, 102,
108
Schools, problems of, 15, 17, 19, 36, 44–45,
50–51, 52, 55; relationship to homes, 7,
17, 28–29, 64–65, 70, 90–91, 94–95,
98–99, 104, 146, 148
Seaman A. Knapp School of Country Life,
21, 33, 97, 98–99, 188n.39
Secondary schools, 23, 42, 43–44, 55, 56;
for African Americans, 64, 65–66
Segregation, 3, 10, 61, 106, 140
Shelby County, 9, 28, 31, 42–44, 64–65, 69,
71, 81–84, 101, 121, 140, 148, 166–
67n.24, 208n.45
Sherrill, Samuel E., 76
Smith, Samuel L., 1; as director of Julius
Rosenwald Fund southern office, 70–72,
75, 76, 81, 89; as state agent for black
rural schools, 45, 47, 58, 59, 62–64, 65,
67, 92, 93, 94, 108–9, 112, 175n.26
Smith-Hughes Act, 91, 93, 94, 95, 96, 98,
100, 187–88n.34
Smith-Lever Act, 33, 91, 95, 100, 105, 106,
108, 192n.11

Southern Education Board (SEB), 2, 16, 17, 19, 21, 23, 32, 36, 61
Sullivan County, 134, 178n.49
Summer School of the South, 2, 20, 26, 29, 58, 92
Sumner County, 32, 124

Teachers, 5, 20–21, 45–46, 57, 94–95, 99–102, 146
Teachers' homes, 75, 81, 82, 83, 88, 92
Tennessee Agricultural and Industrial College, 67, 92, 177n.42 *see also* Tennessee Agricultural and Industrial Normal School
Tennessee Agricultural and Industrial Normal School, 2, 20, 92, 93, 111, 192n.11; *see also* Tennessee Agricultural and Industrial College
Tennessee Child Welfare Commission, 44
Tennessee Colored Women's Federation, 84
Tennessee Department of Agriculture, 6, 31, 147
Tennessee Department of Education, 2, 8, 19, 29, 36–37, 45, 46, 51, 59, 60, 62, 63, 67, 75, 76, 82, 89, 145, 147
Tennessee Department of Public Instruction. *See* Tennessee Department of Education
Tennessee Division of Schoolhouse Planning, 35, 59–60, 147, 171n.77
Tennessee Extension Service, 2, 9, 91, 92, 107–26, 127, 130, 138, 144, 145, 149, 184n.5, 197n.51
Tennessee Inter-Racial League, 76, 78, 84, 177n.42; *see also* Commission on Interracial Cooperation
Tennessee State Highway Department, 5
Thompson, S. H., 36
Tindall, George B., 35
Tipton County, 77, 182n.89
Tuskegee Institute, 16, 28, 67, 68–69, 92, 108

Unicoi County, 32
Union County, 44–45, 123–24
United States Department of Agriculture (USDA), 31, 203–4n.11; Cooperative Extension Service, 33, 91, 105, 106–7, 138
Universal Negro Improvement Association, 77–78, 178n.53
University of Chattanooga, 110

University of Tennessee, 2, 16, 19, 20, 26, 58, 92, 93, 95–97, 98, 99, 107, 111, 125, 187–88n.34

Vocational education, 15, 91, 145; for African Americans, 16–17, 61, 63, 64–66, 70–71, 75, 81, 82, 84, 92, 93, 101, 106; *see also* home economics, Jeanes industrial supervising teachers

Washington, Booker T., 4, 15, 16, 28, 67, 76
Washington County, 77
Weakley County, 116, 133, 196n.47
Wells, Ida B., 3
West Tennessee Normal College, 121, 126
Wheeler, Marjorie Spruill, 18
Wiebe, Robert H., 13
Williams, Charl Ormond, 43, 65, 81, 101, 167n.25
Williamson County, 28, 86, 87, 124, 138, 139, 140
Wilson County, 118, 119
Women, 5, 10, 17–18, 32–33; domestic consumption by, 7, 10, 97, 98, 124, 126, 127–42, 143, 147, 149, 209n.53; as homemakers, 108, 119–20, 128, 130, 132, 133, 134–35, 138, 143, 149; productive work by, 7, 10, 105, 106–11, 123, 128, 143, 149; role in rural reform, 17–18, 29, 85–86, 90–91, 106, 109, 111, 120, 126, 127, 143, 144, 146; school campaigns by, 85–86; *see also* home demonstration clubs, Home-Makers Associations, Home Makers Clubs, Master Farm Homemakers
Worley, Mabel, 141, 149

Rebuilding the Rural Southern Community was designed and typeset on a Macintosh computer system using PageMaker software. The text is set in Sabon and the titles in Futura and Dolmen. This book was designed by Todd Duren, composed by Kimberly Scarbrough, and manufactured by Thomson-Shore, Inc. The recycled paper used in this book is designed for an effective life of at least three hundred years.